I WALKED TO JERUSALEM

e-mail=

tony.dillon46@yahoo.
co.uk.

Phil
Best Wishes
anthony de lyon

I WALKED TO JERUSALEM

A Pilgrim's Trek Across
Europe and Asia

ANTHONY DE LYON

AZARIAH BOOKS
UNITED KINGDOM

This edition published 2015
Azariah Books, 83 Ducie Street,
Manchester, M1 2JQ
United Kingdom

www.azariahbooks.com

ISBN: 978-0-9931864-1-7

This is a work of non-fiction. Where appropriate, names have
been changed to protect the privacy of individuals.

Jacket Design by Daliborka Mijailović

Bible Verses
Based on the New Heart English Bible

Qur'an Verses by free-minds.org

The Battle Hymn of the Republic
First Published 1862, The Atlantic Monthly

To Be a Pilgrim
John Bunyan, Pilgrim's Progress

For the Good Samaritan—
whoever, wherever, whenever

In the midst of winter I did find within myself an invincible summer.

—Albert Camus

Contents

Prologue

Moist. Sticky. Warm. Was that blood?

Something was streaming down my right knee, and it wasn't sweat. I ran further into the dark, feet slipping and sliding on the uneven earth, hurrying toward the bright, dancing lights that filled my eyes. Where was God now? Where was the God that for seven long months I'd learnt to trust and depend on?

Dusk had fallen an hour ago. The great blackness of the Syrian night had swallowed the Levant leaving only chaotic shadows. I glanced back at the irregular triangle of my tent, now abandoned in the gloom of a warm October evening. The lightest in the world, it cost £185—a small fortune. I brushed the thought aside. As I stumbled across the freshly ploughed clods of earth that separated me from the road, I felt no regret at the loss if it saved my life. Again, I turned. Were they still in pursuit?

It had been so different in the beginning. 'You are welcome in Syria!' they'd cried among the copious forest that feathers the northwestern coast. The Armenian grocers I'd encountered had been generous with their hospitality, and there had been plenty to savour. Entire families had happily signed my walking stick. In those early days I'd cause for celebration.

Then. But not now.

I took a chance to pause at the roadside to tighten a few straps on my rucksack. Screaming beams of white and yellow headlight stabbed the night. I stepped out onto the tarmac, dodged a car, then another, and within seconds I was careering across open fields sown, by the reek of the plants, with thousands of tomatoes destined for the markets of Damascus. What should I do? I asked myself. Where could I hide? On the left I spotted a ghostly wire fence. I ran toward it and collapsed in a heap, gasping in short ragged breaths.

Suddenly, a pinpoint of yellow light began to brighten in the distance—another motorcyclist. Blast! Don't these people ever give up? I watched the steady beam grow closer. The bike was crisscrossing in an obvious search pattern. The dread grew.

Too many people had been asking too many questions.

After a few minutes I rose again and decided to track the fence back toward the highway. I'd only managed twenty yards when a huge pile of boulders blocked my path. Even by the light of a quarter moon I could see some were almost a metre across. I quickly sandwiched myself between them. Then, destabilised by my towering rucksack, I clambered awkwardly through the gap until the fence turned ninety degrees right to parallel the road. The words of the Jesuit priest from Homs had transformed into a chilling prophecy:

'Your value to these people, to terrorists, is very high.'

Fate's roaming finger had tracked me across Europe and Asia almost to the gates of Jerusalem itself. After so much effort was my pilgrimage really going to end here?

Five thousand kilometres from my home in England, I undid some straps and dropped the sum of my worldly possessions into the dirt. Alone in the great blackness, I waited.

And I waited for whatever might come.

Into the Winter

'A journey of a thousand miles begins with a single step,' says the Chinese proverb. I'd second that whilst acknowledging any new enterprise carries its fair share of risk. The story of how I marched to Jerusalem with a five-foot walking stick and a trilby hat is not one I thought I'd ever tell, particularly as the bad men of Syria seemed intent on ending the enterprise. True, when I set out in the winter of 2006 neither the hat nor walking stick was yet in my possession. I'd eventually pick up the hat from a department store in Munich, struggle into shorts three sizes too big in Albania, and by the time I reached Greece the generosity of strangers had become so frequent I wasn't surprised when a pensioner gave me the stick over a cup of coffee. Pilgrimage is full of special moments. Full of magic. But I didn't understand that at the start.

The miracle is I got anywhere near Syria, let alone the exalted gates of Jerusalem. Up to then I'd led a modest, unassuming life—nine 'O' levels at sixteen from the local comprehensive, a trio of unspectacular 'A' levels at eighteen, then a few temporary jobs to fill the time. I caught my first break in my early twenties programming computers in the Civil Service. Encouraged by a new wardrobe of sober blue ties, I spent long summers at the keyboard typing in technobabble like:

```
IF VERY-BIG-FLAG NOT EQ "Y"
  PERFORM 2B-ABC-PROCESS UNTIL A-SUB EQ 10.
```

I'll readily admit that deciphering the grammar of the Common Business Orientated Language (aka COBOL) isn't for everyone. Luckily, I discovered a hidden talent for decoding its darker sentences. After my probationary period I felt right at home among the hammering line printers, the ICL mainframe terminals with their sickly green text, the flickering rainbow lights of the data comms cabinet, and the occasional old fellow in waistcoat and pinstriped suit. I enjoyed the mental challenge afforded by the work, and I'd like to think my youthful efforts did some good.

Unfortunately, the little niche of stability I'd found for myself didn't last. What might have been a lifetime of glorious public service ended abruptly toward the back end of the nineties. Prime Minister Thatcher, intent on repairing the UK's dire national finances, gave the Civil Service a damn good handbagging, and it began shedding jobs by the thousand. One of them happened to be mine. So after eleven years I hung up my sober blue ties, plucked out the jeans and frayed T-shirt, and with surprisingly little difficulty moved into the cheery 'We can do it!' world of fundraising. For a while I totally bought the dream. Cue a very wet London Marathon:

'We can do it!' I screamed with clenched fists as the rain fell in torrents and another of our bedraggled runners overtook the red-faced bloke in the fluffy rabbit suit. 'C'mon Mike! Now go for the banana! You're the man!'

Mike's line of vision was blocked by a six-foot banana jogging in skinny pink tights. 'I ca–ca–can't br–breathe,' Mike wheezed, as the banana suit picked up speed.

Poor old Mike. The sixty-year-old from Slough was working his jaw faster than a stranded goldfish, but like a true champ he gamely wobbled on.

'Go on Mike!' I yelled, brutally ignoring his protests. Fantastic stuff. Fantastic commitment. I did worry though when he kept clutching his chest . . .

In the years that followed I continued to prepare fundraising bids and cram runners into jogging vests. I funded everything from space-age cochlear implants at £30,000 a pop to self-help booklets for young women grappling with bulimia. Ultimately, neither the job nor tedious commuting was really my calling.

I might have soldiered on if it hadn't been for an unexpected Internet encounter at 2 a.m. Pilgrimage is a fine old Christian tradition. For centuries, men and women with God on their mind have been plodding around Europe with big walking sticks. I could easily have missed it: a blog-like website, a smiling, red-haired Dutchwoman carrying a rucksack, a list of cities—The Hague, Vienna, Bratislava, Budapest . . . The woman was fifty-two-year-old Johanna van Fessem and the cities mere stopping points on a monumental journey that seemed to defy belief. And yet the story was true; Johanna *had* walked to Jerusalem.

I was blown away by the idea immediately. The travel possibilities seemed amazing: at least ten countries to explore, two great continents, scores of unknown towns. With an itinerary that ambitious you didn't need a stack of *Lonely Planet* guides to realise the journey promised oodles of adventure.

I found the spiritual angle particularly compelling. Notwithstanding some unfruitful forays into Sunday school, aged five, I'd come to see the world differently in my adult years. Once a fully paid-up atheist, in very small steps I'd become a believer. I wasn't sure Christianity held all the answers, but I felt it held more than most, and I'd long been impressed by the wisdom of Jesus. Consider John 8:7:

'But when they continued asking him, he looked up and said to them, "He who is without sin among you, let him throw the first stone at her."'

If there's ever been a more instructive lesson about mercy, I've yet to see it. And I wouldn't have known much about that without my Gideon's New Testament, handed to me at senior school when my interest in all things spiritual was precisely zero. Part of me was surprised I still had it. If, indeed, I was now contemplating a walk to Jerusalem, I was glad I did.

I spent the next few days mulling it over. Like any big decision it was a matter of pros and cons. How much will this trip cost? I asked myself. What about the danger? What about my career? *Think of what you're giving up.* Yep, there's no denying it. When change comes it's always easier to stick with what you know.

In the end, I felt I had more to gain than lose. For a Christian there's something seductive about such a massive statement of faith, of surrendering to the experience and placing yourself in the hands of a higher power. I also hoped synchronous meetings would be part of that spiritual deal. No one knows what fresh insights may be gleaned from strangers, and I expected to meet plenty. As I considered the matter further, the clearer I became about the benefits of following Johanna's lead. Not only had she found the courage to realise her dreams, but in her later pilgrim writings she'd gained a new sense of purpose—a powerful new direction. If I travelled to Jerusalem, could I not find the same?

A question that stupendous just begs to be answered. While I was conscious of the serious aims of the enterprise, the initial planning did produce some lighter moments. I was so fired up I marched straight into my bedroom and started hammering on an old typewriter. I quickly nailed the travel basics:

```
Serbo-Croat: The Essential Phrases
'Bash that Bug!' anti-mosquito spray
1:400,000 map of northwestern Albania
'Monsoon King' self-drying expedition trousers
Can-opener with extra metal twiddly bits
Silver-impregnated antimicrobial travel briefs
'Custer Last Stand' field torch with fold-out,
luminescent spoon (US patent pending)
---
```

Blimey. You know you're on some kind of mission when you throw this lot together.

Shortly after fine-tuning the mega-equipment list came 'The Big Declaration'. It's not every day you announce a 6,000 km pilgrimage to the Holy Land. Reaction ranged from total disinterest, to shock, to abject horror. Old Bill next door collapsed on the sofa complaining of chest pains; he eventually recovered.

Few seemed to believe this magnificent journey would ever get off the ground. My friend Jack was the first to declare. I caught up with him lifting pints at the Anne Boleyn. He put the glass on the bar and began to scratch a sizeable bristled chin.

'Now look 'ere, mate, I'm not sure about all of this. I mean, think about all that kit you're gonna have to carry. You'll need a five-hundred-pound yak to lug all that crap.'

Hmm. That was one way of putting it.

'And your stride length is what, about two-thirds of a metre?'

'It must be about that.'

'Well that's beautiful, mate, honestly, that's just beautiful . . . If the distance to Jerusalem is six thousand kilometres, you realise you're gonna need nine million steps to get there?'

'Yeah, that's pretty much it.'

Evidently sheer terror can be a beautiful thing. I've never seen a man order a triple scotch that quickly. Soon the entire family were wading in.

'Oh, that's nice, dear,' said mum, shoving another baking tray into the oven.

I poured myself a cup of tea, wondering if she'd even heard me. If mum was a Beatrix Potter character she'd be one of those little hedgehogs in spectacles and an apron. The homely pursuits were her domain. Mornings were spent in the kitchen engulfed in clouds of self-raising flour. Afternoons were devoted to the noble art of quilting. If you could bake it, sew it, or roll it flat, she was interested. Otherwise it didn't exist.

I found more interest among the younger generation. A tempestuous redhead with lion's mane hair, my sister Deanne was a modern-day Boudicca who nightly polished her brass breast-plate till it shone and could sack Colchester with a glance. To pay the bills she managed a shop selling camping equipment to out-doorsy types, people like me—'Hey!' she yelled. 'What have you got there? You can put that back!'

I spun round. 'I was just trying out this gadget to see—'

'Now!' she repeated, and began to cross the floor in short rapid strides.

I reluctantly placed the can-opener with extra metal twiddly bits back on the shelf.

She came up beside me, arms crossed and eyes blazing. 'Now look, Ant, let's stop messing about. You'll need this, and this. And ... Oh! This sleeping bag is just *amazing* value.'

My arms started to buckle as she tossed the bag on the growing pile. 'Anything else?' I'd suddenly lost my vision.

She grinned. 'Well, since you ask ... Have you considered the new sixty-litre rucksack with internal bladder and bellows pock-ets? They're on special offer at the moment.'

I hadn't, but it sounded incredibly cool so I bought one anyway. Her sales skills could not be faulted. I staggered out clutching enough kit to make an assault on the north face of Everest.

As summer 2006 turned into autumn I began to make some of the more important decisions. In September I handed in my notice. In the same month I addressed the money situation. I'd been saving for some time, so finance wasn't a problem. I added 5,000 euros to a Post Office money card, withdrew another 500 in cash. I topped up with some AMEX cheques, which seemed like a sensible option.

My final act was to bring some order to the route. In this I was much influenced by the pilgrimage of Johanna van Fessem. In 2001 Johanna had kicked off in Holland, tracking thereafter through Germany and Austria with a brief foray into the Czech Republic. I wasn't sure whether I wanted to dip into the latter but, due to the geography, the first three seemed to pencil them-selves in. It was in central and southern Europe, and what may loosely be called 'the Balkans', that the options began to multiply. Johanna had continued on a straight-ish line through Hungary, Romania and Bulgaria, yet there were other, edgier possibilities. How many people holiday in Bosnia? I asked myself; and when the answer came back 'almost none', I realised a sojourn down the war-torn states of the former Yugoslavia might prove the more interesting choice. Once safely beyond Greece I figured I'd pick up Johanna's path in Turkey, cross the Dardanelles Strait into Asia, meander south toward Marmaris and catch a ferry to Israel's port of Haifa. The service had recently been halted due to an unfortunate upsurge in Hamas rocket attacks. No matter, I thought, with implacable optimism. I'll figure it out.

The grand adventure to Jerusalem began on the morning of 14 November 2006. I crossed the North Sea by ferry, arriving late afternoon at the Hook of Holland. Immigration formalities duly complete, I heroically donned my rucksack for the first time on foreign soil, wondering what the locals would make of a guy camping in the middle of winter. The first person to answer that question proved to be Johanna. We spent a pleasant half hour at the port restaurant, eating Dutch pastries, reminiscing about her pilgrimage to Jerusalem and studying maps that swallowed up the table. Out of the blue she handed me a small cross, roughly an inch long, made from black-and-white plaited string.

'Marvellous!' I said, momentarily lost for anything better.

I took the gift gratefully and listened patiently to her advice. Johanna recommended trimming maps to keep the weight of my rucksack down—a useful tip; and when she told me earnestly that 'people will invite you in', I hoped it would be true. Annoyingly, I'd arranged to be at my hotel at five. I felt uncomfortable and perhaps a little rude when I had to rush off.

I soon had other things to fret about. I spent that night in a creaky guesthouse full of grim dockers in chunky sweaters, then when dawn broke swallowed a typical Dutch breakfast of red-skinned Gouda and cold ham. It was a miserable vista as I trudged east along the coast: vast banks of grey cloud, spinning wind turbines on churning seas, puddled tarmac pinging with rain drops. Everything was blurry as my glasses were dripping wet. I don't know what I'd done to deserve it, but misfortune struck immediately. Within minutes a two-inch blister erupted on the ball of my left foot. Ten kilometres on, near Maassluis, it split asunder leaving me walking on raw flesh. The pain was dreadful.

'And taking care of your feet is most important!' another pilgrim had told me. Yeah. No kidding.

Totally at a loss over how to handle the situation, I limped on toward Vlaardingen and thence to Rotterdam hoping for respite. None came; instead the other foot decided to follow suit. By the time I'd spent another day's effort pursuing the cobbled streets of Dordrecht I was hobbling on a pair of bloodied stumps. My fledgling pilgrimage ended in a soggy campsite a few kilometres east of the city. The whole enterprise had been a catastrophic and embarrassing failure.

It took two weeks for my feet to heal, two long weeks to rake through the debris of a shattered dream. I retreated to the pictur-esque harbours of Rotterdam, finding sanctuary in a youth hostel on Van Vollenhovenstraat. When I eventually arrived home the humiliation was awful. 'That was quick!' someone said unkindly. The humour cut like a knife. I'd told everybody I was walking to Jerusalem and managed only 55 km. Fifty-five! What had gone wrong? Slowly and deliberately I reasoned it out. Lack of fitness was obviously a major factor—for all my noble intentions, I was a pencil pusher, not a marathon runner. And then there was that monstrous rucksack. My sister had done her job well—perhaps *too* well. It was jammed to the rafters with every kind of stupid gadget and still insanely heavy. Why did I need a can-opener anyway? I wasn't carrying a cooker!

The next three months were quite possibly the most important of my life. With the dedication of an Olympic athlete I began to train my legs and feet, walking 20 km a day to improve endur-ance. Reducing the weight of my pack took on new meaning. I became fanatical, sawed the handle off my toothbrush, dumped half my kit and bought an expensive tent with carbon-fibre tent pegs—the lightest in the world. By the last day of February I'd clocked up a whopping 750 km in training. I finally (and tactfully) discarded the can-opener with extra metal twiddly bits. Not even the well-known vagaries of the British Post Office could stand in my way. I don't know whether it was the blessing of Christ or Jim at the sorting office, but the precious overnight ferry tickets dropped on the doormat just in time.

The new D-day for round two of my pilgrimage occurred on 7 March 2007. Once again, the scenes of the previous November played out: doorstep hugs, whispered goodbyes, the taxi ride into town past lighted streets I knew so well. It was a short trip to the station, but I had plenty of time to ponder the wisdom of my plans. Apart from those two weeks in Holland I'd never been to any of the countries on the route. At school I'd bluffed my way through 'O' level German, but that was the limit of my language skills. I was as green as anyone could be without being mistaken for a strip of Astroturf. Was this massive journey really worth the risk?

The railway station was nearly deserted that night. Baskets of purple and yellow pansies dangled from rusted girders. A red vending machine stood near the central pillar dispensing snacks to anyone with a fifty-pence piece. The metallic bench near the ticket office was free. I crossed the concourse in a dozen strides, un-shouldered my rucksack, sat down and dropped it beside me. I checked my watch. A minute later, I checked it again. To this novice pilgrim the route still seemed impossible: Holland, Germany, Austria . . . and was Bosnia still dangerous?

The train of thought leading to the gates of Jerusalem was also a physical one. In a sudden screech of metal, eight navy-blue coaches snaked along the platform. The doors opened, as doors always must. Then carrying my old world on my back, I took the first of nine million steps, and I went looking for the new.

Chapter One

The Netherlands

The Land of Windmills and Waterways

A 500-pound yak willing to lug my kit through fifteen countries would have indeed been helpful. But if you're striking toward Jerusalem in search of deep spiritual truths you don't normally start in the Himalayas. For someone living in England planting two feet safely on continental Europe is the first hurdle. France of course, stands out as the obvious target. Only 34 km distant at the closest point, it's incredibly easy to reach by train or ferry. Belgium offers another possibility, but a one-way ticket to grey Ostend doesn't exactly light up the imagination. The last option is the waterlogged Netherlands, lying east across the North Sea. This is the one I'd set my heart on. It was here in the spring of 2000 that Dutchwoman Johanna van Fessem had left her home in The Hague and, surrendering to whatever the pilgrim road might bring, started walking to the Holy Land. Figuratively, and in some small part literally, I still wanted to follow in her footsteps. There was never any doubt I would return.

It all kicked off again during the evening of 7 March 2007. Although North Sea trawlermen would probably scoff, it was a

1

rough crossing. There I lay under my quilt on the overnight ferry from Harwich, tossing, turning, staring at the ceiling and willing myself to sleep. All I could picture were tall ships anchored in quiet harbours, bicycles with cow-horn handlebars, clanging trams and Rotterdam's zebra crossings click-click-clicking like a mad woodpecker. Dutch shores were fast approaching, and among the clattering coat hangers and low incessant hum of the ship's engines, I felt far from ready. Reality struck at the ungodly hour of 5:30 a.m. Greenwich Mean Time.

'*Dames en heren, zullen we bij de Hoek van Holland . . .*'

The PA system with its officious female voice finished with a trademark hiss-cum-crackle, then the cabin fell back into merciful silence. Blast! Was it really that early? Casio luminescent green screamed 'Yes!' After setting my watch forward one hour, I lay on the bunk and did precisely nothing. I've never been an early riser. Dawn is for gruff farmers in wellies and rosy-cheeked milkmen clinking bottles of Jersey gold top. Surely another five minutes under this deliciously warm quilt wouldn't hurt . . .

Yawning furiously, I reached up for the light switch. An eerie yellow glow fanned out revealing a box cabin of fake panelled wood. Another yawn later, I flipped back the sheets and swung both feet over the side. When my eyes focused they fell on the painting opposite, an old twin-funnelled coal steamer billowing black smoke and foundering quite spectacularly in rough seas. As an advert for the Stena Line, it wasn't overly reassuring.

The routine of the veteran city commuter swiftly kicked in. Showered and shaved, I hovered by the big forward-facing windows, nervously twiddling Johanna's cross now tied to my left wrist, feeling my stomach flip-flop like an Olympic gymnast and momentarily mesmerised by the sight of foreign wind turbines cutting the air. At seven thirty prompt, 44,000 tonnes of Stena Hollandica spun around on the proverbial sixpence. Docking signalled a mad scramble for the exit—a jumble of rainbow ski-hats, bobbing rucksacks, strategically placed elbows and a forty-three-year-old Englishman with a vicious-looking haircut.

It was bitter outside the terminal. For a few seconds I loitered in the car park snorting steam like an Arthurian dragon. The Hook of Holland was much as I remembered: the same breeze pungent with ozone and carrying the lick of blubbery seaweed. Wind turbines in twos and threes lazily cut the sky. Behind me a long embankment of rounded boulders fingered the flickering white crests of a frigid sea. I looked out at the idle cargo cranes, brown with rust, and the containers piled high in blue, yellow, and a neat stack of L-shaped red. Apart from the wind turbines nothing moved in the greyness. The stillness was pervasive.

In twenty strides I was at the railway station. On a grassy hill a pair of brown goats with Chinaman beards stood grazing. I dropped my rucksack beside the noticeboard, blew into cupped hands, windmilled arms in tepid sun. Slowly fingertips began to tingle. Within minutes the train arrived—a two-coach canary-yellow Sprinter. The door swung out with a cobra's hiss, and I gratefully trudged inside. After last year's 55 km of agony there was no need to walk to Dordrecht again; I'd paid my spiritual dues. Half an hour later, I was left standing alone and shivering on the platform at Dordrecht Stadspolders, the place where I'd begun my return journey to England the previous November.

I lingered briefly, thinking back. With perfect clarity I saw myself hobbling through the cobbled streets of Dordrecht, past the art shops selling oil-painted cows and those expensive pink porcelain figurines. Beyond the Stadspolders shopping centre lay the campsite where a dream had foundered. The memory was like treading on razors, but I let it run, recalling that rainy morning when I limped past drizzle-splattered shoppers and with numb fingers searched frozen pockets for coins to push into the ticket machine now standing just yards away. 'It's about taking one step at a time,' Johanna had told me. I'd spent most of the train journey thinking about her advice. I trusted her still.

And for the most part the woman who'd walked to Jerusalem was spot on. Western Holland in early March is not the most stunning landscape, but if you keep taking small steps it does provide a few moments worthy of the camera. To begin with I struck east towards Gorinchem along the banks of the River Merwede. Dutch skies were a foamy, creamy blue; rivers were obsidian, strewn with orange and russet leaves, and patrolled by quacking brown-billed ducks. Straggly willow trees overhung the banks, casting long tresses into the water like maidens leaning over to wash their hair. One, two, three: I counted them off, trudged on half a mile, then stopped to photograph a feather-edged windmill cutting waves of yellowing grass. Wow! A real windmill! Yep. It's amazing how excited you can get over something so trivial.

As expected, I saw plenty of water. In a land where river levels are watched more eagerly than the national lottery you're never far from a canal or daffodil dyke. Crossing bridges is a way of life. Iron-girder spectaculars carry trains and heavy traffic. Little wooden arches grant access to schools that would otherwise be marooned. Especially vulnerable are the low-lying polders, like the extensive grassland of the Alblasserwaard incorporating the magnificent windmills at Kinderdijk. Dordrecht lies just beyond the polder's southwestern tip, and even a city of 120,000 is just one gigantic island.

The excellent network of cycle paths was also a considerable novelty and a great credit to Dutch planners. Many main roads had paths on *both* sides, something you'd never see in stingy old England where you're lucky to find a single sliver of dandelion-infested tarmac, and even then it fizzles out before taking you anywhere useful. Not so in eco-friendly Holland, where every junction signposts the way forward in distinctive red and white. Just remember those nippy cyclists. I was routinely ambushed by middle-class ladies in stiff skirts and blond schoolchildren of all ages gripping cow-horn handlebars and tringing bells.

In timorous steps my induction to the world of pilgrimage intensified. Getting anywhere fast on foot is impossible, so there's no point trying. With twelve hours of daylight to fill I found myself noticing little things, like birdsong at 4 a.m., the dew on a spider's web splitting rainbows, the earthy scent of squelching moss, shadows behind then shadows in front, and how 'yellow' cannot possibly describe the richness of the buttercup, the sulphurous wings of the Brimstone butterfly fluttering against ivy, or the halo of a dying sun dipping beneath the steel-grey barns of the eastern polders. Every second was itself, every moment its own pleasure.

Humour was often part of that mix. Grappling with foreign languages is always fun and uttering monster words like *ziektekostenverzekeringsmaatschappij* can easily dislocate an untrained jaw. Gripped by strange linguistic urges, I realised that learning a few words of Dutch was probably advisable, learnt the word for 'thank you' and proceeded to startle an array of Albert Heijn checkout girls with my brutish Anglo-Saxon accent. I think I mastered the pronunciation eventually. As for the disgraceful lack of public toilets, all those half-litre bottles of cola had to go somewhere ... Once again, I mastered this vital pilgrim skill, nimbly avoiding nosy dog-walkers and outsprinting Alsatians to the choicest trees. I was in Holland striding boldly to Jerusalem. There seemed to be no end to my new talents.

Sadly, choosing the appropriate kit for the time of year wasn't one of them. That first night on the ground swiftly dispelled any triumphalism. Ye Gods, it was cold. My two-season sleeping bag was virtually useless. I groaned mightily and fired off an accusing email to the saleswoman. My sister stubbornly refused to accept the blame. (She was right—I'd chosen poorly.) On the plus side, at least I woke without the need to dress; I already wore a base layer, a T-shirt, a fleece, two pairs of trousers, all the pants I possessed and a set of waterproofs that would be the envy of any North Sea trawlerman. Only the Sou'wester and sealskin cape were missing. I spent each night shivering a few degrees above death. As a layering system, it's not likely to catch on.

'You're gonna love it out there, mate,' Jack had told me, grinning. Tutored by hard experience I was beginning to think 'love' was a bit strong. After wrestling two pounds of slippery canvas into a tiny stuff sack I regained the road and plodded off to God knows where. I was too numb to worry. It takes a brave soul to rise at 4:30 a.m. and a complete madman to enjoy it. Barely three days had passed. I was still clinging to sanity.

The world seemed a better place in the afternoons. It always does with the sun warming the face. Soon a frozen bench became something to prize. Every time I spotted one I'd collapse for at least fifteen minutes and bask like a lizard. This is how walking should be, I thought (while not actually doing any)—easy, unhurried, blister-less. Well, almost. Every 10 km or so I'd feel the pain and stop for a little roadside surgery. Usually, some frenzied cutting followed by a fresh plaster would suffice. I had no complaints. Last year's blisters had been the size of Vesuvius and equally devastating. In comparison these bumps were mere foothills. The daffodils were out. I was ticking off the towns. This time I would get there.

I trudged on through the weak sunshine and sheeting rain. Never underestimate the morale-boosting power of a fully loaded MP3 player. Soothed by the flutes and horns of Dvorak's *New World Symphony*, I threaded my way past tall lancet windows blessed by Christ and regiments of naked fruit trees waiting the blessing of spring. Thus encouraged, I did gain one small victory. I remember well the joy of reaching one of Johanna's stopping points. My diary captured the moment:

> 2 p.m. Where am I? Dunno, but totally knackered . . . new blister bubbling up, not too painful . . . Why is orange the colour of Holland? So much yellow: buttercups, celandines, grass, cheese, trains, butterflies, sunsets, daffodils . . . made Hardinxveld-Giessendam an hour ago! Incredible!

I put down the pen and paper, and collapsed on a daffodil embankment for lunch. Ten precious toes, frostbite free, wriggled in the sun. I couldn't believe my luck. I'd made it to Hardinxveld-Giessendam—a small achievement, but in those early days it carried the weight of Jerusalem itself. I was an innocent abroad with a mountainous rucksack and a bucketful of hope. I didn't know any better.

Thirty kilometres on, I chanced upon another campsite. It was the usual deal, i.e. muddy and heavily waterlogged. The Dutch are great at building artificial islands off the coast of Dubai, but obviously don't give a damn about walkers with small tents. I gritted chattering teeth and avoided most of the larger rivers. My induction to the arcane world of pilgrimage became complete just after midnight. When you see a guy march off clutching a trowel it's not polite to ask questions. I dug rapidly, trying to ignore the lashing rain. One by one the garments fell.

Waterproofs were tentatively lowered.

Two pairs of trousers came down.

Five pairs of pants were the last lingering line of defence.

At 12:05 a.m. I descended stoically to answer the call of nature. 'Blimey!' I gasped. 'I never expected this!'

* * *

Whilst patiently awaiting those astonishing synchronicities and moments of profound spiritual insight that are surely the right of anyone wielding a muddy trowel at midnight, I spent most of that first week gently easing myself into pilgrim life. If I'd thought squatting over rainy holes was the end of my induction, I was disabused of the idea a day later outside an orange-brick chalet at Dodewaard. A snarling poodle is not something you see every day. Nor is a sausage dog leaping three feet into the air, foaming at the mouth. Before a pilgrim can hang up his boots he is likely to see both. Why? It's an incontrovertible law of nature: dogs and pilgrims just don't get along.

The early evening drizzle had stopped by the time I pushed open the gate. The growling next door hadn't.

Blast that stupid dog! I grimaced and continued to limp up the rose-brick path. I was tired, hungry, damp and nursing another blister. Will . . . you . . . shut . . . UP!

The Alsatian carried on barking as it was no doubt trained to do. I glared at the creaking fence. Without those six feet of featheredge there would have been a murder of some kind. I crept slowly up to the glass door. Homely yellow lamplight seeped through a side curtain. Would these people allow me to camp in their field?

I had high hopes; the adjacent grass was nearly waist high and almost certainly unused. I squinted hard, searching the growing dimness for lurking goats and the menace of hidden cows. Thankfully, none materialised. It looked ideal.

At the door I came to a halt, stomach in knots. A trembling finger hovered over the bell. My opening line seemed ludicrous even to myself: 'Oh yeah, I'm a pilgrim walking six thousand kilometres to Jerusalem, you know how it is . . .' I was about to turn away when the door swung open—but only a foot—and a pair of suspicious eyes appeared in the gap.

'Hello,' I said, 'do you speak English?'

A man's face: glum-looking, greying hair with matching sideburns, silver-rimmed glasses; blue eyes cautious and wary.

'My name is Tony. I'm a Christian from England walking to Jerusalem . . .'

The face blossomed into a puzzled frown.

'. . . I'm sorry to disturb your evening, but I would be grateful if you could let me camp in your field.' I pointed at the patch of grass now shrouded in darkness.

The frown intensified, which in renewed drizzle I struggled to identify as a positive sign. Then, suddenly behind the glass there was movement and the query of a woman's voice. Before I could react, the man's head slipped from view, the door swung outward with a swish—missing my own head by inches—and I found myself smiling nervously at a plump, snowy-haired woman in her sixties, wearing a chunky cream sweater and brown cords.

Right from the start I sensed Heleen was eager to help. Alas, the same couldn't be said of her husband, Frans. There was something of the no-nonsense farmer about this big Dutchman,

8

and that suspicious frown still lingered. While she bent his ear with soothing words, I shifted uneasily on frozen feet. The fight seemed totally lost when suddenly she gave his arm a loving squeeze, turned to me and said, 'You are a Christian walking to Jerusalem?'

I nodded stiffly, wondering how to prove it. I lifted my wrist, revealing the little black-and-white cross Johanna had given me.

Heleen's face broke into a motherly smile. 'Come now—' she said, stepping back, 'come inside. It is very cold.'

Frans moved aside fixing me with an appraising stare. I could sense his uncertainty.

'Come inside,' she repeated. I was still glued to the doorstep. 'You must be hungry. Are you hungry? You are lucky. We have a spare room upstairs. You can sleep there if you wish.'

I limped across the threshold in a daze of euphoria. 'People will invite you in.' Incredibly, Johanna van Fessem had been right.

Frans and Heleen turned out to be generous hosts. You'd think the prodigal son had returned. At seven we took supper in the kitchen, an arm's length from rows of winking chrome spatulas and shelves of thin glossy cookbooks. Frans sat at the table's head in a red checked shirt, back ramrod straight, face impassive and hands clasped in silent prayer. I sat to his right maintaining a respectful silence as Heleen bustled around us. Soon the air swam with the aroma of red-skinned Gouda and freshly ground coffee. Fatted calves were temporarily out of stock, but there would still be plenty to eat.

'Would you like some stew?' she asked.

I certainly would.

'Cheese? Ham? A glass of milk?'

You bet.

'Some coffee, Tony?'

Of course!

For the next hour I sat eating and drinking everything placed before me. Mugs were emptied and politely refilled. The table rang with clinking spoons and the clatter of white china plates.

Heleen, speaking the better English, asked most of the questions. I did my best to oblige.

'It's hard to say exactly, perhaps I walk twenty-five kilometres a day . . . Yes, blisters are always a problem . . . The cross? Oh, that was given to me by Johanna when we met last year . . . No I won't walk back to England, I already have my plane ticket.'

Curiosity satisfied, Heleen tilted her head and shot me another of those motherly glances. But not Frans.

'So,' he said roughly, 'blisters are a big problem for you.'

'Unfortunately, they are.'

'They must be. I saw you limping outside.'

What? Was that scepticism in his voice? Keeping my voice matter of fact, I turned to face him. 'Yeah, I know. There's a huge one on my left foot right now. It's still quite painful.'

He's right, I thought, as his face tensed. Despite the agonies of last November, I still wasn't taking proper care of my feet. I would have to do better. For a few seconds the table fell into awkward silence. Then came the question that had been burning in his breast right from the start.

'And how long have you been a Christian? One day? Two?'

Ahhh, so this is it. Ignoring the obvious insinuation, I placed my cutlery onto the plate and, keeping my voice calm, looked him levelly in the eye. 'About five years or so. Yep, five years sounds about right.'

The big Dutchman's forehead began to crease. 'So, about five years, you say . . .' The words trailed off, and his gaze drifted up as if weighing their truth. He didn't seem very convinced.

After supper we cleared away the dishes and prepared for Bible study. To be brutally honest I hadn't expected this. Heleen smiled and slid a thick leather book across the table. 'We always read something afterwards,' she explained.

I picked it up and started to casually leaf through. The book was a battered English hardback: rich maroon vellum, scratchy gold lettering on the splintered spine; the smell of old paper was unmistakable. We began proceedings with a passage from

Mark. I'd spent the previous night shivering in a soggy field by the railway. I wasn't exactly at my best.

'It's after Matthew!' snapped Frans, flipping his page back and forth.

I know that! While Heleen read in Dutch, I traced my finger across the page in a vain attempt to follow. By the end of the passage I was hopelessly lost. Luckily, neither of them appeared to notice.

Heleen brought her hands together closing her Bible with a thump. With an encouraging smile, she said quietly, 'And now you shall read.'

Err . . . I shall read? Only four days ago I was in England. Now I was sitting around a table in Dodewaard, guzzling big jars of frothy goat's milk and listening to Bible readings in Dutch. It wasn't my normal Sunday evening.

Under the scrutiny of Frans' unremitting stare, I scoured the tiny print for inspiration. Where should I take this? There were so many great passages to choose from, perhaps too many. My mind went frighteningly blank, then suddenly cleared. Thumbing through miles of crinkly pages, I at last found it—St Paul's famous words from 1 Corinthians:

> Love is patient and is kind; love does not envy. Love does not boast, is not proud . . . Love never fails. But where there are prophecies, they will be done away with. Where there are various languages, they will cease. Where there is knowledge, it will end. . . . But now faith, hope, and love remain these three. The greatest of these is love.

Without saying a word, Heleen rose from her chair, went to a drawer, pulled out something thin and paper-like, and returned to the table. Glancing down, I could see the front was embossed with a pair of silver bells, like those on a wedding anniversary card. I was right: it was. I'd chosen the same verse—in fact, *the very same words*—that Heleen had written ten years earlier for her husband. For a moment there was a hush, a pregnant still-ness, everyone sifting and weighing their thoughts.

Frans broke the silence first. He slapped his palms down onto the table and said, 'Now I feel better about us helping you!'

The tension in the air dissipated alongside the spiralling coffee vapour. I was only too eager to echo the sentiment.

Hobbies dominated much of the later chat. Every man has one, so I wasn't surprised. For some of us it's the beautiful game of football and the agony of watching England lose a vital penalty shootout. Others declare a peculiar fondness for trainspotting. Wearing their trademark snorkel anoraks, they stand for hours in the pouring rain outside Clapham Junction, scribbling serial numbers into soggy notebooks. One can only imagine the in-credible pleasure seeing the 8:10 from Waterloo must convey. Or for that matter, the wonderful world of goat breeding . . .

'Yes,' I assured him, 'a superb specimen.' Like a good guest I nodded politely and placed the deluxe copy of *Goat World Inter-national* back on the coffee table. There it joined *The Joy of Goats* and about thirteen others.

Frans finally broke into a smile. Having farmed goats for a living, he knew everything about them. Fifteen books later, so did I. Goats you see, were his hobby.

Never be surprised by anything that happens on pilgrimage: it's a very short walk from 1 Corinthians to *The Joy of Goats*. In the lounge Frans and I sank three inches into enveloping arm-chairs as Heleen shuttled in cups of coffee from the kitchen. I took mine gratefully with trembling hands, desperate not to spill any. Apple pastries quickly followed, flaky and oozing cream. In between these tasty delicacies I jabbed excitedly at giant atlases and flicked through Frans' magnificent goat book collection.

The evening was coming nicely to a close when out of the blue Heleen said, 'Seeing you here reminds me of my past.'

I glanced up. 'Oh, really?'

She peered at me over her cup. I leant forward expectantly searching her face for clues. Even Frans had looked up from his mountainous pile of goat books. Heleen put her cup down on the side table.

'Well, you will understand this is many years ago. It was after the war, and our family were very poor. In those days there was little food, and everyone was hungry. On one occasion I remember a man came to us from Rotterdam. He was travelling around by bicycle, like people did. He needed somewhere to stay. My mother let the man into the house, and I remember he had two bags'—she spread her arms wide—'two big bags, and inside one was a huge loaf of bread. The stranger gave it to my mother for her kindness. My mother, of course, yes, she was very pleased. We all were. We children were always hungry in those days.'

She fixed me with a mysterious smile, and said, 'So this is the reason I decide to help you. As a child I learnt that good things can happen if you help a stranger that knocks on your door.'

I didn't catch on at first. For months I'd been thinking about the deep spiritual insights a pilgrimage might offer. When they hit me in bed around midnight I needed a few moments to work it through. A comparison of the facts seemed startling. The man in Heleen's story had come from Rotterdam; I'd also come from Rotterdam. He'd been a stranger in need; I'd also been a stranger in need. He'd knocked on a door seeking shelter, and despite enormous reservations and a faltering voice, I'd done the same. The similarities were obvious. Yet it was her final sentence that really gripped.

'As a child I learnt that good things can happen if you help a stranger that knocks on your door.'

This was the crucial point. Long ago a traveller had appeared planting a seed in Heleen's young mind. Fifty years later, I'd arrived under similar circumstances, and because of previous events—*and those events alone*—also found acceptance. Consider this, I asked myself: was it really an accident you arrived at the right place at exactly the right time? I fell asleep convinced of the answer. Somehow Heleen's life and my own had been joined to realise this moment. It felt like an incredible synchronicity, and who could have arranged that, except God, the Creator, the Almighty?

I slept well that night but contrary to natural inclination rose early. Heleen's revelation had fired me up. Blisters or not, I was eager to press on towards Nijmegen. Our breakfast was another wonderful spread: more ham, more coffee—the full works. There was no end to their generosity. Frans had also caught the new mood. His initial suspicion had faded. Fun was on his mind.

Heleen opened the fridge door and pulled out a small carton of orange juice. 'Would you like this?' she asked.

I was about to respond when he jumped out of his chair, ran into the adjacent pantry, and re-emerged with a whopping two-litre bottle of lemonade. He brought it level with his shoulder, grinning from ear to ear. 'Would you like *this*?'

Heleen's hands shot to her hips in wifely exasperation. 'Oh, Frans . . .'

Laughing, Frans returned it to the shelf and quickly retook his seat.

'The orange juice would be great,' I told her. She smiled and placed the carton beside the freshly made sandwiches.

'For you everything here is free,' said Frans, tapping the table with his finger. 'Outside you must pay, but here it is free.'

Yes, I thought, he's a changed man. I nodded politely and ate heartily, thanking God for the faith of these good people.

After breakfast we gathered on the porch. I'd been dreading this moment. I'm not good at farewells, and this one was already pushing the emotions high. Heleen was the first to arrive. I let my giant rucksack fall to the ground, then Frans appeared in a blue padded jacket. The air carried the combined chill of early morning and early spring. My own fleece was zipped right up to the chin. He'd chosen well.

'Frans,' I took his hand in mine, 'thank you for everything, for all you've done for me. I really appreciate it.'

A gentle shake of the head. 'Tony, do not thank us—'

'No, I really mean it.'

'There's no need to,' he repeated. His face became thoughtful. 'You have given us a great deal to think about.'

Something in his voice told me we were parting as friends. I was glad. We shook hands quickly, then I turned to Heleen still immaculate in her cream sweater. She took my hand lightly: a woman's grip.

'Thank you, Heleen. I don't know what to say . . .'

Her cheeks flushed. Perhaps it was just the chill in the air. 'Here—' she said, holding out a small parcel neatly wrapped in brown paper.

'Oh, great.' I took the sandwiches from her hand. 'I forgot to pick them up.'

Her face broke into a soft smile. 'Now don't forget,' she said cheerily, 'you can come and visit us anytime.'

I reached down, pulling the rucksack onto my back. At the gate I was still fighting back the emotion. I paused to wave, they waved back, then the gate fell back onto the latch with a click, and I rejoined the road to Nijmegen, and beyond that the frozen fields of Germany. From start to finish the whole experience had been completely unreal.

I trudged on, sweeping past the overgrown field that had led me to their door. The previous evening I'd passed by dozens of possible camping sites, but it was the home of Frans and Heleen I'd been drawn to. Their deep faith, their willingness to help, Heleen's experience as a child—it was just too perfect to be coincidence.

Ask, and it will be given you. Seek, and you will find. Knock, and the door will be opened for you.

Could those famous words from Matthew 7:7 be more warmly honoured? Mighty Germany beckoned.

I went east, itching to find out.

Chapter Two

Germany

The Land of Order

Such were the momentous events of the early twentieth century across Europe that it's a rare person who undertakes their first visit to Germany without reflection. I arrived at the border on 13 March, two days after leaving Frans and Heleen. I immediately found myself mulling everything from Dunkirk to the Battle of Britain. What history couldn't provide, geography was more than happy to. During the spring of 1945 the surrounding forest was part of the Allied Rhineland Campaign, and Canadian units advancing with their British counterparts ran into fierce German resistance. As a result, the trees of the Klever Reichswald hide as many bad memories as they do delightful hiking trails. A few of the more adventurous locals advised me to dive in and start exploring. I decided against. Instead, I stuck to the boring highway, eager to embrace the next bit of civilisation. Somewhere a hotel bed beckoned with fresh crusty rolls served as *Frühstück*. I'd been a fully fledged pilgrim for the massive total of four days. I was still holding on to the familiar comforts.

The crossing was a strangely underwhelming kind of experience. There were no checkpoints. No border guards. No one to leaf through passports and cast penetrating stares. The watery Netherlands merged seamlessly into Western Europe's economic powerhouse like a patch expertly stitched onto a dress. What remained of my Dutch-inspired euphoria carried me to Kleve, a typical German town where church spires rise from immaculate brickwork, plaster Jesus figures stand behind benches, window shutters resemble heraldic shields, and if you look hard enough you can find a medieval castle somewhere.

Accommodation-wise, I chose to hit the hostels first. Having missed out on that spectacular backpacking experience boasted about by gap-year students, I was now on a mission to make up for lost time. Meeting 'amazing people like you from around the world!' was exactly what I needed. That, and a cheap bed. I had my twenty-euro note out even before I pressed the doorbell.

The L-shaped building of the local *Jugendherberge* was all cold glass and annoying silence. I was beginning to think the bell was broken when the door swung open, and a balding head appeared in a beige zip-up cardigan.

'Do you have a card?' he replied, in answer to my polite request for a bed.

I struggled to think. 'You mean, perhaps a credit card?'

'No, no, your membership card.' Grey eyes narrowed. 'Are you a member of the Hostel Association?'

'Actually, I'm not. I didn't know I needed to be. Look, can't you make an exception? It would great if I coul—'

The manager shrugged. 'I'm sorry,' he said, and began to pull on the handle. 'Try one of the hotels. Perhaps they can help.'

The door closed with a deeply unsatisfying clunk, and I was left standing in a gathering blizzard. It was at least five minutes before I could bring myself to walk away.

Reluctantly, I trudged back to the town centre. By the time I arrived, Kleve had become almost Dickensian in the dark. Along shadowed streets iron railings with arrowhead tips zebra-striped the pavement. Yellow lanterns hung from every porch. Hollow owl calls were haunting guttered rooftops, and sleet was in the skies flaking the hair of stick-like figures walking briskly, heads down, coats drawn tight around their necks. I was the eternal outsider looking in at lighted windows and smiling faces. The cheer of others seemed to mock my own misfortune. I was about to march back out into the countryside when I saw a single spire needling the sky. Great! A church!

I'm still not sure what gave me the audacity to step inside. But the stories of other pilgrims—nostalgic tales of sleeping on cold stone floors echoing the suffering of Christ—probably had something to do with it. I at once took reassurance from familiar trappings. The air was fruity with lemon-oil polish. Dust motes danced above the wooden lectern where an opened Bible—a wedge of gold-edged paper—lay winking beneath a dull yellow bulb. Eight wooden benches were the width and length of this diminutive chapel. Black hardboard hymnbooks rested on a shelf running behind the pews. Where should I sit? The rejection at the youth hostel had sapped my confidence. Being an English Protestant in a German Catholic church, I decided to make for the safety of the back.

Slowly, the latecomers began to settle. A curly-haired teenager unwrapped her rainbow scarf, eyes aflame with religious fervour. Four rows back, a grey figure stooped in years and swathed in widow's black gingerly made her away across creaking pews. In between, ten gloved hands pulled at toggled coats and woollen hats. The congregation was small—fiercely loyal, cradle-to-grave Catholics every one. They must have been to brave this dreadful weather. The group sat down. I sat down. Backs ramrod straight, we waited in respectful silence.

We didn't wait long. The German insistence on order and effi-ciency abhors any kind of delay, and religious services, as trains, run like clockwork. At 6 p.m. prompt the Mass began with a reading by the female deacon. For the next hour we rose, we sang, we sat; we repeated the same procedure about ten times. In an astonishing display of bravado I mangled the German hymn like no Englishman before or since. I'm amazed no one noticed. After the final solemn reading, we rose again for the Communion Rite. The singing for the most part had been tepid;

now the throng murmured affably. This is what they had really come for.

Gradually, an orderly queue began to form at the front. One by one these vassals of Rome stood hands-cupped before their priest, a sober giant in white vestments draped at the shoulders in royal purple. I've never been very fond of excessive displays of piety. While deference is pleasing to the Lord, does he really want us to grovel? The third worshipper—a glossy brunette in a white silk blouse—had no such qualms. Indeed, instead of taking the wafer in her hand, as others had done, she sunk dramatically to her knees and gazing upward with rapture began to sway like a dying swan. The priestly brow creased with exasperation. I could almost hear him say it, 'Next!'

For all the devotion on show, there was no loitering at the end. The giant priest left first. Without thanking any of his flock he simply turned and fled down a passage on the far side of the church. Twelve parishioners hurriedly re-buttoned their coats and followed suit. This was the opportunity I'd been waiting for. I picked up my rucksack, stepped into the aisle and dashed to the front.

The deaconess was a dowdy sort: prim lips, beehive of blond-grey hair, heavy pleated shirt. She glanced up from the lectern, a flurry of pink fingernails and darting eyes. I was a Christian on pilgrimage needing somewhere to sleep. If anyone could help me, it was she.

'Excuse me, do you speak English?'

Blue eyes swivelled round, but the fingers carried on working. 'Nein. Was wollen Sie?'

Her tone of voice said it all. Only a few moments ago this woman had been singing hymns and praising God with great fervour, yet when asked for a simple act of kindness showed no interest in anything beyond her candlesticks. Surely those in the service of the church had an obligation to do better?

Two hours later, cosseted in expensive hotel sheets, I was still obsessing. Much as I tried, the parable of the Good Samaritan wouldn't go away. I kept seeing a blond woman with pink finger-nails crossing the road, bypassing the man on the ground. That man was wearing a rucksack. That man was myself.

After another hour oblivion came. It was without doubt the best thing to happen all day. As sleet flecked the windows, I slept uneasily, remembering the words of James the apostle: 'To him therefore who knows the good he ought to do, and does not do it, to him it is a sin.'

Once more I saw the deaconess falter.

And in that far-off land where dreams are made, and quite often broken, there was no one who would come to my aid.

✳ ✳ ✳

Two unexpected rejections in a single day hadn't done much for my belief in the goodness of man, but it didn't lessen my appetite for novelty. A day's march south of Kleve lies one of the most important Marian Shrines in Europe. Each year 800,000 mainly Dutch and German pilgrims arrive in Kevelaer eager to squeeze themselves into a three-foot alcove. Some might consider that a miracle. If it is, it's not the one they come to see.

The true miracle of Kevelaer began in the winter of 1641 on the road to Geldern. Few of us will ever hear the voice of the Blessed Virgin while kneeling by a roadside crucifix. Fewer still on three separate occasions. 'Build a little chapel for me!' cried the purple-heathered moors. On the first occasion Dutch peddler Hendrik Busman was understandably dubious. But the voice was insistent. The third time he collected his tools and obeyed.

Busman's wife, Mechel, held the key to what happened next. One morning the following Easter, she'd awoken to recount a dream to Hendrik. Perhaps he'd taken her hand, enthralled by the white light she'd seen glowing around his humble chapel and an unusual portrait of the Blessed Virgin resting inside. No one can be sure. What is known is that two German soldiers had offered to sell her a similar picture and she'd refused, thinking the price too high. For the God-fearing Busmans, the divine meaning of the dream was clear: acquire the portrait from the soldiers, and place it in the newly built chapel.

So they did.

It was the event that put Kevelaer on the spiritual map of Europe. Pilgrims arrived by the thousand. Then the miraculous healings began. Soon the lame began to walk, the seriously ill became seriously well and souvenir sellers grew seriously rich. A jubilant church built a lot more churches, including a splendid neo-Gothic basilica that dominates the holy square and is itself well worth a visit. Sadly, Busman's original chapel has since been lost to history. In 1654 it was torn down to be replaced by the current hexagonal Chapel of Grace.

Miracle or not, on a wet afternoon in mid-March I was privileged to see the interior myself. Ignoring the benches and two bowed heads on either flank, I focused on the crimson-draped altar and the gilt doors of a cabinet quartered with pastel-pink saints. All that gold begged to be photographed. I un-popped a belt stud and took careful aim. One hurried shot was all I got.

To my left, a muffled cough. I turned to face the sound. It was a glum-looking priest dressed in a black robe.

The shrine is behind,' he whispered, extending a bony finger towards the golden cabinet.

I nodded gravely, not wishing to offend. He replied by holding a finger to his lips; then I skirted the altar, dipped under a wooden arch and slipped awkwardly into the alcove.

The memory still gives me the shivers: a glass panel strung with pearls and amber, and glinting silver rings; a smudgy 7 × 5 inch postcard resting in the centre: the Blessed Virgin wearing a crown of 5 six-pointed stars, clutching a sword and sporting bizarrely long hair under a billowing cloak—it wasn't the most flattering likeness. For several timeless minutes I stood glued to the glass, lost in winking silver, amber and miracle.

Three hundred years.

Eight hundred thousand pilgrims.

All looking at this picture.

The creak of the chapel door broke the spell. I crossed myself and turned to leave. The movement was almost imperceptible. Nah. It can't be.

Our Lady of Kevelaer gazed back, Our Lady was full of Grace, but never once did Our Lady speak.

* * *

'So, do you think I could place my tent here?'

I tapped my rucksack and brought my fingers together to form a triangle shape. He kept shifting back into German. I wasn't sure he understood.

Franz-Otto Smits was a rosy-cheeked beekeeper in blue over-alls tinkering with a brown Volkswagen in the frost-tipped grass of Kerken. Eight hours' march from the miracle of Kevelaer, past electricity pylons humming in the drizzle, had brought me to the crest of a frigid hill. My base layer was literally pasted to my back. I badly needed to camp and dry off.

'Pilgrim, eh?'

He rose, huffing, on one knee, placed one hand on the bonnet and winced slightly as he straightened up. Then, with narrowing eyes, he jabbed a spanner at the cross dangling from my wrist.

I nodded and gave him the warmest smile that five degrees above zero would allow.

He glanced at me thoughtfully. '*Ja, man kann aber . . .*' Snapping his fingers, he walked up beside me, touched me lightly on the arm and said with a wink, '*Kommen Sie mit.*'

We took a hard left toward a clearing. Silver birch trees stood naked, outwardly dead. The beekeepers' hut sprawled beneath, an oblong of crudely cut timbers eyeing the frost-blue sward through two panes of filthy glass. A blistered green bench gathered raindrops beneath the rightmost window. I was beginning to see his intent.

'You can put your tent here on the ground but . . .' He waved his spanner airily at the hut. 'This is *besser*, no?'

I let my eyes roam the cobwebbed windows. It was bound to

be warmer. Compared to the frostbitten ground, I guess it was a little *besser.*

It says something about my mood that day that at first I wasn't overly thankful. An unheated hut without water or a toilet, and teeming with more creepy-crawlies than London Zoo does have a few drawbacks. The inside was in keeping with the exterior: a long table filmed with dust, six spindle-legged chairs shoved against the walls, stale air reeking of damp wood. There was a noticeboard to the right pinned with photos: children holding plastic cups and laughing in orange and pink, cone-shaped party hats—a joyous summer's occasion.

After a quick tour Franz-Otto went outside, and I drew up one of the chairs and began to settle in. While he tinkered with his car, I scribbled notes in my diary, unfurled enormous maps, cursed myself for not buying more food and quietly wondered if I would live to see Cologne. Thirty minutes later, I heard him gun the engine and watched the Volkswagen roll down the slope back to the main road. His return was as unexpected as the basket he placed in my hands.

'Here, for you—' he beamed, kicking open the door with a muddy welly and marching straight toward me.

I looked up with astonishment. He was smiling paternally, like a toy-store Santa. I peered inside: white china plate, knife, four crusty rolls, cheese triangles, beef pâté in foil-wrapped tubs, a big bottle of orange juice and another of still water. Even a red-and-white napkin had been included. There was nothing missing that might prevent the enjoyment of a meal. Not one thing. I stammered a 'thank you' and began placing the items on the table.

But do not forget to be doing good and sharing, for with such sacrifices God is well pleased.

The words of Hebrews 13:16. One moment I was standing in a frozen field with nothing. The next I was the richest man on Earth. I felt more than a little humble.

I rose early the next morning, shivering and stiff with cold, but it was the previous day's feeling that prevailed. The business back at the church with the deaconess had upset me more than I thought, knocked me off my stride. Now something good had happened unexpectedly, and I was glad.

On the table there was still plenty to eat. I opened another cheese triangle, buttered a crusty roll. I decided to leave the rest as I didn't want to appear greedy. Before departing I dropped a note in the basket: *Vielen dank für alles* (thanks for everything). Trying to add more would have been beyond my German and made me look foolish. It would have to be enough.

Trudging on toward Cologne, I saw many crucifixes of wood and stone standing tall and proud in northern fields. Each one always reminded me of Franz-Otto Smits, the Good Samaritan of Kerken. My stay with Frans and Heleen in Holland, the surly deaconess in Kleve and now this . . . at each step other souls were also being tested. It struck me, then, that this great adventure of mine asked as many questions of them, as it did of myself.

And now I saw the truth: right from the start this is how God had wanted it.

* * *

For three weeks I carried these new insights south, ticking off towns and villages like a Roman general bent on conquest. The British love to moan about the weather, and I'm not about to break the tradition. A heavy blizzard between 22 and 23 March forced me inside for a day, and on the cycle paths at least, there were few people to converse with. Those that were seemed programmed like a drawstring toy: 'How far do you walk each day?', 'How heavy is your pack?', 'How will you get home?' and sometimes an incredulous 'Are you trying to break a record?' After a while, the answers came without even trying. When I finally rediscovered the gift of spring, outside the walled town of Vellberg, another 500 km had vanished underfoot. It's amazing what you can achieve if you really try.

I took a simple approach on the map. From the beekeepers' hut I drew a vertical line to Mainz on the Rhine, then a southeasterly one running from Darmstadt through Vellberg, and thence to Munich in southern Bavaria. Cologne and Bonn were the initial targets. The plan looked brilliant on paper: two big cities brimming with history and culture, a decent mattress to sleep on, a basin to wash dirty clothes. The latter is not to be sniffed at (in this case quite literally; everyone needs to wash their underpants eventually). Alas, plans can easily go awry. For a novice pilgrim learning the ropes, the price of these creature comforts only became clear when I tried (and struggled) to leave Cologne. City exits are primarily for cars, not walkers. In these situations an autobahn flyover is definitely worth its weight in gold.

I found a greener Germany beyond the suburbs. Despite heavy industrialisation, 30 per cent of this substantial country is still carpeted with some of the finest forests in Europe, and they're great for getting lost in. The Heiderhof was the first to test the compass. A dark and hilly country, it's ideal for wild boar, closet masochists and anything else fond of walking in huge concentric circles. All the trails are marked by coloured shapes, a fact that hardly helps when they fizzle out—which is all too often. If you can't tell a red triangle from a yellow square from a black blobby harp, you'll be wishing you could, and the colour blind will be doomed right from the start. Cursing is futile. Screams for help will only startle the woodpeckers.

Once back in civilisation I found much to praise. Organisation, order and efficiency are the German virtues. I found them all in abundance. Youth hostels are methodically swabbed down with antiseptic. Church bells ring on the hour *every* hour. Shops are famous for closing promptly on Saturday afternoon (a fact that left me hungry more than once). Most villages have information boards leading you to the town hall, and park hedges are always neatly clipped. Graffiti is disturbingly absent, as is litter. Even the nation's frogs are expertly woven into the national plan. Halfway to Limburg I encountered a crew of woolly jumpered eco-types laying down miles of roadside netting. 'It gives us a terrible pain to see them squashed,' declared a bearded bloke on the verge of tears.

Uniting the landscape was the rich Christian heritage. I never seemed far from a field-side crucifix, a mass-produced plaster Jesus, a church or a calvary like the one at hilly Hesselbach. On a rare sunny day I clambered past fourteen stone Stations of the Cross, rewarded at the top by a hexagonal sandstone chapel. Inside were rows of red candles and on wall-mounted marble the Wallmanns, Webers and Weidmanns chiselled in neat black lettering among the names of fallen soldiers. As expected, the whitewash was impeccably clean, the wooden pews polished. In all these kinds of places I lit votive candles, dropped coins into donation boxes. It might have been naked self-interest, but I got into the habit of crossing myself before every church.

Then, at the end of March while closing in on Limburg, once again I left the road and what had been threatening to happen, finally did.

I got lost. Big time.

To be honest, it wasn't difficult. Never enter a German forest without three weeks' rations, a Bear Grylls survival guide, an air ambulance on call at a moment's notice and a personal hotline to God. It's fatal. When the trees broke into clear sky, I spotted a group of cottages and an old guy in blue jeans, leaning on a gate and chewing a piece of straw. Frustration had been building for hours. I almost ran to the spot.

Kornelius Moll was there to shake my hand that day. He was a friendly sort with a caterpillar moustache sitting above an anvil jaw. I gave him my implausible story. He gave me part of his. Before retirement he'd managed large teams of men who did macho stuff with big tractors in Africa. I never did find out what.

'*Ja, ja,*' said the craggy-faced Moll, still lounging on the gate. 'What you are doing is tough. I like that.' Kornelius, I quickly discovered, admired tough guys.

'Yeah, well. There's still a long to go way.' Cheeks burning,

I glanced down absentmindedly at the map. I was still hopelessly lost, which isn't very cool for a tough guy. Just where, I asked myself, was the road to Görgeshausen?

After the initial buzz the conversation fell into one of those awkward lulls. I thought about pushing off, but I badly needed those directions. I hovered by the gate, hoping he was going to oblige. He did.

'Come inside, and then we walk together.'

Just not in the manner expected.

I raised both eyebrows almost to the hairline. 'Are you sure? I don't want to put you out.'

'No problem,' he said, grinning, and sweeping my astonished face through the gate. 'I walk to Limburg many times.'

He was seventy, slippered and probably had better things to do in his potting shed. Don't you believe it. Nothing could stop him. Five minutes later, he was reaching for his cowboy hat and walking boots.

It was a splendid day to clown about in the forest: warm sunshine yet refreshingly cool on the brow, crispy golden leaf litter flecked with crimson, woodpeckers knocking on hollow boughs. Speckled Wood butterflies, flashing polka-dot brown and ochre, bravely defended every leaf, chasing us away. And the air ... forest air will always beat city smog. There's no contest. I inflated my lungs like a pair of bellows and instantly felt a zillion times better.

We were an odd couple. Kornelius led the way in his massive Stetson, marching strongly with unnatural vigour for one so ancient, sucking in air like a turbo-charged Hoover. I slithered along behind, gasping, panting, grabbing at treacherous Germanic vines, every muddy inch of the forest seemingly clinging to my boots (but not his, I noted with annoyance). Every so often we'd stop, and he'd frown anxiously at the trees. I'd wait patiently, look hopefully at that chiselled jaw and then we'd spin ninety degrees and disappear down another soggy, rutted track.

He was a fund of unlikely stories. I don't know what the hell he was doing with those tractors in Africa, but it involved men doing mad things with ferocious animals and quite a lot that sounded impossible. I listened dutifully to his ramblings.

'*Ja, ja,* that guy from Zimbabwe was really tough. What was his name again?' There was a wheezy pause for the name that never arrived then, without turning around, 'I watched him wrestle a thirty-foot crocodile, open his jaws and pull a beer bottle clean out. Dammit. He was the toughest guy I ever knew.'

I grunted politely, trying to picture something that was clearly insane. A sudden muddy slope did nothing to stop the flow.

'*Ja, ja, ja,* the South Africans, now . . . *they* are the tough guys. I knew a man once,' he wheezed, 'South African, you know. In twenty-four hours he drove three thousand kilometres in a jeep. Boy,' said Kornelius, shaking his head in disbelief, 'he was a tough guy.'

Another tall tale. I did the arithmetic and quickly realised that was impossible. Even for a South African. Even for a really, really tough one.

'He–must–have–been,' I gasped, pulling hopefully on a slippery vine. Diplomacy is a useful skill. It's not helpful to contradict your guide, especially where he's nearly as lost as you are.

Red-faced and breathless, I staggered defiantly on. In the mind of Kornelius I was the ultimate toughie, an unholy trinity of Schwarzenegger, Vin Diesel and the whirling fists of an ageing Steven Seagal. He was undertaking a 20 km round trip to help me. I couldn't disappoint. By the time the forest broke we were both caked in mud.

'Kornelius . . .' I croaked. I wriggled out of my rucksack and collapsed feebly by the kerb. My boots had morphed into a pair of twiggy bird's nests. The tough guy was totally spent.

Kornelius spun round. He dropped to his haunches and shook my shoulder. 'What's the matter? Are you hurt?'

I shook my head and smiled wanly. 'I need a few seconds, just let me catch my breath.'

He grinned; we were still friends. For a few minutes I sat in a heap, scraping forest gunk off my boots, wondering if we were anywhere near Görgeshausen and grumpily gulping air.

When I finally rose Kornelius was pointing at a three-storey pillar of glass. 'Would you like to eat?' he asked.

We'd just trudged our way through 10 km of the foulest mud in northern Germany. I was ready to devour anything, even a charging boar.

We cleaned up as best we could, then climbed the winding stairs. The restaurant was at the top: brown leatherette seating, panoramic views of endless arrowhead trees, a steamy kitchen plus regiment of red-faced cooks in white smocks. A four-piece band in black tuxedos was strumming and drumming something waltzy for the ballroom crowd. A sour-faced waitress gave me a frosty look and ordered me to leave my rucksack by the table. I didn't waste time arguing.

Food was the top priority. Kornelius handed me a plate of vegetables and meatballs swimming in gravy. We crossed to the window, leaving the minimum of muddy footprints. The dance floor began to sway with silver-haired couples joined at the hip, spinning like tops. Not all these respectable retirees appreciated our dishevelled company. He didn't care and nor did I. What else could we do? We smiled. We ate heartily.

We decided to tough it out.

* * *

From Kornelius' muddy boots it took a further two weeks to complete my 500 km march to Vellberg. Even though the seasons were starting to turn for the better, like a true Briton that didn't stop me complaining. As I left the state of Hesse behind clammy March ticked over into sunny April, then Baden-Württemberg approached, swelling green on the hills and dotted with stone crosses. In the villages that necklace the Odenwald forest, oak-beamed *Gasthäuser* were waiting to tempt me with soft beds and freshly baked crusty rolls. I wilted badly in the warm afternoon sun and often gave in to temptation.

Moans apart, I think I had good reason. The first week of April was hot and the second scorching. Almost overnight the temperature rocketed ten degrees. The heat was so intense even the campsite owners were bitching. 'Our shop is just not ready yet!' complained one, jabbing at empty shelves. For weeks I'd had the cycle paths to myself; now I had to compete for leg space. They were a mixed bunch: cyclists gyrating uphill in rainbow spandex; well-to-do women in navy tracksuits, twittering like birds and swinging trekking poles briskly down gravelled lanes; golden Labradors, tongues out and panting, trotting beside their owners with well-drilled efficiency.

Spring accompanied this glorious heatwave. At last! I thought. This is the Germany I'd come to see! Buds opened tentatively. Pink blossom appeared on cherry trees. Grass seemed two tones greener. I started to see pale legs in shorts (the surest sign of all). Then along came Easter. Gold-foiled chocolate bunnies began to fill village shops. In the greenery above Mudau's fountain I spotted looping coils of red-and-yellow plastic eggs. The Easter theme continued in Osterburken. Slumped on a bench, I watched a procession of rosy-cheeked kids march single-file around the town. The solemn leader—a pony-tailed girl with freckles—held a wooden cross and couldn't have been older than ten. I wasn't the only one taking a rest.

'Giss a drink,' wheezed the drunk in his best slurred German.

I've never inhaled 100-proof carbon dioxide before. I recoiled from the fumes, the three-week facial bristle, the dirty grey mac, the empty bottle of Smirnoff. A match here would have meant certain death—for both of us. I rose giddily, trying to clear my lungs of vaporised vodka. I still felt dizzy an hour later.

Once sober again, I resumed my assault on the Odenwald—the great forest knitting Baden-Württemberg, southern Hesse and Bavaria into a giant wall of trees. It's splendid hiking country. Timber watchtowers rise above fields shifting with mist. Grey squirrels scamper up mossy boughs, peer down at waist-high ferns, lost pilgrims and caterpillars wriggling in silken webs. Fir trees run for miles, arrowheading the sky. I was following a trail of blobby red circles that afternoon. They soon vanished.

'Excuse me,' I asked them, 'do you know the way to Vellberg?'

A pair of silver-haired ramblers in padded jackets burst into excited German, looked at me as if I was mentally deficient, then ordered me to follow the red circles.

Marvellous.

In the end, I followed the jagged bank of the River Bühler, tiptoeing across slime-green stones, dipping under overhanging branches keen to pop my eyes out, following a muddy trail that carried the footprints of others, so surely must lead somewhere. It did: a huge deserted car park. The day was going pear-shaped when another muddy rambler emerged from the thickets. God bless that man. Minutes later, I was standing under Vellberg's clock tower fighting teenage rollerbladers for a strawberry cone.

And I'm glad I did. Any walled town where circular towers pirouette up the corners has got to be worth exploring. Among the ivy-covered ramparts crumbling steps spiral down to grassy walkways, and if you're brave enough to follow you'll either find impressive forests of silver birch or absolute terror—they're not a great place to have a panic attack. The inner courtyard is much the safer. Orange Koi carp sleepily circle the pond. Gargoyle faces dribble water. Medieval timber houses abound. I'd seen dozens of these *fachwerk* houses before in Montabaur and Michelstadt. Charming assemblies of X-, V-, and W-shaped beams with grey shutters and lots of claret paint, their preservation is exceptional. This is German order at its finest. One hundred years from now I know they'll still be the same.

I spent that night in one of the hotels. It was an easy decision. Rough camping was becoming a chore, and after several nights on rock-hard ground, you long for a shower, a firm mattress, the smell of coffee . . . anything to make you feel human. Vellberg fitted the bill. When I woke the next morning it was to the sound of muffled cries below the window. Crikey, I thought, tourists with dripping cones are already on the battlements.

With no chance of a lie-in, I quickly dressed and went looking for breakfast. Half an hour passed. Then the waiter sauntered in: white smock above pleated trousers, crumpled hair, a newspaper folded under the arm. He was clutching a brown paper bag full of rolls and had eyes like bloodshot eggs. I could almost smell the hangover. He was completely subdued until I mentioned my itinerary.

'You are travelling through Bosnia Herzegovina?'

'Yeah, that's the plan. Get there around June, then work my way down the Balkans. I've already been walking for a month.'

Inhaling deeply, the waiter lifted his head and as it dropped let out a long languid breath.

'Hmm, for you I think it will be okay. Just be careful in Bosnia. There is still bad feeling due to the war and sometimes people are taken into the forest. Such people are never seen again.'

Nice. Thanks for telling me . . . I unfolded a map of the area and stabbed a few places to see what he'd say.

'What about Albania?'

'All robbers and thieves.'

'And Croatia?'

'Houses there are very simple. Family upstairs. Animals below. I grew up somewhere like that, and it wasn't nice.' He ran a hand through his hair and looked down glumly. It sounded like a shitty childhood; I decided not to press it. He brightened considerably when I mentioned Ellwangen.

'When you get there try the old pilgrim monastery, they may help you, but'—and at this point he became emphatic—'ask directions first otherwise you might waste time going to the castle, which is on the opposite hill.'

I smiled pleasantly, and then his eyes began to shine as if he'd suddenly remembered something. 'Okay,' I said, 'I'll do that. I've never stayed in a working monastery before, should be good.'

'Do you like wine?'

'Sure . . .'

He quickly returned to the table, cradling a large dark-green bottle. Although some of his advice sounded like prejudice, you don't look a gift horse in the mouth. Heck, what did I know about the Balkans anyway? The bottle was a monster, far too heavy to carry. On the other hand, it *was* wine. I gave in without a struggle. Six days later, I was still sipping the dregs.

After breakfast I cracked on, fuelled by two mugs of coffee and some doorstep ham sandwiches (another gift from the waiter; he was a generous sort, if nothing else). I made Ellwangen just before dusk. He was right about the church-cum-monastery.

'Of course you may stay!' exclaimed the voice.

But wrong about the help.

'That will be thirty-five euros, bitte!'

The Pilgrim Church of Schönenberg wasn't in the business of taking in guests. The grandiose hotel opposite did nothing else. Reluctantly, I paid up.

As I plodded upstairs I couldn't help feeling let down. I'd expected to see monks in flowing robes wandering silently through cloisters, deep in contemplation. Instead, I found a pimpled teen chewing on a pencil. Oh, well. At least the disappointment didn't last long. After several generous cupfuls of medium red, I was dancing with Jesus, Mary and the Saints in the Milky Way. Hell, even John Lennon was there, and I thought he was dead.

'Glad you could make it!' said the winking Lennon.

* * *

I gawped. Heights always make me dizzy, but I'd felt safe climbing the creaky stairs. The final room was hexagonal and dusty, box windows in every direction, a lone table with long bevelled legs in the corner. We reached the top breathless. The tower of St Blasius was higher than I thought.

'Great view,' said the boy behind me with a tinge of pride.

'Fantastic.'

I peered out through the cobwebbed glass. I was an eagle soaring over red-tiled roofs and miles of looping telephone wire. Bopfingen looked tiny.

'In old times this tower was used to spot advancing soldiers.'

'Yeah, I can see why.'

'Would you like to sign our guest book?'

I turned to face the voice. My guide was the priest's son, a curly-haired teenager in jeans. We'd begun our tour downstairs ('. . . and this section of the altar is by the artist Friedrich Herlin . . .'). His knowledge was impressive. Something told me he'd done this before.

'Sure. Do you have a pen?'

'There should be one there.'

I crossed to the table and lifted up the book, a black hardback shaped like an accountant's ledger. He was right; the biro was underneath. I flipped back the cover and started to leaf through the entries. Gothic German. Some scrawling Dutch. Nearly all were unintelligible. I grabbed the pen and began to scribble:

Anthony de Lyon, a pilgrim walking from the Netherlands to Jerusalem, wishes to thank the priest of St Blasius and his family for their kindness and generosity.

I added the date as a footnote: 11 April 2007. It was the day after my stay at Ellwangen.

At eight we gathered for dinner. Despite improving navigation skills, I was the last to find the dining room; the parsonage seemed bigger on the inside, much like Doctor Who's TARDIS without the threat of imminent Dalek attack. Our table was a polished mahogany beauty that went on forever. A piano stood to the right, lid closed, awaiting someone with the skill to play.

We were six in total. At the head sat the priest of St Blasius: chrome glasses, navy sweater—a man in his forties greying at the temples. Bernhard's wife, Andrea, sat beside him, auburn-haired to the shoulder, smiling in an orange-and-white banded cardigan. Three pink-faced kids shamelessly ogled the mysterious guest. At the front door I'd hesitated, fearing another Kleve brush-off. I was glad I'd found the courage to knock.

'Nina cooked the spaghetti,' said Andrea proudly, tilting her head toward her daughter.

All eyes focused on the young cook, who slipped a little lower in her chair.

I smiled at her. 'They're good, Nina, really good.' I was twirling my fork with gusto. I hardly ever eat Italian and struggled to keep up. In between the clatter of plates, I explained the who, what, where and 'how far' of my pilgrimage.

Nina gasped. 'Have you really walked from Holland?'

'Yes,' I replied; but in answer to the obvious question, 'I'm not walking back!'

From here it seemed natural to discuss issues of faith. Bernhard spoke about their annual pilgrimage to the summit of the Ipf (a table mountain north of the town). I rattled on about my hopes and dreams. We established that I was Protestant, Bernhard was Lutheran and there wasn't much difference between them. While familiar with some of the saints, I'd never heard of St Blasius. Just who was he?

'Well, it is believed,' said Bernhard, 'that the monks of Cluny brought his story to Bopfingen. Of course, that was long ago. You should know that here in Germany his name is associated with many miracles.'

'Interesting, I've always been fascinated by miracles.'

'So,' and shifting in his seat he turned to me, 'you would like to hear about the miracles?'

'Sure, I would like to hear it all.'

'Then you shall.' With elbows on the table and hands clasped together, he continued smoothly, 'It is said that St Blasius once saved a small boy who was choking on a fishbone. That was the first miracle. The second was that he could talk to animals, and on one occasion he told a wolf to release a pig. His third miracle, however, was the greatest.'

I stopped wrestling with my slippery spaghetti and looked up. 'And what was that?'

'He was seen walking on water like Jesus.'

'Really? That's amazing!'

Bernhard nodded gently.

'So what became of him? I mean, how did he die?'

Crikey, that sounded a bit morbid!

Luckily, Bernhard took it in good humour. 'The governor of Cappadocia ordered St Blasius to be tortured, and he was killed because he would not renounce his faith.'

Saints. Yeah, they invariably come to a sticky end.

After dinner the mood became considerably lighter. Talk was of ice cream, snow-choked Austrian passes and, to my surprise, steam-driven traction engines. Bernhard sauntered over, and we both peered into the glass case. There were dozens of them, miniature models with green funnels and red-and-black spoked wheels. They reminded me of all those Airfix kits I'd thrown together as a child. You can have a lot of fun with two hundred bits of plastic that never quite fit together.

'So,' I said breezily, 'you are a fan of traction engines?' I'm an expert at stating the obvious. His face exploded like a firework. He was besotted. 'You have a lot of models. Where do you get them from?'

Bernhard smiled, sensing interest. 'Oh, mostly through magazines, including some from England. In fact, there might be one here somewhere . . .' He dropped to his knees, rummaged around in a cupboard, then rose and handed me a copy.

I began to leaf through. Funnels. More wheels. More funnels. 'Is this one really worth twenty thousand euros?' I tapped the page under a black funnel ringed with brass.

Bernhard lifted his glasses and peered down at my finger. 'Yes, I think . . . yes, I would say so.'

'But it's tiny!' I said, as they fell back on the bridge of his nose.

'It is small,' he agreed, 'but a fully working replica.'

'Hmm. Let me find another.'

At that moment, Nina quietly closed the piano lid. She crept up behind her father and gave his shoulders a teasing squeeze. 'Papa loves his traction engines more than the church!'

Bernhard reddened and turned to face his daughter. 'Now, that's not true!'

With our lips still chilled by ice cream, it wasn't long before we turned to geography and the considerable obstacle of the Alps. Great. The Alps—now there's a prospect to blanch the face of any walker. Peak after peak of rock, snow and ice. Legs turning to jelly. Mountaineers with forbidding stares and impressive beard stubble reduced to snivelling wretches. I'd never been to Austria before. All I could think of was snow, and lots of it.

'I'm sure it will be fine,' said Andrea. She pulled out the chair in front of the computer desk. 'Let's take a look at the webcams.'

For the next hour we huddled around the screen, switching between grainy images that took an age to load. I stared intently, examining every pixel for specks of snow. After five minutes I was already imagining the worst: me suffocating under an avalanche, me freezing to death in my two-season sleeping bag, me striding manfully up craggy peaks in the famous *lederhosen*. The latter vision was particularly disturbing; knobbly knees never look good in shorts.

Eventually, we returned to the dining table for a final check of the map. Andrea spoke first.

'Tony, I know you are thinking of going through Austria, but have you considered the Brenner Pass?'

'The Brenner?' I looked up. 'Doesn't that lead into Italy?'

'Yes, but the pass is clear right now. We believe it could be better for you. Don't we?' She glanced at Bernhard, who nodded affably. They both seemed pretty keen on the idea.

I stared at the map, unconvinced. I'd always planned to enter Austria at Salzburg. Did I really want to tackle Italy as well?

In the morning I marched on to Mönchsdeggingen clutching another bag of sandwiches. A new feeling had joined the familiar gratitude, and it wasn't a pleasant one. For the first time on my journey I was overcome by a horrible creeping guilt. Just why *did* I deserve support? After all, I had plenty of money. There were several hotels in Bopfingen. This early in the season I could easily have acquired a room. I didn't need to knock on church doors. I didn't need anyone.

I had to wait almost until Bavaria and a fragrant meadow of shifting grass before I found the beginnings of an answer. Perhaps the reason lay elsewhere: in the multitude of ways people were responding to my journey, in a synchronistic event that might damn a life or save one, in the book some were urging me to write. Perhaps, in the years ahead, a stranger at their own private crossroads might read that book, and on walking their fingers across the pages think: 'Yes, I'd like to do that. I want to see what you have seen.'

Who knows? Perhaps someday someone shall.

It took two weeks to reach the Austrian border. Thanks to the vagaries of geography I'd saved the best till last, for the state of Bavaria lay in between, big, brash, beer crazy and—in the eyes of the free-thinking locals at least—supremely different. If you're unconvinced by a quaint fondness for twelve-foot alpenhorns, the dubious fashion merits of *lederhosen* and a distinctive white sausage that by tradition must always be consumed before noon, try the murky world of politics. The state parliament never ratified the 1949 West German Constitution, nor did the last king—Ludwig III—ever formally abdicate. The popular saying goes thus: 'Bavaria is not part of Germany, it's near it.'

They have a point. More brass-cowbells-and-Alpine-meadow than fuming Rhineland, the commanding landscape proclaims Bavarian otherness. When the first mountains appeared they arrived suddenly, powder white and snarling at fleeing clouds. The one-hundred-foot firs riding their skirts were mere feathers. I must have been overwhelmed by the romance of the moment. Everywhere, timbered rooftops seemed to be fluttering on the rise, swooping like the wings of an eagle caught on the downward beat. Forty years earlier the opening scenes from *The Sound of Music* were shot beneath these snowy mounts. As

I strode through the buttercups, with piebald horses grazing quietly on the lawns, I could well see why.

One by one the villages fell. Mönchsdeggingen: painfully hilly to the south, with an old dust-and-gilt *Klosterkirche* buzzing with pink plaster cherubs. Eggelstetten: a campsite of bowling-green turf ruthlessly trimmed with German efficiency. Then came the outskirts of Biberbach, where dainty fritillary butterflies danced among boughs purple with violets. It was around here I joined the *Jakobs Pilgerweg*—the road to Spain and the pilgrim Cathedral of Santiago de Compostela. For a few brief kilometres I tracked the famous cockleshell signs. Thousands had already done the same, plodding west with sticks and rucksacks, and questions for the Divine. I felt both their kinship and disappointment when I finally turned away.

I did little in Augsburg, other than sidestep clanging trams. Drugged by the heat, I bought a map of Austria then, chased by wasps, retreated to a campsite where I mistakenly pitched in the area reserved for display tents. Unsurprisingly, there were some interesting moments when prospective buyers peered in and found me staring back, semi-naked, clutching a Jaffa Cake. Yes, it's a disturbing picture ... Somewhere in all this craziness I stumbled onto the so-called Romantic Road—the tourist honeypot that knits vineyards, labyrinthine forests, Wagnerian castles and walled towns with a three-star hotel and trilling cash register waiting at the end. I might have enjoyed the journey more without those chugging tractors. The stench of pig slurry in a high crosswind rarely puts me in the loving mood.

I made Munich on 19 April, scarcely believing it. The line on the map I'd followed since Darmstadt had at last petered out, and Austria was only a week's walk away. To celebrate I marched straight to the nearest hostel, hoping for a blood-pumping hot shower. On posters grinning backpackers lifted frothy tankards, urging me to 'Feel the vibe!'

'Just the one night, please,' I said to the receptionist.

'Oh, sorry!' she gushed, grinning broadly. I felt my face crash.

The wretched woman could at least stop smiling. 'It's a new rule', she said. 'No one over thirty allowed!'

Three chunky Australians in orange-hooped rugby shirts and floral shorts sat sniggering in armchairs. I was thirteen years too late to feel anything except embarrassment, and certainly not 'the vibe'—whatever that might be. With a wounded sniff, I grabbed my passport and spent my last 20 euros in the adjacent hostel.

There was only one further incident of note that evening. It's a dramatic moment when you shove your Visa card into an ATM and nothing happens. The second time it's deeply worrying, and the third may lead to a vigorous outburst incompatible with the teachings of Christ. When I'd run out of curses I took a deep breath and rang my bank. After ten layers of menu, Mr Singh in Bangalore politely explained that I'd entered the wrong PIN number three times, and he'd very helpfully frozen the account: 'To protect, sir, your very, very good interest.' Oh, and would I like to purchase some house insurance? I was standing hungry and penniless in Munich. It wasn't top priority.

The Bavarian capital is a gigantic city. It took ten hours to escape the interminably long Münchner Strasse and find a pitch among the spongy moss and towering firs that edge Oberpframmern. A new goose-feather sleeping bag made the night almost bearable, and for once I no longer woke wearing every item of clothing. Four days later, with Cyndi Lauper blasting encouragement in my ears, I limped toward the outskirts of Austrian Salzburg. Although I'd arrived in Germany far too early in the year to witness the country's natural beauty, I had many fond memories. My only regret is that I didn't stay longer in Augsburg, or indeed Munich. There surely would have been much to see.

I must have been 5 km from the border when the last MP3 battery ran out. My left knee had begun to seize up like a rusty bolt, but it hardly registered. On the bank of the River Salzach I found my lips unexpectedly curling around the old Bunyan hymn. Wow! Where had that come from? It's amazing what you can dredge up from your schooldays.

I started tentatively. *Then fan-cies fly a-way.* Fifty paces to the bridge. *He'll fear not what men say.* Stop to tie a shoelace. *He'll la-bour ni-ight a-nd day.* Halfway across I suddenly found my voice:

'*To—bee—aaaa—piiiiil—griiiiiim . . .*'

Crikey, I thought, I've just walked to Austria.

It wasn't a bad way to leave country number two.

Chapter Three

Austria

The Land of Mozart and Mountains

If you've ever visited a country with preconceived ideas (and let's face it, who hasn't?), you're by no means alone. Although the popular *Lonely Planet* guides have revolutionised our knowledge of travel, there's still a few of us clinging to outdated national stereotypes. On the day I walked into Republik Österreich I had them all lined up like ducks. What could Austria be, other than a land reverberating with sounds of music, where tight leather shorts are worn without embarrassment and every second girl is called Heidi? Oh, and what was the name of that ultra clever composer fellow? I think it began with M . . .

By the final week of April I'd spent seven weeks walking to Mozart's birthplace. Having arrived there, my first instinct was to immediately leave Salzburg. It seemed like a good idea at the time. I've got no idea what the Austrian statutes say, but it must surely be a crime against nature to do anything other than camp in the magnificent countryside. As I limped off toward another wigwam on the map, I was already embracing the vision: snow-capped peaks, Alpine meadows dotted with buttercups, cuddly cows with clinking neckbells nibbling impossibly green grass. 'Crikey,' I huffed, 'this is going to be fantastic.' Perhaps there really would be a girl called Heidi, a blond, blue-eyed maiden with plaited hair and aproned dress, shouldering sloshing milk buckets. I was still living the fantasy at the traffic-choked round-about: *Campingplatz 18 km.* Umm. No such luck.

I spent a good hour walking back. Lost in a maze of tall thin townhouses, I did what anyone would do after a wasted journey. I swore heartily, begged divine forgiveness, found a crumpled twenty-euro note and blagged my way into the nearest hostel.

It could have been worse. The first choice of those on a fag-end budget, hostels have always been brilliant fun. Half the world can be found swapping tall stories in these places, and the stereo-types usually apply. Brash, shouty Americans. Rugby-obsessed Australians. The excitable French. The most exotic specimen will be lurking morosely on the topmost bunk—a skeletal ex-Soviet émigré in a flak jacket from somewhere radioactive ending in –stan. The resultant gathering often resembles a mini United Nations, minus the self-righteous speeches.

Naturally, the fun doesn't end with the nervous handshakes. Since the time of Adam the female form has played havoc with the male fig leaf. In mixed dorms it's not that easy getting ready for bed without revealing too much flesh or, for that matter, *seeing* too much. I can only guess at the number of pink-faced Christians who've foundered while slipping into their pyjamas. Throw in the menace of deadly foot odour, unmedicated snoring disorders and the selfish guy that always bags the only radiator for drying his towel, and you have that 'unforgettable' experi-ence backpackers like to brag about. As I trotted into the hostel lobby, this Christian was getting ready to brag big time.

For once I was glad of the disappointment. I've stayed in some awful hostels, but the YOHO wasn't one of them. With its four matronly bunks and gleaming taps the dorm would have graced any private hospital. Seeing the room was empty, I kicked off my boots, showered lazily, then grabbed my diary and slumped on a bunk, scribbling notes. I'd just unpeeled a banana when the door swung open, and a short guy with lank hair and pallid, pockmarked cheeks sauntered in.

What the hell is that guy carrying on his back? He had the tiniest rucksack I'd ever seen. For that reason alone he deserved to die.

'Is this one taken?' asked the sullen newcomer, pointing at the nearest bunk.

'Nope.' I'd been watching him with curiosity. Backpackers are notoriously territorial animals.

He nodded without speaking, mind clearly elsewhere. While he began to unpack, I munched quietly on the remainder of my banana. When I looked up again, his bed was strewn with neatly rolled socks and from that tiny rucksack he was pulling out an enormous blue towel, like a rabbit from a magician's hat.

'I need a shower,' he muttered to no one in particular, and with towel in hand ducked into the bathroom. Thus, on the fifty-second day of my pilgrimage, did I meet Magnus, twenty-three, from the concrete suburbs of Helsinki.

Hostels have many advantages, but choosing your roommates isn't one of them. Magnus was by far the most depressing individual I'd ever met. We only spent a few hours together, and by the end I was staring deep into the abyss. Every word he uttered was shrouded in gloom. In the dark world of Magnus there were only endless snow-driven wastelands, cold graffiti-ridden tower blocks, stupid professors who ignored his brilliance (he fancied himself as an academic) and Helga, that beautiful blond girl who slipped through his fingers at eighteen to marry his best friend. I guess with a life that rotten you're entitled to be pessimistic.

Nevertheless, hostel tradition still required the courtesies be observed. After he'd bagged the only radiator with that humongous towel, the inevitable took place. We rose sheepishly from our respective bunks, shook hands, exchanged email addresses and promised to stay in touch. If I remember rightly, he had a degree in Medieval Viking Poetry or something equally obscure. When the chat hit a lull I decided to open up. What did Magnus think about a pilgrimage to Jerusalem?

'I'm not sure that's a good idea.'

And my route through the Balkans?

'Have you considered the danger . . .'

The length of my journey?

He raised an eyebrow. 'Won't you run out of money?'

Fifteen minutes later, I'd sunk into a pit of depression I never knew existed. Stiff leg or not, I had to get some air.

It was a brilliant day to be in Salzburg. Gauze cloud filtered golden sunshine; the air carried the freshness of snow-blown peaks. I walked on past haughty townhouses: sky blue, frosted peach, milky lemon and rosy pink—a rainbow encasing Georgian glass. For those new to the city, the Getreidegasse is the place to be. In narrow side streets wrought-iron cockerels hang above doorways. Hands pick through glossy postcards. Then nostrils twitch and catch the scent. Every second shop is a confectioner's Mozart shrine, all pink ribbons and red bows like a Valentine's display gone mad. Praline and marzipan *Mozartkugeln* crowd the windows in their distinctive violin-shaped boxes. Twelve pieces cost about 16 euros. They make a delicious treat.

On curling avenues I dodged horse-drawn carriages with their clippity-clop and swishing tails. Two raven-haired women with sunglasses in their hair clattered past, beaming like royalty. They weren't alone. Tourists regularly outnumber the locals, and the Japanese outnumber everyone else. As usual, they were out in force, shouldering the coolest camcorders. Salzburg's remaining foreigners were posing beside Getreidegasse 9—the six-storey townhouse where Mozart was born. Beneath the mustard hues of its Georgian façade I felt my back shiver in quiet acknow-ledgement. He wrote his first concerto at the age of five. I still couldn't play the recorder. True genius: it deserves respect.

Then, through three great portals, at last came the cathedral.

Dry air immediately cools the brow. Tourist fingers point, and not just at Mozart's baptismal fount. A dome seventy-one metres high is not readily forgotten, nor are the many frescoes depict-ing the Passion. When Italians Mascagni and Solari stood brush in hand on their scaffolding, they did an excellent job. Colours are rich and earthy: crimson cloaks, olive-green robes, mustard tunics. It's four hundred years since the paint dried, but one can almost smell the blood and feel apostle anguish. White stucco forms much of the rest, and it's far from tedious. Chubby-faced cherubs and period figures wearing breeches swarm around the murals, all in exquisite detail. Before moving on, I took a final look at the organ's massive silver pipes. A young composer once played here and could make them sing like no other. That guy's name was Wolfgang Amadeus Mozart. Of course, it had to be.

I was still buzzing when I returned to the hostel. Salzburg's got a bloody history, and there's much more on offer than over-priced sweets. Coveted by mad archbishops and grasping dukes, the city's been in and out of Bavaria, parcelled off by Napoleon to one of his chums and was famously acquired by the corporal from Linz during the 1938 *Anschluss*. I glanced up and on the heights glimpsed a chalky-white fortress peppered with rows of tiny black windows. They must have plenty of stories to tell and not all of them pleasant. It begged to be explored.

Back at the YOHO business had started to pick up. Hovering by the counter were three new ponytails, one green sombrero and two baseball caps, each with a mountainous rucksack and a commendable eagerness to fight for that only radiator.

'Oh, thanks, have you been to Salzburg before?'

A woman's voice. That must have been the receptionist, now imprisoned behind a wall of heavy-duty cross-stitch. It was a tight squeeze. I was easing myself around the last bobbing roll mat when those dreaded words struck the tympanum.

The lanky American pulled off his sombrero, revealing a mop of unruly blond. 'No, Ma'am, I haven't, but I've heard *The Sound of Music* tour is big here, right?'

I smiled and began to climb the stairs. Yes, very right. In fact, monumentally right. The simple truth is this: no one can possibly enter Salzburg, or for that matter leave it, without hearing those awful four words:

The Sound of Music.

I hate musicals. I've always hated them. If I had to sing the nauseating *Edelweiss* I would probably gag. If I had to sing *Do-Re-Mi* I might temporarily lose my mind and take up crochet, vote Liberal Democrat or seek to build a 1:40 scale replica of the USS Nimitz with nothing but a pile of matchsticks. Worse still, if I had to watch the *entire* film I might go bonkers and agree that Keanu Reeves really is an actor. (Yes, I know he isn't in it.) All these things are possible, which is why I avoid musicals at all costs and this one in particular. And here's why:

Cue some unnaturally green grass and a milky-faced Julie Andrews singing lustily in a navy-blue aproned dress. Aargh. I think I'm going to be sick.

It was 1965 when Miss Andrews and the disgustingly cute von Trapp children took to those buttercup slopes near Lake Fuschl. No one can doubt the genius of Rodgers and Hammerstein who penned the songs. The Broadway musical was a huge hit in the fifties, and the film smashed box office records to smithereens. Many of the movie's iconic scenes took place in Salzburg. Ever with an eye to profit, the city's hotels and hostels are happy to keep the dream alive. They all push the coach tours hard knowing that tourists like nothing more than a fanatical rendition of *Do-Re-Mi* as they career across the Austrian countryside. For me, ignoring the hype was rather easy. Watching *The Sound of Music* is like gagging on a tablespoon of liquid sugar. Liberally doused with syrup. And an awful lot of chocolate. Enough said.

I spent two nights in Gothic Salzburg. Sightseeing aside, due to a rapidly stiffening leg it could easily have been more. The Alps lay ahead, ripping skies and frightening in their grandeur. How would I make it across? I felt far from confident.

It wasn't until the second evening I really confronted the issue. Planning a route in these parts is all about percentages, and the percentages that matter are marked on the map with little arrows and a two-digit number. These are the gradients of the dreaded mountain passes. The arithmetic is simple: 12 per cent is bad, 15 does strange things to the vertebrae and 18 will crush you like a grape. Comprehensive travel insurance including air ambulance is strongly advised. While Magnus buried his nose in a book, I began to add some tentative check marks. An hour later, I'd sketched a route all the way to Slovenia. It looked like a nine-day walk, maybe ten.

I reached for another Jaffa Cake. What did Magnus, wannabe Viking poet and depressing know-it-all from Helsinki, think?

He closed the book with an exaggerated thump and began to swing his skinny legs over the bunk. 'Actually,' he said, letting out a sigh, 'I didn't want to tell you this before.' No, of course not. 'But fifteen per cent is nearly impassable.'

Wha . . . ?!

He dropped to the floor, and I watched him trot barefoot to the small radiator beneath the window. He had that enormous towel in hand. Yep, he was going to hog it again. As my mind searched for a witty retort, steam vapour began to spiral up.

'Well then,' I answered mildly, 'I'll just have to cope.' There was no way I was going to let his pessimism drag me down.

Magnus shrugged. Brushing a strand of greasy hair from his pallid brow, he returned to his bunk and, picking up a Viking novel the width of a doorstep, proceeded to ignore me for the rest of the evening. After he fell asleep his towel magically disappeared from the radiator. Mine miraculously replaced it. Bless the Lord. He certainly does work in mysterious ways.

✳ ✳ ✳

'*Schönes, schönes Österreich!*' cried the gap-toothed old lady, grinning beside me.

From a wooden bridge spanning a snaking river clearer than any glass, between sandy white tracks hedged by brilliant green, I looked up at skies torn asunder. Flint grey and deeply veined, the twin powder-white peaks seemed almost two-dimensional, like a painted backdrop for a movie. As I stood slack-jawed before a billion tonnes of rock I half expected to see a director arrive and shout, 'Cut!' No director came, for this was God's work, and no man could remove it.

'*Schönes Österreich!*' she cried again. The old woman spoke the truth. With our hands gripping the railings, we stood together. We just stood and *looked*.

From the hostel it took less than three hours to reach woman, mountain and bridge. I set out just after dawn, mind fuzzy with half-remembered concertos and the taste of Mozart-inspired chocolate. Magnus was fast asleep, which suited me fine. We hadn't got on, and we both knew it.

With a new map in hand, I made good progress navigating Salzburgian streets. By seven I was already tracking the S-shaped River Saalzach out of the city. Georgian houses the size of minor palaces hugged the curling banks. A pair of beady-eyed seagulls sat on lapping waters, preening ragged feathers then taking to the skies in search of breakfast. When the valley finally opened I found myself at Golling, surrounded by timbered chalets with low swooping roofs and long polished verandahs dripping in pink blossom.

If that marvellous vista at the bridge was the beginning of the seduction, then this confirmed it. Austria is built on the kind of chocolate-box scenery that makes you wonder whether you're living in the right town, or for that matter—the right country. Greens are five tones greener. Yellows are blinding. Buttercups swarm on every slope. I defy anyone to pull on a rucksack and simply walk, to spend even a single hour here and not feel the same way.

The purity of the water seemed astonishing. I dropped to my haunches and in the slower reaches of the River Lammer saw myself looking back more clearly than in any mirror. I stood up and glanced left. Alpine meadow was awash with purple and yellow blooms. Swordtail butterflies swooped between slender green saplings. Tiny Orange-tips fluttered weakly past. Clouded Yellows speckled the grass, like gold coins dropped from the purse of a passing giant. The scent of Eden was on the breeze, and it roamed the valley's gape, finding release in clouds and ferocious white peaks jagged and hungry for the sky.

It must have been several hours before the riverside trail petered out. Then I was back on the tarmac, climbing high and sweating. I was halfway up another soaring hill when two guys in black wetsuits dropped into view.

'Yes,' said the taller, shouldering a dripping oar, 'Abtenau is this way. But I think you must visit the canyon first.'

Must? I scanned the canoeist's face and took a swig of water. It was too hot for a major detour. 'Is it far?'

He shook his head and grinned. 'No. Not far. It is closed now though you can still get down.'

His advice was sound. The turnstile leading downward was unmanned, but a stout push saw me through. It was narrow inside the canyon, particularly at the top; I had to remove my rucksack to navigate the wooden platform clinging precariously to the wall. Curling grey rock rose on all sides. Below was a torrent of roaring white surf—a tumble here would have made an unusually refreshing experience ... I was turning to leave when suddenly on the right a pair of canoeists appeared in red helmets, furiously spinning oars and whooping like Indians. They slipped through the crack in seconds.

Each day provided similar adventures. I woke at dawn not knowing where I would eat, drink, sleep or camp. I might meet with disaster or good fortune; I might meet a sinner or a saint. Uncertainty was the only certainty, and she promised nothing more than a sunrise, a sunset and a hard day's walk. Can mere words capture the freedom and excitement of the open road? I'd argue against, and in saying this I'm sticking my neck out because some truly amazing individuals have tried. Consider the story of Ibn Battuta. Six centuries ago this splendid Moroccan spent nearly thirty years in constant travel. By the end, he'd collected ten wives, dozens of concubines and more first-hand experience of the Islamic world than anyone else. His carefree lifestyle struck a chord. When I was free of blisters and wading through buttercups it seemed possible I might never go back.

For five days I pushed steadily toward the first mountain pass, following gravel tracks around curling rivers. I took my time, averaging no more than 20 km a day. If you're about to scramble up huge mountains, you need to be in tip-top shape, and one good leg and a bit of flailing flesh rigid beneath the knee hardly qualifies. I met few people to converse with, but all were friendly. I remember a small boy greeted me with a chirpy *'Grüss Gott!'*, and the surprise I felt says as much about the English as it does the Austrians. On the aloof streets of England, initiating conversation with strangers is rarely undertaken, and for some Britons even an innocuous smile on a bus can be tantamount to an assault. I guess national stereotypes cut both ways.

In between laboured gasps I continued to take photographs, trying and failing to capture the grandeur, knowing that with each new step the inevitable approached. Three great mountain passes stand between Salzburg and Slovenia. In order: the 15 per cent Radstädter Tauern, the Katschberg and finally the 18 per cent man-killer known as the Wurzen Pass. On the fifth day I stood in the wildlife park at Untertauern, gazing pensively at velvet-brown stags pawing the ground. After nibbling a hastily improvised sandwich, there was nothing left to do but climb.

Due to the Tauern Tunnel there isn't much traffic nowadays on the B99 Katschberg Straße that crosses the Radstädter Tauern Pass. Even so, caution is advised. The metal barrier is wafer-thin and beyond that lies a screaming drop into wooded oblivion. I was standing goggle-eyed beside another cascading waterfall when an open-top sports car screeched to a halt. Out jumped a pair of giggling tourists. The woman pushed up her sunglasses. She tilted her head seductively, 'Would you mind?' Fluttering hazel eyes can work wonders when you're starved of oxygen. They linked arms and gave me their best cheesy grins. I snapped once, they took the camera back, jumped in, then sped on up the pass. Lucky them.

It wasn't so easy for me. With every step the air grew colder, forcing me back into my gloves. Halfway up my heart began to piston wildly. Near the summit it went berserk, turned traitor

and tried to rip open my ribcage. By the time I spotted Obertauern's welcome arch both legs had turned to jelly. Desperate
for something to collapse on, I wobbled to the bench that lies
beneath. Unfortunately, at this height it was far too chilly to
loiter. I rose unsteadily, joints stiff with cold.

'I didn't want to tell you this before. But fifteen per cent is
nearly impassable.'

Really, Magnus? I mentally shook a fist at his pockmarked face
and shivered defiantly on. Proving that misery wrong almost
made the ascent worthwhile.

And almost is about right.

If you're seeking a bed for the night, May is not a great time
to visit a ski resort that only opens in November. I looked up at
the spectacular hotels—Alpine cathedrals with tinted glass and
cherry-hued balconies dedicated to the worship of money. Snow
slopes bristled with soaring roofs the span of a jumbo jet. Not
realising the situation, I stupidly began banging on doors. 'Try
Tweng,' answered a pair of fire-flushed cheeks devoid of pity.
Wasn't Tweng 8 km away? After an ascent that brutal it might
as well have been 800 ... I dropped my eyes and slunk away,
pitching instead among a lonely fir grove. Far below, frosted
pasture glittered like blue sequins. At twilight the roar of camping gas rose to meet a web of glittering stars. I sipped greedily
from a mug of steaming black coffee. I was cold and hungrier
than I could remember, but it was better than nothing.

When morning arrived I packed hurriedly and rejoined the
chocolate-box landscape leading up. If you haven't figured it out
yet, everything in Austria is immaculate: the timber hotels, the
verandah-and-flower houses, the virgin-white peaks, those little
sheds stuffed to the gills with neatly stacked firewood—*alles*, as
they say, very definitely *in ordnung*. Within minutes I ran into
a guy in blue overalls condemned to brushing piles of immaculate dirt from the resort's single immaculate street. I've never
held a conversation with an Austrian road sweeper at 5,700 feet
before. It's not something I'm likely to repeat.

'Congratulations!' said the strapping lad, pumping my hand with startling vigour. He jabbed at my chest. 'You are the first walker through Obertauern this year!'

I laughed. 'Well, yeah, that's great.'

He released my hand, and we started chatting. It wasn't long before I realised his knowledge of English might have a few limitations.

'Where is the nearest shop?' I asked him.

'Yes.'

'Err Max . . . How far is it to Mauterndorf?'

'Yes.'

And the biggest question ever to vex the popcorn-munching moviegoer, 'Is Keanu Reeves really an actor?'

A troubled frown, then a beaming smile and a mighty:

'Yes!'

The last one was the clincher. No one who understood the question could possibly agree.

I crested the pass soon after. I'd never felt greater relief. While talking with Max had been fun, I was running on sugar vapours and I knew it. Fifty metres ahead, a black Land Rover pulled up. The door swung open, and a blurry figure shot across the pavement. Could it be a shop? The intuition of a starving pilgrim screamed 'Yes!' Desperate for calories, I sprinted to the spot.

Five minutes later I collapsed on a bench and began to snack on flaky apple strudels. Sheer heaven. Every finger was numb. My teeth were chattering. I was high as I could be without doing something dodgy with white powder and a syringe. I didn't care. Despite Magnus' gloomy prediction, I'd bested the Radstädter Tauern Pass. I was a pilgrim walking to Jerusalem.

And at 5,700 feet, 500, or 5 million, that was *still* the only thing that mattered.

* * *

For the next 110 km I travelled south toward Villach near the Slovenian border. The road offered an interesting selection of little hamlets, each clinging to a slightly obscure moment in history. Mauterndorf: a market town once home to Luftwaffe chief Hermann Göring. Gmünd: birthplace of the Porsche sports car first built here in 1948. There was nothing so profound in St Michael, but after I'd plundered the supermarket for roasted chicken wings it did herald the start of another serious climb. Over the space of three hours I blew several hundred calories clambering over the 5,384-foot hill known as the Katschberg Pass. Like Obertauern, the summit was another phantom ski resort. Not even a road sweeper shook my hand.

I spent five days making the trip. The journey wasn't without considerable danger. In a world carved out by foaming rivers and great mountains it's what lies between you need to worry about. A victim of geography as deadly as it is beautiful, on the road to Seeboden I became trapped between the rushing River Lieser and a wall of solid rock. What were supposed to be two generous lanes of tarmac were more like one and a half. Every second vehicle from behind was a juggernaut. After six wheels whistled past my left ear I took fright and fled into the adjacent slip road.

The clouds hung dark and heavy for the remainder of that afternoon. I hadn't travelled far before torrential rain sent me clambering into my waterproofs. Up to now very few drivers had offered lifts. Would the grey Audi pulling over with flashing windscreen wipers be the exception?

'Thanks for the offer,' I spluttered through a mouthful of rain, 'but I think I'll walk on.'

The driver's eyebrows hit the roof. Visibility had dropped to a miserly ten metres. I guess I could understand her reaction.

Villach politely appeared on 6 May after the kind of 30 km slog you don't want to undertake too often. I found nothing unexpected. If you've seen as many Austrian towns as I have, you'll know they're all cut from the same cloth. Wrought-iron cockerels hang over doorways à la Salzburg. There's invariably a Catholic church, several beery *Gasthäuser* offering food and lodging, a plate-glass river, a bridge, and a bunch of flags fluttering the red and white stripes of Austria. Mountain peaks are powdered a crowd-pleasing white 365 days a year and usually visible from every direction.

As expected, Villach was all of the above, minus the delicious *Mozartkugeln*. While the city had been bombed flat during the Second World War, you wouldn't think so now. Three- and four-storey tenements parade down the main square in pastel shades: Seville orange, aquamarine, lemon yellow—all very regal and very grand. The ground floors house glassy boutiques selling chiffon dresses, leather handbags and all those pretty things that women with money like to buy. A yellow M-shaped sign hangs over the high street. No surprise there. If they could plant a McDonalds on a floating ice sheet, they probably would.

I spent two nights in Villach preparing mind and body. It was a time to take a break from the endless walking and undertake some essential housekeeping. Tattered old maps from Germany needed to be sent home. Something smelling quite badly in my rucksack needed to be dealt with, and quickly. Washing clothes is a nasty job, but it does have to be tackled eventually.

I had mixed results with the accommodation. The first night I flopped down in the back room of a noisy *Gasthaus*, the second rather more cheaply in one of those pine-smelling, antiseptic youth hostels so typical of Germany. Everything was great until a team of German American-football players turned up (yes, they do exist) and decided to male-bond very loudly at 2 a.m. I was outnumbered ten to one and for some reason had forgotten to pack my shoulder pads. On the whole, this didn't seem like the right moment to step out into the corridor with a cheery *'Grüss Gott!'*

I devoted the last afternoon to a hunt for maps and trying to get a sense of the place. As much as the stunning geography it was the 1919 Treaty of Saint-Germain-en-Laye that shaped this marvellous country. After the First World War the defeated Austro-Hungarian Empire was effectively asset-stripped by the victors. In Parisian smoke-filled committee rooms Lloyd George and company sat around huge maps parcelling out bits of land. There wasn't much for the new downsized Austrian Republic to cheer about. There never is for the losers. Polish and Hungarian smiles welcomed independence. The gritty Slovenians were given a tiny backwater called Dravograd. Czechoslovakia picked up the Sudetenland (though probably later regretted it when German storm troopers goose-stepped in). The jubilant Italians inherited more ski resorts, acquiring Trieste, the South Tyrol and a bunch of other pretty buttercup places. Villach remained staunchly Austrian with a whiff of Italy persisting in the latter-day Italiener Strasse and a clutch of spaghetti restaurants. As the Italian border stands only 15 km away I guess that isn't too surprising. Slovenia is even closer, though you wouldn't necessarily know it.

On the way back to the hostel I stopped at the bridge. Two old women in washed-out grey sat cross-legged holding polystyrene cups and gazing up at passers-by with desperate eyes. Had these Gypsies crossed the border from Slovenia seeking a better life? Their harsh existence seemed at odds with Austria's chocolate-box image. I never expected to see beggars here.

✳ ✳ ✳

Of all the Austrian challenges I had to overcome the last is the one I feared the most. No official statistics exist for the number of walkers brutally eliminated by the force of nature known as the Wurzen Pass. If a figure did exist, it would probably make grim reading. For those who studied biology, it's the ultimate instrument of Darwinian evolution designed to weed out the weak and irresolute from the strong and chisel-jawed. A blue rectangular road sign showing a car on a slope announces the start: *18% 3.5 km*. Worryingly, the little car seems to be slipping back under the pull of gravity. It's not a reassuring sight.

As the sun blazed down on the sixty-fifth day of my pilgrimage I stood at the base, windmilling my arms in a mock show of strength (who was I kidding?) and sucking in air like a boxer preparing for a title fight. Adrenalin was pushing up heart rate, opening big throbbing veins, preparing me for 'fight or flight', though there was no chance I could run from this; Slovenia lay somewhere over those mountains, and I knew I just had to get there. Before kicking off, I took a final look at those two lanes of chaotic tarmac shooting toward the sky. So far I'd bested the highest Austria could throw at me. Surely the climb couldn't be as bad as the locals made out?

I'm not sure there's a polite answer to that question. Conquering the Wurzen is all about faith, or stubbornness, or a mix of the two fortified by occasional expletives and frequent drags on bottled cola, or whatever pumps sugar into your veins in the fastest possible manner. I guess it really doesn't matter as long as you make it to the top.

Enclosed by spiky conifers I circled upward, gasping in tiny pathetic steps. Traffic was light that afternoon, just the odd car and rumbling lorry. Occasionally, a motorcyclist in black leather roared effortlessly by. I let the envy fade and quickly sussed out a plan. At ten-metre intervals there was a plastic reflector strip rising from roadside. I'd make for one, get out of breath, stop, then drink some more and carry on. Every five minutes I'd take a longer break, drop my rucksack and stretch back muscles knotted like rope. I was going to win by salami-slicing the ascent.

Ha! Ha! Ha! Was that divine laughter in the trees?

Two hours later, the road appeared to level out. 'Hallelujah!' I gasped, sensing victory. The euphoria was exquisite, but short-lived. A few metres on I spotted another of those wretched road signs: *18% 600m*. What the . . . ? I snarled and began to robotically work my legs. Instantly something exploded in my right hip. Every joint clamoured for rest. Three thousand feet up an enormous hill, I guzzled the last of my cola. I tossed the bottle away, cursing myself for littering such a pristine wilderness, but even more so for running out. It had taken three hours to reach this point; surely the summit must soon be within my grasp?

Nope. Not at all. Not in the least.

'It's always darkest before the dawn,' goes the saying. I don't know the name of the genius first imbued with such wisdom, but they must have been standing red-faced and panting where I was when they discovered it. Up ahead, I spotted another of those infuriating blue signs: *18%*. And still no end in sight.

Once again, I began to clamber toward the heavens. The road rose higher, mocking every step and daring me to admit defeat. Round and round and round we go ... Would I ever escape these blasted trees?

At 4 p.m. on a bright May afternoon, what I thought would never happen, finally did. The winding road began to level out and became straight like an arrow, funnelling a lone pilgrim on foot and what little traffic had braved the pass toward the long-hoped-for border with Slovenia. Gasping for air, I wobbled up to a traffic sign that simply read: *Wurzenpaß Seehöhe 1073m*. I'd lost contact with my legs hours ago. All the same, I might have whooped with joy if I'd had the breath.

There was a final restaurant before the checkpoint, a charming hunting-style lodge crafted from rough timber. I spent my last twenty minutes there, drinking my favourite cola and deep in thought. I'd felt safe walking through Western Europe. Most people I'd met had spoken English or German, and the ability to be understood is always reassuring. Now, barely thirty metres away, lay the former Yugoslavia, an unknown land scarred by ethnic and religious conflict. Nothing good came to mind. The moment seemed like a turning point, something to be savoured, remembered and quite possibly feared. Had mighty Caesar sitting by the banks of the Rubicon felt the same?

I lifted the glass, swallowed and glanced at the border sign: 'Slovenija' in blue, circled by twelve golden stars. Love it or hate it, the mark of the EU is instantly recognisable. There was a whitewashed bollard underneath chiselled with 'St Germain 10 Sept 1919'. History casts longs shadows. Lloyd George and all those that made the peace were dead, yet their legacy lives on.

I carried on lazily drinking. A glass cabin split the centre of the tarmac, home for a bored customs official with nothing to do except check passports. Hundreds of feet above were more jagged peaks, more mountains. Thinking back to the heights I'd already scaled brought to mind the words of Matthew 17:20:

If you have faith as a grain of mustard seed, you will tell this mountain, 'Move from here to there,' and it will move.

I moved no mountains that day, but by the summit I'd shifted my dishevelled presence over three high passes totalling 15,000 feet—about half the height of Everest. Despite the negativity of Magnus, I'd always believed I would make it. For two weeks in the Alps I walked with one hand in the heavens. Was it God's I now felt on the other side?

I knocked back my drink and slammed the glass on the table. I could have done with another, but it was getting late and I still had to descend the Slovenian side of the pass. Who knows how long that might take?

I was about to rise when a girl in her twenties appeared from nowhere. White apron, blond plaited hair, eyes like finely cut sapphires: she strode across the lawn, smiled, lifted up my glass and proceeded to nonchalantly wipe the surface with a cloth. Could this Aryan beauty be the mythical Heidi? I glanced at my watch. Perhaps I could linger for a bit longer . . .

'Excuse me,' I said, looking up at the girl with sparkling eyes.

Chapter Four

Slovenia

The Land of the Heroic Statue

I didn't stay long with Heidi. Actually her name turned out to be Lena, which just goes to show the limitations of national stereotypes. I bought another drink, left a tip and after a final wistful look at Austria, began to descend the Slovenian side of the pass.

I was largely ignorant of what to expect. It is, after all, a rare tourist that arrives in Slovenia with any great knowledge of the country. The nation seldom figures prominently on the international stage. Outside of Central Europe its leaders and politics are largely unknown. Even the geography is a mystery. Prior to picking up a map, I had this tiny western-looking republic firmly in the Monaco-Liechtenstein-Andorra group, i.e. located someplace in Europe but nobody's quite sure where. My sole point of reference was a bunch of half-remembered news reports from the Balkans wars of the nineties. The Republic of Slovenia, born out of Yugoslavia's chaotic and bloody collapse that left 130,000 Europeans dead across five countries, seemed a dark place where dark things might happen. The abiding feeling was of leaving safety behind and walking into the unknown.

I think I was right to feel cautious, at least to begin with. The history of the former Yugoslavia is a salutary lesson on what can happen when a federated state disintegrates. The six socialist republics had always been a quarrelsome group: Serbs, Croats, Slovenes, Montenegrins, Macedonians, Bosniaks, and in Kosovo several million Albanians reluctantly scratching out a living as an autonomous province of Serbia. Looking back, conflict was inevitable. Why? It's an iron law that antagonistic populations can only be held together by strong government, and only then if kept permanently in place. When President Tito—Yugoslavia's strongman—died in 1980 the national will began to falter. Divided by religion and ethnicity, it was only a matter of time before this unhappy fraternity of brothers tore itself apart.

They waited eleven years to get started. Though nationalism figured strongly, as much as anything else it was empty supermarket shelves that drove the push for freedom. By the nineties Yugoslavia's command economy was about as useful as those rusty iron statues of heroic men and women littering the town squares. Change arrived suddenly in 1991. Slovenia's chance to break free came in the spring. Its leaders saw an opportunity and bravely took it, eventually declaring independence on 25 June after fighting a brief war with mercifully few casualties against the Yugoslav National Army.

Unfortunately, other parts of Yugoslavia didn't get away so easily. When Croatia tried to leave a second war erupted, then another in neighbouring Bosnia Herzegovina. Media coverage became frenetic. Reporters with telephoto lenses sought out detention camps, eager to photograph the most emaciated bodies. Newsreaders in Britain talked solemnly about 'ethnic cleansing' and a faraway place called Kosovo where bad things were happening to Albanians. Here, and all across the Balkans, women and children were going for walks in the forest. Many never came back. As the violence escalated, a bewildered Europe rediscovered long-forgotten phrases—'war crimes', 'genocide' and 'concentration camps'—unsettling words that created a queasy feeling in the stomach and an unpleasant sense of déjà vu.

So it was during the dying embers of a May evening I descended into Slovenia, wondering what I would find at the end.

Given this background of violence, I wasn't surprised that the first person I met was a former soldier. At the foot of the pass lies the village of Podkoren (or Wurzen in German; this part of Europe is a battlefield, and everywhere has at least two names). Of special note for trekkers is the farmhouse-cum-youth-hostel awaiting foot-weary guests. If the upstairs kitchen looked well lived-in—it was. The coffee pot was charred black, and every pan carried the remains of a meal. The management ethos was nicely summed up by a notice taped above the greasy cooker:

I'm not your mama!!
Do your own washing up!!!

Strongly put. However, that the rules of the house were being blatantly flouted didn't seem to bother the boyfriend-girlfriend team putting up the notes. Of the two, only the male part was available to welcome me that day. A giant Croat with a red scar on his right cheek and an armour-piercing stare that could halt a T-55 battle tank, Ziga told me he had recently left the army and served with NATO in Afghanistan. I glanced at his razor haircut, green combats and black army boots, tightly laced and gleaming. There was a tin of polish and a pile of rags lying on the floor. I sensed the guy was still in transition.

'My friend!' he boomed, suddenly throwing his arms open like an opera singer reaching for the high note, 'My friend, of course you can stay!'

I instantly felt my shoulders relax. At least the hostel wasn't full, which was my main fear.

'Will you stay more than one night?' he asked.

I shook my head and stifled a yawn. 'I don't think so, I only need somewhere for tonight. In the morning I'm going to push on towards Ljubljana.'

'Okay, but please understand we were not expecting you. Let me fix up your room with fresh sheets, and after we can drink coffee.' Then, scooping up the polish and rags, he marched off into one of the back rooms.

While Ziga got to work, I decided to kill some time in the hallway. A row of aluminium pedal bins adjoined the wall. One had been labelled for plastic bottles, another for waste paper; clearly someone was eager to save the planet. Near the banisters there was a long oak table covered by tourist leaflets. I unfolded one at random—a street map of the capital Ljubljana. Scattered words leapt from the grid of claret squares. '*Cesta*' dominated. My guess was it meant 'road' or something similar. I was about to pick up another leaflet when he emerged from the darkness and ushered me down the hall.

I swear the sight would have driven a German backpacker to suicide. Where the disorderly kitchen led, the sleeping quarters naturally followed. A handmade wardrobe with a Pisa-ish five-degree lean to the left, a small scratched oak table, a spindle-leg chair: the room was full of junk. At least there was a mattress, two plump white pillows and a double bed to go with them.

We went into the kitchen to grab some coffee, then returned to the bedroom so I could finish the process of unpacking my limited possessions. Cradling a steaming mug, I talked about my pilgrim experiences, fed him some mildly amusing stories about Austrian road sweepers and long-distance walkers chased by dogs. In reply, he revealed that he and his girlfriend had always wanted to walk across Africa. It sounded something contrived for my benefit, but who knows, it might have been true.

I thought twice about asking potentially awkward questions. Ben Nimmo, writing about his 2,000 mile walk to Santiago de Compostela, said mentioning Struthof in France is like shouting 'Auschwitz!' in England. In the former Yugoslavia the massacre at Srebrenica holds similar dread. During the summer of 1995 Serbian forces murdered 8,000 Bosnians, mainly men and boys. The word genocide was used. It still is. The German waiter I'd spoken to in Vellberg had been muttering darkly about Bosnia. What had he told me?

'There is still bad feeling due to the war and sometimes people are taken into the forest. Such people are never seen again.'

At the current rate I would be there in less than three weeks. I leant back against the window and let my fears spill out.

Ziga looked up from the spindle-leg chair, face impassive. He spoke calmly; there was no Auschwitz effect here.

'What you are talking about happened many years ago. You will find things quieter these days. There were many problems before, during the war, as you say.'

'That's reassuring. I've heard a lot of bad stuff about Bosnia, particularly concerning the fate of the Muslims.'

He nodded coolly. 'The Serbs caused big problems for all of us. They didn't like the Muslims, and they still don't. For tourists, though, the situation is very different. I'm sure no one will harm you.' He glanced down at his watch and slapped his thighs. 'And now, my English friend, I must leave you.'

Ziga rose from the chair and stopped by the bed to scoop up a pile of crumpled sheets. At the doorway, he turned and said, 'I don't think you will have any trouble. When you get to Bosnia you will find the people friendly. All Balkans people are friendly.'

I spent the rest of that evening penning a guide for surviving the Wurzen Pass, chilling out to an exquisite MP3 of *Jerusalem* and praying Ziga was right. By the third mug of coffee I'd mellowed considerably. Although German antiseptic was obviously anathema to the management, for all its faults the decrepit hostel felt homely. It felt *lived* in. And home, what was that? Just some place now so very far away.

✻ ✻ ✻

I took breakfast alone in the morning. Far from being full with messy guests who refused to wash their dishes, the hostel was surprisingly empty. I sat at the kitchen table munching toast and drinking coffee which been my habit in England before setting off to work. I sensed the feelings of the previous evening sneaking up on me. Staying too long in the same place can make you think twice about moving on, and anywhere reminding you of home (even loosely) definitely will. I hadn't fried an egg in over two months. Fourteen euros: it seemed a small price to rekindle the memory.

Pleasantly full with fried food, I struck east along the highway towards Ljubljana. The spectacular geography I'd witnessed in Austria was largely unchanged. North were the blue crystalline peaks of the Karavanke Mountains snapping at cotton clouds; south, the jigsaw greens and labyrinthine boughs of the Triglav National Park. Slovenia has plenty of wild parts—and there are more than you think. Aided by Ziga's whirring laptop I'd learnt that 50 per cent of the country is forest, and there were upward of four hundred bears between myself and Croatia, though I seriously doubted any would find their way onto the handy D2 cycle path. Cocooned by juicy green leaves, I crossed brooks flashing silver in the sun and an old iron girder bridge burning red with rust. A few of the splintered boards creaked underfoot, but God was still with me, and their rivets held.

What is it about statues and socialist countries? It's a question I often asked myself. Slovenia is littered with all kinds of heroic figures. Men are muscular and chisel-jawed. Women are heavy-bosomed with broad hips—perfect material to bear children and farm land in accordance with the peasant ideal. I found an intriguing exception at Mojstrana: a blindfolded man, tied to a stake and sagging at the knees. His silent scream was forever cast in blackened bronze. A couple of elderly locals passed by. Was he a victim of the Yugoslav Wars of the nineties? No, they said, a brave partisan executed by the Germans. It's hard to know what to say in these situations. I nodded sagely, keeping my face respectful and grim.

I spent that night in Jesenice taking a room in Pivnica Kazina. It was a poor choice. The bathroom mirror had a crack like fork lightning. There wasn't a trace of hot water, and the windows were devoid of curtains, which meant stripping off would no doubt amuse the neighbours who even now were peering across from their dingy tower blocks. Gluttony was an even greater hazard—food was absurdly cheap. In the evening I gorged on several pounds of strawberries from a Mercator supermarket, then feeling sick promptly regretted it.

I returned to sleeping in a tent the next day with the usual mixed results. A few miles from Jesenice is the big campsite at Šobec. I do recommend a visit, but be aware that among those shady fir trees the holiday camp spirit dominates. Screaming kids clamber over the caravans, the washrooms and practically everything else that will hold their weight. Potbellied old men in string vests wander around, clutching shaving bags and shouldering towels. Avoiding the worst of the bedlam, I slept well in a quiet corner spot, enjoying a hot shower before trudging back to the road. Kranj was the next big target, but where was it? I slumped on a grassy verge, pulled out my map and wondered . . .

'Hello, can we help you?'

It was the woman's voice that brought me to my feet. Their car—a flash of gleaming white—had pulled up seconds earlier. I ran to the left door and glanced inside: a man, square jawed and broad shouldered, sitting quietly at the wheel and staring ahead; a woman smiling affably, strawberry complexion, blond hair curling under the ears.

'Actually, I'm looking for the way to Kranj, I think this is it—' I jabbed into the distance. 'Although I'm not really sure.'

The main road was swollen with early evening traffic. The woman leant out the window, almost yelling.

'We live there and we're on our way home. It's not far, would you like a lift?'

My refusal only seemed to stoke their interest.

'You're walking to Jerusalem? Look,' she persisted, 'we have a spare room in our house. It's not large, but you are welcome to stay with us.'

Seconds later, I had their address in hand and was marching towards Kranj in search of new friends. Much to my shame I nearly messed it up. A few kilometres outside the city I took the railway path as they suggested. After that: absolute disaster. Somehow the paper fell from my grasp, and I had to backtrack a hundred metres to find it. 'There is nothing lost that cannot be found,' declared Edmund Spenser. I'll second that. Never were truer words muttered while knee-high in gorse thorns.

It was with more gratitude they could ever know that I finally took my place at the dinner table. A trio of platinum-blond children had joined the adults sitting before the glittering, neatly arranged cutlery. I put the eldest boy at eight, the youngest girl at three. To my right, a bookcase towered above us, overflowing with a collection of gold hand-tooled tomes, silver-framed photos and most notably—the thin edges of maps. Clearly this was a couple who understood the value of travel.

Rok cleared his throat. He glanced at his wife with questioning eyes, and then back at me.

'We don't always do something, but since you are here and this is a special occasion, perhaps the guest will . . .'

I instantly saw his meaning. I bowed my head, giving a short speech thanking God for the food on the table and all the good things of the Earth. Somewhere in the mix I threw in a speculative plea for peace in Jerusalem. Given the nature of Middle Eastern politics, I wasn't overly optimistic.

'You were lucky,' said Irena, lifting her glass, 'today we were late collecting our son from school. We were debating whether to stop. Isn't that right, Rok?' She took a sip of red liquid, and he nodded in agreement.

I looked down at the roasted meat on sticks, the steaming greens, the heaps of fries. She was right: I was incredibly lucky. The wine itself was deliciously fruity. I was midway through my second glass when I decided to mention the statue of the blindfolded man I'd seen at Mojstrana.

'Ugh . . .' Irena's face crinkled. 'Those ugly statues. I wish they would go away.'

Rok laughed and gave his wife's hand a gentle squeeze. 'Well, hold on a moment, we have to be patient. The older generation still have a lot of power. Once they are gone things will change.'

'Sure,' I told him, 'and I guess Slovenia must have seen many changes since becoming independent of Yugoslavia. What's the situation like now? I mean, would you say younger people are better off?'

'I would say so,' said Rok. 'Slovenia is slowly becoming more like Austria and Italy. The rest of the Balkans region is not so good. Croatia is maybe ten years behind us. Bosnia is probably another ten.' He took another sip of wine, then said pointedly, 'You should know the roads are very bad there.'

His words carried the ring of truth. Slovenian supermarkets, at least, were well-stocked, and I'd already seen one new highway being built. There was also the D2 cycle path running out of Podkoren. Any country with money to spend on cyclists can't be doing that badly.

'Again,' Rok continued, 'it is different for the older people.' He chuckled wryly. 'I'm always arguing with grandfather about this. It's true that in Yugoslavia there were many benefits. The government really did look after the people. Workers got paid even if they didn't work.' Then, with an exasperated shrug, 'But the whole system was uneconomical, and it couldn't last. I still don't know why he can't see it.'

We ate until all the dishes were picked clean. Then the three children reluctantly retired to their bedroom. We drank more wine, talked about Jerusalem and leant over maps so large they overlapped the table. Irena reached up to the bookcase and pulled down a photo album showing pictures of smiling faces on the beach at Galilee. Seeing them reminded me how far I still had to travel. Rok must have sensed my mood.

'I do not think you will have any problems in the Balkans and certainly not here in Slovenia.' He looked me straight in the eye. 'Tony, you should not be afraid to knock on doors if you need help.'

I nodded, finding comfort in his quiet confidence. He knew these people better than I did. Perhaps I wouldn't 'disappear' in a Bosnian forest after all.

I was left alone for most of the following day. 'We have to

take our son to his confirmation,' they explained, and roared off to Ljubljana. With plenty of time to kill, I wandered around the town centre, bought an indecently large map of Croatia, took some fuzzy-ish pictures of bronze statues resting on blocks of Soviet-era concrete. They were the usual worker-cum-peasant figures, i.e. muscular men and women glaring at unseen capitalist aggressors. The most memorable moment came in the parish church where I gate-crashed a wedding. Only when the bride was blushing in the doorway did I realise my mistake. I looked up. The huge bouncer in the black tuxedo narrowed his eyes, 'Do you have an invitation?' Actually, the Slavic languages were never my forte. It could easily have been something less polite.

It was shortly after dusk when the family returned. The evening air was sweet with cherry blossom, warm and still, and far too pleasant to stay inside. Clutching long-stemmed glasses, we descended the narrow staircase in single file and made our way to the garden's leafy pergola. Unbeknown to me, my new friend Rok had been burning the telephone lines. Three faces half my age were already chatting around the table.

'Look at this man!' bellowed Rok. Six startled eyes focused like lasers. 'This is the guy I told you about. This is the guy walking to Jerusalem who refuses to take a lift!'

It was a tub-thumping introduction worthy of the pope himself. I momentarily sank into the ground, wondering how I could possibly match the build-up. After regaining my composure, I sat down opposite a twenty-something couple, grinning ear to ear and linking arms. I should have guessed immediately . . .

'We're planning to get married in Jerusalem,' they told me, gazing dreamily into each other's eyes.

They asked very few questions, but as I rattled off my story listened politely and gawped in all the right places.

I felt more in tune with the bloke sitting beside them. Sandi was a young man sporting a wispy goatee who liked to 'get away' and walk alone for weeks among the high limestone mountains. Alpine air drawn from ice-blue peaks, dawn mist weaving among mossy boughs, silver moons at midnight, and better still, no one to fight for the only seat on the train—his life seemed infinitely better than the one I'd just left. As for Yugoslavia . . . there wasn't a rabbit mound where he hadn't placed his boot.

'What about these guys here?' I lowered my glass and jabbed a finger at a village called Debar. For a naive Englishman it looked the ideal crossing point from Albania into western Macedonia.

'Hmm. Let me see . . .' Sandi leant over the table, rubbing his goatee and squinting under the bulb's dull yellow light. After a pause he looked up and said with serious eyes, 'This is a mixed area. Some villages are Christian, others Muslim.'

And never the twain shall meet, I thought, recalling the religious affiliations of those involved in the horrors at Srebenica.

'They are peaceful right now, but they don't mix, and they don't like each other.' He smiled at me. 'Perhaps this place is not so good for you.'

'Okay. Perhaps you're right.' I dropped my eyes to the map. If I followed Sandi's advice and abandoned my Debar plan, I would eventually have to approach Macedonia from the north. That meant taking a trip through Kosovo. If reputation was anything to go by the latter was like Bosnia, but a hundred times worse. The question loomed. Dare I walk across Kosovo by myself?

I had little time to worry about the implications or make an informed choice. The morning of 13 May was clear, blue and bright, and for all its promise came far too quickly. I was standing next to Rok in the front yard, mentally rehearsing another goodbye speech, when Irena suddenly appeared on the balcony.

'Oh, you are leaving!' she shouted, and cradling her daughter rushed down to join us.

The rituals of parting must be played out. Rok's ninety-year-old grandfather volunteered as official photographer, became momentarily confused about the correct button to press, was set straight by a few words from his grandson, then the rest of us drew together for a cheesy group shot on the driveway. After the second attempt it was time to shake hands.

Rok remained typically upbeat. It was his openness and positive outlook that had impressed me the most.

'I will never forget what you told me about the Dutch woman,' he said, gripping my hand. 'How good things can happen if you help a stranger that knocks on your door.'

I recall feeling pleased he'd remembered the story.

So with camera in hand I left another family standing at the gate. Our time together had been short, but in those two days I'd seen faith propel people toward higher good. For Rok and Irena the words of James 2:26 were more than eight-point type on lifeless paper:

As the body apart from the spirit is dead, so faith apart from good deeds is dead.

One moment in May I'd been sitting lost and alone on a kerb. The next I'd found two new friends I never knew existed. Who among us could have asked for more?

Which man or woman deserved any less?

There's something adorable about Slovenia's capital in spring. Although dulled by fatigue, I felt it immediately. If Ljubljana is the spiritual heart of the nation, then to be in Preseren Square is to feel its pulse. Regal in his frock coat, solemn in mood, the statue of France Preseren stares down at the milling crowds. Beyond the poet's gaze, colonnaded houses boast of power and the threads of lost nobility. Under balustraded bridges white as chalk, the emerald waters of the Ljubljanica dance and swing, then flee south in search of blooming green. Churches embrace curling streets. Spires blot out the skies. Gothic belfries soar, feeding the sunshine with tick and sleepy tock. By day, lemon yellow meets virgin white; salmon pink melts into clotted cream. By night, onion spires turn grey and burn red against a dipping sun. And above it all stands the Madonna—the Immaculate

Heart steadfast and true—crowned with burnished gold, pinned sea green against fleeting clouds, rising imperious over this most Catholic of cities.

It's the sacred duty of every writer to whet the appetite of the reader. So with an introduction that magnificent you might think I'd be dancing my way in. You'd be wrong. Diarrhoea is never fun at the best of times. On a lonely gravel track in the middle of the countryside where hot water and toilet paper are non-existent, the experience is terrifying. Seconds before the third explosion I hurtled into a nearby copse. I'll save the gruesome details for the *Daily Mail* serialisation, but the resulting cleanup by a muddy stream wasn't pretty. When the last sliver of emergency soap was gone I emerged to face the world humming John Bunyan's inspiring hymn:

There's no discouragement
Shall make him once relent
His first avowed intent
To–bee–aaaa–piiiiil–griiiiiim

I'm not sure the great man was referring to diarrhoea, but hey, it made me feel better.

From Rok and Irena's house it had taken eight hours to reach the city many call the 'new Prague'. Under the low grey cloud of a dismal May afternoon I found myself on the outskirts, tracking the railway down the long diagonal Celovška Cesta. I quickly noted some familiar icons: for the communist East, two bronze statues of heroic young women angrily shaking their fists at decadent imperialist aggressors (everyone in the old Yugoslavia seemed to be heroic, or angry, or both); then, representing the capitalist West, a McDonalds restaurant packed with bobbing heads chowing down on burgers. My decadent Western stomach gurgled enthusiastically. I plodded past the window mesmerised by sesame seed buns dripping with red ketchup.

Drawn by the cast-iron promise of a soft mattress and with

frequent nervous checks of the map, I meandered toward what I hoped would be the safety of the eastern suburbs. Despite the euphoria of chalking up my first European capital, hunger and fatigue grew with every step. That's not really surprising. Long-distance walking is demanding, and pilgrims are even more so. We need constant feeding. We need watering. We need some-where to wrestle with maps the size of a duvet. In the Middle Ages blokes with shoulder-high sticks and muddy feet rampaged across Europe like locusts devouring every last cabbage. Not much has changed since then, though personally I draw the line at brussels sprouts. I'm finicky about my greens.

Luckily, I found everything I needed that night a short walk from St Maria. The church that reassured me I was plodding in the right direction was typical Ljubljana: salmon-pink stone-work adorned with strips of lacy white plaster; pushing upward were the traditional twin bell towers ending in copper-green cones the shape of a witch's hat. Apparently, the next family to be my hosts lived nearby. Rok's female friend had fixed it up the night before; and when he'd told me 'Tony, you must thank this young woman', I had, squeezing her dainty knuckles with frightening fervour. Now I was standing on another doorstep, grinning at three strangers and exuberantly shaking hands.

'Hello, hello, I'm Tony...'

I hastily scanned the assembled faces: a middle-aged woman in a purple blouse, blond curls, arms folded and smiling; a man's tortoiseshell spectacles sitting above a neatly trimmed beard; beside them a teenage girl with long dark hair standing quiet and thoughtful in a navy tracksuit.

'I'm Sonja,' said the woman offering her hand.

'Janez,' said the man briskly.

'It's Anja,' replied their daughter.

And with my towering rucksack we stepped inside.

I always got a big lift when I stayed with a family, but I have to be honest, once you cross the threshold you never know what to expect. My latest benefactors were by all accounts a typical Slovenian family: house, car, dog, plus traitorous cat that mysteriously disappeared until mealtimes. Rok and Irena's kids hadn't batted an eyelid when faced with my brutal, army-style haircut. Not so Sonja's powerful shepherd dog.

'Stand back!' she said. 'He's frightened of you!' as the simpering hound was dragged off into a backroom.

The hound was frightened of me? He had the shoulders and waist of a small horse!

Ultimately, it fell to Sonja's considerable culinary skills to put the pilgrim-host relationship back on track. For the third time in forty-eight hours I gratefully sat down to an excellent cooked dinner. We discussed the former Yugoslavia at length. That was my idea. I couldn't pass up the opportunity to ask questions, to find out what people thought and how they really lived.

'Was life better for you under the old system?' I asked, casting off caution and immediately getting to the heart of the matter.

There were a few seconds of confused silence, a Sonja-Janez exchange, and when the translation from Anja came back—'for the older people it is not so good, but perhaps the young have more opportunities'—I realised that when change comes there will always be a range of views. In between the questions I was firing in all directions, seventeen-year-old Anja tried to teach me how to say 'good day' in Slovenian. 'No,' she said firmly, then laughed and shook her head. 'It's *Dober Daaaaan*.'

I finally got it on the seventh attempt. From this minor linguistic challenge we moved seamlessly and rather surreally to the Middle East and the vexed question of Iraq. I was pleased to note, as we all began to relax around the table, that G W Bush was as popular in Slovenia as he was in England—which is to say not at all. My opinion of Slovenes rocketed.

I retreated to my room a few hours later. The meal had been a delight, yet an even greater pleasure awaited. Before turning back the sheets I made straight for the shower for a long overdue cleanup. Steaming water, peach blossom soap and the miracle of scented toilet paper: 'Ahhh.' Could it possibly get any better?

With hindsight the answer turned out to be yes. I'm not a natural sightseer. When I arrive in a foreign city I don't feel the need to scrutinise every monument and art gallery. On the other hand, when the inclination strikes I'm more than willing to pound the *cestas* to prove I'm not a total Philistine. I set off at around eight that morning clutching camera, spare batteries and wallet, and in Ljubljana, which is a compact city, it took surprisingly little time to tick off the major landmarks. By 11 a.m. I already had half the good stuff in the bag. I sat down on a bench and took another peek at the map. The Dragon Bridge? Yeah, got it. The Triple Bridge? Yep, done it. Preseren Square? Check, sitting under France Preseren's statue right now. The biggest draw seemed to lie just below the clouds: rows of dark, soulless windows and pyramidal turrets flashing burgundy.

I think I was a fetching shade of burgundy myself by the time I made the summit. I don't know what the weather reports in Slovenia normally look like, but on a warm day in May walking in huge concentric circles will knock the stuffing out of anyone. Once my heart rate had quietened, I felt well rewarded. Ljubljana's castle is one of the better-maintained chunks of Balkans stone. Cross-slitted ramparts once buzzed by Ottoman arrows jut out over plunging slopes, and on a breezy day the city's green-and-white flag billows from the clock tower and is visible for miles around. It's popular, too. Red-faced tourists disgorging from stuffy coaches routinely mingle with parties of schoolchildren bickering on the benches. The main attraction for the lovestruck lies underground. Hidden within the castle's bowels is the popular 'marriage room'—the perfect location to enjoy a moment of pure terror before embracing endless bliss.

I was hot, thirsty and still unmarried when I traipsed back down to the Triple Bridge. There wasn't a great deal left to see around Preseren Square. From the bridge's chalky balustrade I glanced up at mauve skies stitched with layers of gauze cloud. Beneath the bottom seam the sea-green statue of Mary still hovered protectively over the city. From the rooftop I let my gaze descend the strawberry façade tramlined with clotted cream paint. At the base I spotted two flights of stone steps leading up to a pair of panelled doors. The Franciscan Church of the Annunciation and 350 years of Christianity lay beyond. I was a pilgrim walking to Jerusalem. I couldn't pass this up.

At first I struggled to see. Eyelids blinked in the dimness. Nostrils flared in the dry, musty air. To my right, two imploring eyes atop a grey beard sat cross-legged, demanding money. I dropped a few fifty-cent coins into the beggar's outstretched palm and moved on.

Okay, I thought, focusing the camera. Those statues in the side chapels look interesting.

White flashlight split ancient gloom—snap: pink plaster Jesus in gold loincloth flanked by cherubs. Snap: medieval maiden with head shawl looking demurely down. I was about to squeeze off a third when the ambush occurred. Out from the shadows stepped a burly Franciscan monk: coarse brown robe, knotted cord belt, basin haircut, an old scar on his right cheek. I'm sure he was a lovely guy, but it wasn't a face I'd like to meet down that proverbial dark alley. Nine hundred years ago this fellow might have been on the battlements of Old Jerusalem swinging a broadsword with Raymond of Toulouse. No prisoners were taken then, either. The monk scowled like a true Crusader and led me to the door. Alas, it was closing time.

✳ ✳ ✳

On a long-distance pilgrimage you can get used to soft living. Arguably a bit *too* used to it. Having had the pleasure of sleeping inside for three straight nights, I powered east out of Ljubljana toward the village of Stična intending to throw myself on the mercy of the church. The focus of my effort in the ensuing rain turned out to be commendably protected. Very little of the locally famous monastery can be seen from the approach road, just some faded pink paintwork, a clutch of high, chimneyed roofs and a single onion spire topped by a golden ball. During the fifteenth century Ottoman armies regularly plundered the surrounding lands, and the twenty-foot-high stone wall blocks detailed scrutiny as well as arrows. The wall must have held. Centuries later a small community of Cistercian monks still live at Stična, and they still don't talk at breakfast. How do I know?

Because I joined them.

My improbable induction into the monastic life began in the reception area to the left of the main archway. It was a simple office: wooden desk floating with paperwork, a pair of spindle-legged chairs, swivelling stands of glossy postcards, grey plastic telephone with an old-fashioned finger dial; when the receiver was handed to me with an invitation to converse in German, I looked at it with disbelief. The line itself seemed plugged into Outer Mongolia.

'Err . . . *Guten Tag*,' I stammered into the ancient mouthpiece. '*Ich bin*'—crackle—'*ein Pilger*'—crackle—'*aus England*'—crackle.

Another furious crackle, then a voice gruff and completely unintelligible. A yellow warning light started to blink furiously on the phone plate. Blimey. What the hell is that? Red-faced and dripping rain, I blathered on.

'*Ich gehe*'—hiss—'*nach*'—crackle—'Jerusalem'—crackle.

A night in a working monastery was at stake. In the ensuing melee I threw in every German word I knew relating to God, Jerusalem and warm beds. It was all a little desperate and not wonderfully coherent. Was the Almighty still with me? The call ended abruptly with the words '*Ich komme*' and a distant click. Within the halls of the great monastery a very patient German-speaker was on his way to greet me. Apparently, God was.

Ever since the first stones were laid in 1132 there's been a Cistercian presence at Stična. I spent a single night in one of the functional yet comfortable guest rooms, and fuelled only by a vivid imagination, the basic layout was much as expected. At ground level traditional vaulted cloisters with arched windows ring a central rose garden, bristling with red blooms. Polished marble floors suggest diligence; virgin-white walls symbolically echo the discipline of celibacy. Wandering around the cloisters, I looked up at hooplike ribs painted pastel yellow, tan brown and aquamarine—it was a strange palette, to be sure.

As far as I could tell, guests tend to reside on the upper floors. Here slabs of medieval oak meet modern bathrooms fitted with primrose tiling and gleaming mirrors. Although the monks live austerely, they bathe in facilities worthy of any three-star hotel. Silence, of course, is the order's golden rule. It clings to every doorknob and plaster saint like dust. Only the occasional slamming door and hollow footstep breaks the ethereal stillness. How many monks lived among these hallowed walls? Ten? Perhaps twenty? It's hard for a casual visitor to know. Those I saw were solemn fellows with placid eyes and faces calm like still water. With crossed arms and hands resting inside their white lambswool sleeves, they glided past as if on wheels, lost in thought or the enjoyment of some private reverie.

And but for the assistance of one of the order's more youthful converts that might have been the sum total of my experience at Stična. Despite Europe's ageing priesthood, a few young men are still called to service in the church. Father Nikolaij was one such man. Intelligent, slight and deathly pale, with a keen grasp of history, in the empty dinner hall I soon found myself grateful for his company.

'We don't normally talk at meals,' he whispered, as we sat down at the long dining table. Gripping each handle with white cloths, he gingerly lowered the steel casserole dish, which was full of beef stew, and placed it beside a pair of steaming mugs. 'But as the others have gone I think this can be an exception.'

'I'm grateful, father, for all of this. Do many pilgrims come to Stična? I mean, I didn't think that—'

'Actually, pilgrims are not that uncommon. Once we had an American couple, arriving on bicycles I believe, yes bicycles. They telephoned ahead from America to ask permission to stay, it wasn't necessary.' A half-smile fluttered on his lips, then fled just as quickly.

'How are you finding your room?' he said, dabbing his mouth with a napkin. 'Are you comfortable? The room we gave you is quite special.'

'Oh, how so?'

'It was home to the last Trappist monk in Slovenia. Do you have the Trappists in your home town?'

I mumbled a few polite words in response, mostly to try to hide my ignorance. Southend-on-Sea is richly endowed with Baptists, Protestants, Catholics and Methodists all marching in different directions for Christ. I'm pretty sure Trappists aren't among them. I felt on surer ground talking about myself. I was in full flow, extolling the virtues of pilgrimage and all the good things that follow, when he pushed back his empty bowl and turned to face me.

'That is fine, but what will you do if bad things happen?'

'Bad things?' I shifted uncomfortably. 'I think that depends. I don't think events will go that way, but if they were really bad I might decide God didn't want me to reach Jerusalem.'

He looked at me quizzically, demanding more.

'Well, for instance, if I was attacked or in some way became seriously injured.' I shrugged, not knowing what else to say.

'And then?' he asked.

'And then . . .' I inhaled deeply and all the fight just flowed out of me. 'I guess I would have to return to England in failure. And after that, I don't honestly know.'

Yes, return to England and do . . . what? Stack shelves in the local supermarket? Become an accountant and dedicate my life to the pursuit of money? I had no idea where this journey was leading, or what waited on the other side, but I was more determined than ever that this wouldn't be the final outcome.

I met Father Nikolaij for the penultimate time at breakfast. The huge dining table was spotted white with china bowls. Once again, it was frugal fare: watery cabbage, crusts of bread, cups of honeyed tea, and was that pasta? The monks really did live simply.

I found eating in silence to be a strange business. Talking is an important part of human interaction, particularly at mealtimes. Father Nikolaij sat opposite, nibbling on a dry crust, face impassive, yet eyes bird bright and alert. All around me elderly men in white lambswool robes were lifting spoons, chewing quietly, getting up and sitting down; there was plenty of clinking cutlery and enthusiastic slurps, but no one spoke. Did the other monks mind my presence? No one appeared to. Every so often I caught the father's eye. What was he thinking now? Did he have any regrets about joining the priesthood? Did he harbour any doubts? Did he secretly long to speak, to tell me more about the history of this great monastery?

After breakfast it took only a few minutes to pack. The skies were a miserable grey, the air scented with wet grass when we finally stepped into the courtyard. I sniffed nonchalantly. More rain seemed likely. For only the second time since we'd met, Father Nikolaij smiled . . .

'I made you some sandwiches,' he said. 'Here—' And he handed me a shopping bag bulging at the seams with what I assumed to be oranges. 'You do eat meat?'

I forced a tepid grin. 'Yes, father, that's no problem.' I took the bag and shouldered my rucksack. We shook hands—a stiff and rather formal goodbye. Then, after a final wave, with two rounds of ham sandwiches and a handful of oranges, I was gone.

Three days later, the Croatian border approached. I was still pondering events at Stična. The monastery had been a generous host accepting me in a way that other churches hadn't. I found myself conflicted by the gratitude I felt to the order and the kind of observations people invariably make about others. The virtues of their community were obvious: charity to strangers, humility, self-control, obedience, a diligence not for oneself, but for a greater good. Courage must also be added to that list. The Ottoman armies of the fifteenth century had failed to dislodge them, and there are many from the secular world that could learn from their steadfastness in time of danger.

And yet . . .

In a community where laughter has no purpose and words are deemed unnecessary, where does humanity find expression? When does humanity speak to itself? If a young man like Father Nikolaij could still take pleasure from describing the portraits of the former abbots (and I'm convinced he did), what then can be said of the older monks? Maybe it was only visible to an outsider, or perhaps with greater knowledge I would have concluded differently. But the older members of the order seemed withdrawn beyond the needs of mere contemplation. I sensed no joy in their endeavours, only a steadfast commitment to their vows. And as I walked on to Croatia a little wiser than before I realised that much may be gained in the service of Christ.

And perhaps something else is always lost.

Chapter Five

Croatia

The Land of Two Germans

When Yugoslavia fell apart during the nineties, putting an end to a country that had previously stretched from Austria in the north to Greece in the south, Croatia was one of the former socialist republics that found new life as an independent state. Partially fuelled by Father Nikolaij's excellent ham sandwiches, I spent the next three days getting there. The final kilometres provided much that was familiar: a free room, supper and complete acceptance at a Franciscan monastery, then a decidedly un-Christian brush-off at Kostanjevica na Krki (the priest's wife—a shrill woman with pursed lips and accusing eyes—had all but slammed the door in my face). I also discovered something else. No matter where you are in the world, how good you look in a small travel mirror, or how much God loves you, the ability to read a map is essential. I'd just spent seventy days crossing four countries. If only someone had told me . . .

'Mr de Lyon,' said the voice, and the words were accompanied by a sharp intake of breath. The Slovenian border guard leant casually forward on the wooden rim of the kiosk window. Cold blue eyes beneath a peaked cap raked my face. 'This is not an international crossing point.'

My jaw dropped. 'Are you sure? I have the map right here—'

He held up the flat of his hand. 'I'm sure. Look, we will let you pass, but it's very likely the Croatian side will send you back.' He straightened up, and with my passport in outstretched palm said, 'It's up to you.'

Such had been my good fortune I wasn't averse to taking a gamble. The Croatian guard sitting in the next kiosk was a tubby guy with flapping red jowls, crammed into a uniform two sizes too small. It didn't seem to be my day. He wasn't smiling, either.

'Mr de Lyon,' said Tubby, swivelling on his seat to face me, 'I have to tell you this is not an international—'

'Crossing point?'

Tubby narrowed his eyes.

'Yeah, I already know. The Slovenian guy told me.'

'That man was correct. This road is for local people, Croats, Slovenes and so on. I'm sorry,' he said, his voice suddenly picking up speed, 'but you cannot cross here. You must go back.'

'Back?' I heard my voice crack. 'That's going to put me into a lot of difficulty. Couldn't you please make an exception?'

'Well, I—'

'I've walked here all the way from Holland, I'm a Christian on pilgrimage walking to Jerusalem. Look—' I lifted my hand and began to wave Johanna's cross around like a talisman.

The guard licked his lips. There came a long pause pregnant with every kind of imagined disaster, and then:

'Bah.' He waved me away with a flick of the wrist. 'Go on, get out of here, just go.'

Rarely have nine words been more gratefully heard. I hastily took back my passport, shoved it down my shorts and quickly moved off before he could change his mind. And so it happened that on 19 May 2007 I managed to blag my way into Croatia.

If God is for us, who can be against us?

In the words of Romans 8:31, definitely not a bad-tempered fat bloke near Dobova.

From that troublesome border with pedantic guards it's an entire day's walk to the capital, Zagreb. I lost no time marching straight there, and boy, Rok was right about the roads. As soon as I crossed into Croatian territory they began to crumble. Potholes abounded—some large enough to satisfy the most intrepid cave explorer. Village pavements were crude affairs of crushed rock and sand, but not a trace of tarmac. I nimbly skirted the assorted debris with a new respect for solid British flagstones.

The walk took much longer than I expected, and the sun had set by the time I hit the suburbs. Although I don't recommend wandering around foreign cities in the dark, I can't deny it was a splendid evening. The moon was one half of a gold sovereign caught in fourth-floor windows, and twilight had turned the tramlines of the central zone into twin rivers of flowing silver. The ancient trams were regular if not noisy. Every few minutes another string of eerie yellow windows came screeching down, scaring flocks of ghostly pigeons from shadowed rooftops. Like swerving caterpillars the antique rustbuckets came on, chewing their way hungrily through the thick and heavy dusk.

I don't know how many hours I spent traipsing along Ilica—the endless street that bisects the city west to east—but it must have been several before I saw the spluttering red sign: Hotel Ilica. Hmm. Not very original. Normally, I would have been banging on church doors or checking out the hostels, but the lateness of the hour argued against.

Given my vast experience of crap Balkans hotels, I should have known better. The lobby had all the usual three-star accoutrements: a gleaming chessboard floor, a vulgar gilt-edged mirror to add a bit of class. Standing between mirror and counter was a uniformed receptionist in dire need of anger management.

'Three hundred and ninety-nine kuna?' I said, with a steadily rising voice. 'That seems expensi—'

She slammed her pencil down on the counter. 'Mister, are you joking? For a magnificent hotel right in the centre of Zagreb it is cheap!'

The receptionist continued to glower, a shrill and humourless blonde pouting in pink frosted lip gloss. There was more red and gold tassel on her shoulders than a five-star general in a banana republic.

Pink Lips shrugged. 'The best I can do,' she said, 'is give you a fifty kuna discount,' and picking up a nail file, she began to work her fingers, blowing lightly at the tips.

'Okay, I guess that will be fine.'

'Excellent!' Pink Lips put the file on the counter and threw me a plastic grin.

'Where do I sign?'

'Oh,' she said, and slid a ledger forward, 'here will do.'

I found 349 kuna in notes and coins and spread them out. Without thanking me, she scooped up the money, counted it like a nimble-fingered bank teller and began to rummage in a key box. While she did so, I scouted the lobby. Now that my eyes had properly adjusted I had a better view of the garish décor. Every inch spoke of seventies horror flicks: blood-red drapes shielding hidden monsters, brass gargoyles with protruding tongues, the menacing tick-tock of a grandfather clock winding down to the next bloodcurdling scream.

Pink Lips straightened up and pushed a key toward me. 'Here— Mr <insert something unpronounceable> will help you.'

Though I didn't catch the surname, it sounded like a Scrabble player's nightmare, full of Ps, Vs and at least one Z. Great for a triple word score, but a disaster in the latter stages of the game. Pink Lips dropped her arm under the counter and pushed an unseen buzzer.

SWISH! A pair of blood-red drapes parted. Cue some heavy breathing in the gap.

A few seconds later, the bellhop from hell stepped forward. Pink Lips took two steps back. I remained frozen to the spot, wondering if I'd blundered onto the set of a new Frankenstein movie.

This guy was the real deal, a worthy assistant to anyone insane with a white coat, a pile of twelve-inch bolts and an unhealthy interest in dead body parts.

The Igor-figure looked up at me. That wasn't hard; he was at least a foot shorter. I gazed back: at the shabby grey uniform, at a face square and cruel, at those tremendous shoulders, at two brawny arms dangling six inches longer than the average *Homo sapiens*. The latter was either an unfortunate congenital defect or too many years spent lugging heavy suitcases. There was no way this knuckle-dragger was touching my rucksack.

'Err . . . that's okay, mate. I got it.' I smiled as sweetly as I could at one so hideous. Crikey, I thought, I wouldn't like to rattle that guy's cage.

With a nod, Igor gave me a near-toothless grin, then vanished behind the drapes to get the lightning rods ready. As he slunk away I could almost hear the unspoken script: 'Yes, Master! The new head is ready! There will be a very big storm tonight!'

I didn't hang around long after that. Not wishing to have a twelve-inch bolt hammered through my neck, I scooped up my key and stumbled out the door toward the single rooms. On the way a group of elderly gents drinking and laughing raucously in a side room handed me a bottle of Karlovačko beer. It was a timely gift: those arms, that face . . . I needed something to steady my nerves.

Despite the thunder and lightning (which bizarrely did make an appearance), I awoke surprisingly refreshed. Breakfast was a decent buffet laid out beside gilt and velveteen chairs. I munched on a few crusty rolls, sipped some lukewarm coffee then, with camera and street map in hand, headed out to see the sights.

The obvious starting point was Ban Jelačić Square—named in honour of a nineteenth-century hero largely forgotten by anyone who isn't a historian or travel writer. A lifelong soldier serving the Austro-Hungarian Empire, Count Josip Jelačić spent the most important part of his career suppressing the 1848 Hungarian Revolt, and in so doing hoped to win favour with the Austrian monarchy to gain greater independence for his native

Croatia. While some of Jelačić's political aims succeeded, and others were frustrated, his loyalty to the imperial court didn't go unnoticed. In 1866 the Austrian authorities named the square in his honour and threw up an impressive black bronze statue. The statue remained the square's centrepiece until the 1940s when President Tito of Yugoslavia (ironically a fellow Croat) declared the statue to be 'ideologically unsound' and ordered its destruction. Fortunately, not all commands are obeyed.

One hundred and forty-eight years after Jelačić's death I took my own place by the reassembled monument. On top of a stone plinth a warhorse dramatically paws the air. Riding the horse is the scowling general in braided uniform and felt hat, his sabre drawn and face steely as Japanese tourists cluster around the stirrups. The square's grander structures mostly lie to the north and east. Here one can find wrought-iron balconies, convoluted floral stonework and, given Croatia's long association with the former Austro-Hungarian Empire, perhaps a sense of lost greatness. One of these lovely old buildings appeared to be a newly converted bank. Another, labouring under renovation, had been draped in a fifty-foot poster showing a blond woman in a bikini holding a credit card. The effect was utterly tasteless.

Then, as now, I'm not sure what I expected from Zagreb. One hundred years ago moustachioed hussars would have been gliding around chandeliered ballrooms, clutching women in white silk gloves—the fabulous architecture does much to spark the imagination. Since the end of those imperial days, it occurred to me the city has taken a massive step back. Beggars brazenly rummage through trashcans in newspaper-blown side streets. Everywhere, black graffiti is angry and chaotic. Crumbling concrete gathers in neat piles awaiting a broom that never comes. The pavements are so narrow on Ilica that many pedestrians have to walk down the central zone. As for the decrepit trams, they were probably delivered in the 1960s when Soviet leader Khrushchev was still in power.

And yet, my brief visit was by no means a disappointment.

Frantic photography is not the only reason to run around the upper town, but it's a jolly fun one. The national parliament is there—a large colonial building where members of the Croatian Party of Pensioners moan about dwindling savings. You can't get in, but it's worth a snap. On the ecclesiastical front, the roof of St Mark's Church—struck from a playschool palette of red, white and blue—is the one to gawp at. Seemingly constructed from a box of Lego bricks, the effect does strange things to the eyes if looked at for too long. The choicest bits of architecture are best seen from the garden beside St Catherine's Church: in the distance a copper-green onion dome decorated with floral gold; and rising from scaffolding, two needle-thin spires threading their way through ruffled cloud. Everything about Zagreb's twin-spired cathedral appeared to be leaning five degrees to the left, à la Tower of Pisa. Despite numerous attempts, I never did get a decent shot.

One night in Hotel Ilica had been enough to satisfy curiosity. I ended my second evening in the hostel on Petrinjska, scanning blurry images drawn from eight hours of manic plodding. Not even insults could spoil the mood. Before drifting into sleep I glanced at the black scrawl on the bunk above:

British scum leave Ireland now!
Seamus woz ere 2003

God bless you, Seamus, for my great-great-grandfather was Irish, you know. And with that, under a wafer-thin blanket peppered with cigarette burns, British scum fell fast sleep.

✳ ✳ ✳

For most of the next day I marched to Vukovina, some 25 km to the south. The long walk out of Zagreb's imperial streets began at 8:45 a.m. outside that awful hostel on Petrinjska. With a face full of sunshine I turned toward Ban Jelačić Square, grateful I no longer needed to shower behind an unlockable door full of holes plugged with newspaper. The showers had been a breeding ground for some creepy Swedes seeking out the bathroom for all the wrong reasons. I was glad to be rid of the place.

If the day began well, it quickly faltered. I don't know what possessed me to tie up so much money in AMEX cheques. The commission charged by most European banks would make a New York mugger blush, and despite bellicose advertising to the contrary, I've never seen any of those commission-free places they always trumpet about.

The teller took the usual generous cut. Then he methodically counted out several hundred Bosnian marks. I scooped them up, glad to have some local currency. Nevertheless, I could feel the unease growing. Only fifteen years earlier tens of thousands of people had died on Bosnian soil. When I closed my eyes nothing good came to mind. (Emaciated figures staring blankly behind barbed wire formed a particularly vivid vision.) The reality of modern life may have been different, but I had no first-hand experience and nothing except outdated news reports to go on.

The exit from Zagreb took longer than I hoped. Leaving a big city is usually harder than getting in, and it wasn't until late afternoon and travelling some very straight roads that seemed to go on forever that I finally arrived at Vukovina. It's a strip of a village: twentieth-century houses on one side, the odd pile of sixteenth-century thatch on the other. The church sits on the corner where the road spins off to the right, and outside stands the most cunning soul south of the River Sava—a bespectacled, silver-haired granny in a knitted shawl selling all the trappings of worship. For the price of two yellow candles this sweet old dear also sells directions to the house of the priest. Exulting in the mysterious workings of the Lord, I slipped her a few worthless kuna and marched straight up the front path.

That day I learnt something vital: never try to short-change sweet old ladies in the service of the church. It's suicide. The only thing bigger than the priest's residence was the hungry Alsatian that had been quietly dozing in the corner. I must have fled twice as quickly.

Having struck out spectacularly at the church, I had no choice but to camp. It actually wasn't a bad option. The area around Vukovina is an agricultural mosaic of cabbage-like greens, strips of dirt, rutted tracks imprinted with tractor tyres and metallic barns bouncing the sun. I was standing in a field, pondering the best place to pitch, when a tiny tractor broke a line of distant trees and came hurtling towards me. What's this? I thought, and wondered whether to flee.

Eventually, a tonne of smoking scarlet metal stuttered to a halt. An elderly woman in a purple headscarf jumped down, followed by an old gentleman wearing a straw hat and red checked shirt.

'*Wie geht's?*' said the man, with a crunching grip my hand will never forget.

I *geht's* pretty well thank you.

Alas, most of the ensuing German went straight over my head, and I could do little else except stand there like a dummy. I was bracing myself for a good ticking off when I started to recognise a few of the smaller words, like 'you', 'sleep' and 'house'. Wow! Was I hearing this right? Ever the optimist, I inserted 'in my' to create the most glorious of all phrases: 'you sleep in my house', and after that, I achieved an entirely new level of euphoria. But if my translation was correct, how exactly would we get there? Joseph grinned and tapped the rear mudguard. In the forty-third year of life I was about to make my debut . . . on a tractor.

I have to admit at this point that I'm not really an agricultural type. Just looking at a trowel gives me chronic backache. Anything I spray with a watering can promptly dies. Ditto any plant I repot. My deathly touch even extends to cress seeds, which as every child knows are notoriously easy to grow. I remember it well, a five-year-old boy staring at a piece of dried-up cotton wool on the windowsill. 'Where's the cress?' I asked mum, before exploding into tears.

With a warm bed in the offing this didn't seem the right time to voice embarrassing childhood failures; a clever pilgrim knows when to keep schtum. Joseph dumped my rucksack into the rear lifter then marched to the front and clambered into the seat. His buxom wife and I settled anxiously on opposing mudguards—it looked like a long drop to the ground. Suddenly, black smoke erupted from the turret as Joseph gunned the powerful engine. There was another flurry of good-natured smiles. Then we spun left and made for the road. I was still beaming pleasantly right up to that first scream.

Not all madmen are called Hannibal Lecter and dine on fava beans and fine Chianti. Two kilometres outside Vukovina, sixty-two-year-old Farmer Joseph suddenly morphed into Michael Schumacher, revved the throttle and stepped on it—hard. We never did reach the relative safety of the main road. Instead, we turned left again and took a narrow dirt track. That was the start of it. Croatian dirt tracks are like their roads, but worse, far, far worse. I'd not been this frightened since kissing Aunt Lil's fuzzy top lip. That was over forty years ago when Slade always bagged the Christmas number one. The memory still haunts.

Nothing in recorded history could have prepared me for what happened next. Shuddering and rattling, we hurtled up the track, dipping, rising, swerving around huge mounds of earth, accelerating past imaginary competitors in a dash to the finish. Some of the potholes would have swallowed a train. We dodged them by a hair's breadth then went even faster. Wind tore through our hair, whipping insanely at the wife's headscarf. I quickly caught a mouthful of smoke, coughed, spluttered, struggled to find something to breathe. For twenty seconds I was doubled up and too busy suffocating to scream.

'*Ja, ja, alles gut!*' shouted Joseph, turning to face me.

Alles gut? Why isn't he watching the track!

I glared at his back. One moment I was praying for his death, the next that he would live forever—or at least long enough to get me to the house. On the mudguard there was nothing to hold onto, not even a sliver of muddy straw. I hastily improvised and deployed my buttocks like a massive vice. For ten long minutes my life depended on a seriously out of shape gluteus maximus.

After narrowly missing the race's largest spectator—a dandelion-munching cow that had foolishly blundered into our path—we turned the final bend in triumph and took the chequered flag just outside Joseph's gate. Remarkably, all four of us would live to race another day, bemused cow included.

To the hungry victor go the pork schnitzel spoils. For all the oft-celebrated romance of pitching camp at sunset you can't beat sleeping on a firm mattress; and besides, a shower and hot meal are always worth fighting for. The wife was an excellent cook and trained not to let a guest leave the table until completely stuffed. After dinner I virtually rolled into bed.

When morning came I caught up with Joseph tinkering by the tractor. He put down his wrench and rose unsteadily clutching his back.

'*Mann muss dem Menschen helfen,*' he said, hand in mine.

Man must help man. Two rheumy eyes looked down, and at once I knew he meant it. He'd been a true Samaritan. I wouldn't forget.

A few hours later, while travelling the Vukovina-Sisak-Petrinja highway, I spotted a pair of buzzards riding the currents, spreading their wings as they circled joyously in the infinite sky. The wind suddenly freshened, drawing the spinning birds higher. I was still thinking about my fortuitous meeting with Farmer Joseph, a man I would undoubtedly never see again. Could this be the moment when I finally let go of doubt?

The two buzzards soared again. And in the company of feathered wings faith climbed a fraction higher on that blue bridge before Heaven's gate.

✳ ✳ ✳

The churches of Europe have a surprisingly large number of unhelpful priests. I discovered that for the third time near Sela. A day's walk south of Vukovina, the village is a strip of rickety fences surrounded by golden wheat and seemed deserted like one of those dust-blown atomic test sites in Nevada. The only time I saw life was on the top of a telephone pole. I glanced up, drawn by a pair of red bills, and was confronted by two orange-legged storks standing incongruously in a nest big enough for a man to sit on. The birds were the king and queen of all they surveyed. They made a fetching couple.

I had to return to the highway to find the priest's house. The old building was a Tudor mix of oak beams crisscrossing black paint and whitewash. I knocked eagerly, again feeling hope rise. I couldn't help myself. Another church meant another door and another chance for God to show his blessing.

Two minutes passed. No answer. Then the door swung out, leaving a miserly six-inch gap. A pair of darting eyes squinted through the crack. I could see the white ring of a clerical collar. Would this kind priest in the pay of the church and pledged to help the needy offer a pilgrim shelter?

A mouthful of ridiculous bluster, and then: 'Try Sisak,' he said coldly. 'You will find a bigger church there.'

I felt the disappointment bite. While it was clearly his right to turn me away, the decision seemed inexplicable given the huge resources at his disposal. I looked up at the windows of his ten-bedroom home. A community building stood behind me, which looked twice as large again. Surely I could have rolled out my sleeping bag there?

That evening I pitched camp in an apple orchard layered with straw. After leaving the church I'd blundered into a built-up area, and it was the only place that appeared remotely suitable. The son of the owner was a young man, blunt in manner, with dark, accusing eyes. His mother had given me a bottle of water. Then, shortly before dusk, the son stopped by. He was driving into town and asked me if I wanted anything.

'No thanks,' I answered. 'I'm fine.'

The son cocked an eyebrow.

I smiled. 'No really. And by the way, huge thanks for this.' I lifted the bottle, a wonderfully cool two-litre monster.

He laughed, hands on knees, rocking gently on his haunches.

Straw crackled underfoot. 'Why thank us? We only gave you water.'

'I did try the priest at the big house on the road, but he wasn't very helpful. The guy actually told me to walk on to Sisak.'

The son snorted and reached down into the straw. 'Oh him,' he said, and began to twiddle a stalk between finger and thumb. 'We know all about *him*.'

'How come?'

'We are Catholics and that place is our church. He's new here, arrived a few months ago.' The teenager clucked his tongue and shrugged. 'No one likes him. The old priest was much better.'

It was a pretty emphatic statement of discontent. Ask, seek, knock: sure, it often worked, but there were always exceptions. I lived in the real world, and the world was full of cold hearts. Unfortunately, quite a few had made their way into the church.

It was at rotten times like these I often thought back to the experiences of other pilgrims. The facts might seem surprising, but at any minute of the day someone will be walking to Jerusalem—or thinking about it. Tens of thousands more will be taking the Way of St James towards Santiago de Compostela in northern Spain. There will be many reasons for setting out: a deep-felt obligation to promote world peace, the desire to highlight cherished political causes, the search for the inner self, or perhaps a desire for new direction. A few may simply be enjoying a pleasant walking holiday, and despite the heavy spiritual connotations of 'The Way', there is nothing wrong with that. Going is what really matters, and by the end everyone will have a story to tell.

Mony Dojeiji, a fellow pilgrim hailing from Canada, was one such individual. I remember corresponding with her by email as I travelled; and when I told her 'I always thought priests had a responsibility to help pilgrims', she replied 'I had the same belief to begin with.'

'So what happened?'

'I learnt to knock without expectation.'

The advice was particularly relevant to my current situation, coming as it did on the heels of another priestly rejection. But it was the rest of her story that strengthened my belief in the Divine and encouraged me to persevere. Travelling initially to Santiago de Compostela, this former Microsoft executive found much more than a desire to advance world peace. Unbeknown to her a Spanish artist named Alberto Agraso had set off in the same direction. In 2001 their worlds collided at Cape Finisterre on the coast of Galicia. Since then, they've both walked to Israel, become man and wife, emigrated to Canada and started a family. Which just goes to show on the pilgrim road you never know what lies in store.

Of course, not all tales end so well, and not all start in the same fashion.

For those unfamiliar with the world of volunteering, Raleigh International is a well-respected charity providing opportunities for young people to work abroad. In 1998 Ben Nimmo had been a twenty-five-year-old team leader in Belize overseeing a variety of ecological and community building projects. Conditions in the jungle were primitive, groups were close knit and friendships the kind that last. Disaster struck out of the blue. A fellow co-worker building classrooms in San Pablo went missing. The news was both sudden and painful—she'd been murdered.

In the immediate aftermath Ben and his team carried on working. To have done anything else would have been a victory for the killers; and no one wanted that. In time, the volunteers returned home. Raleigh set up a fund, and Ben decided to begin a fundraising walk in her memory. For nine months he busked to Compostela, shouldering a huge trombone. It was a noble and selfless act. It was also a test of endurance. Remember, I'm the weight fanatic who sawed the handle off his own toothbrush. This jazz-loving pilgrim was made of sterner stuff. His spirit seemed indomitable. Whatever this guy had—I needed it now.

By 25 May I'd put the disappointment of Sela behind me, and I was closing in, albeit with considerable trepidation, on the

Bosnian border. In those final days the shadow of the Yugoslav Wars was never far away. The region of Croatia horseshoeing around the northwestern edge of Bosnia Herzegovina used to be the Republic of Serbian Krajina, and it's one of the darker stories of Croatian independence. The republic was originally created in 1991 by local Serbs as a means of self-protection. It didn't take long for events to take a sinister turn. In the cryptic language of the times the land was 'ethnically cleansed' by the Yugoslav National Army aided by Serbian militia. Thousands of Croats were expelled from their homes; hundreds more killed defending the city of Vukovar. As military fortunes changed Croats responded with crimes of their own, including the Gospić massacre which was nothing less than cold-blooded murder. Although roughly a hundred Serb civilians are thought to have died, vested interests on both sides mean the exact number remains hotly disputed. The full truth of who did what to whom will probably never be known.

Today, as a political entity at least, nothing remains of the Serbian Krajina. The self-styled republic only lasted five years before being destroyed in 1995 by a revitalised Croatian Army. The physical scars are still visible, however, for those walking cautiously beside white-boughed trees. I saw several bombed-out houses: blackened concrete shells, roofless and choked with creeping vines. They very eloquently testified to the carnage. And there were other buildings, too, that jogged the memory of past conversations:

'Houses there are very simple. Family upstairs. Animals below. I grew up somewhere like that, and it wasn't nice.'

The German waiter I'd met at Vellberg had been a fount of semi-useless information. These two-storey dwellings had no windows, no doors and a flight of concrete steps ran up the outside, presumably to the living quarters. Did oxen and pigs normally live underneath? The houses looked half-finished, as if the owners had suddenly ran out of money or fled to UN safe havens that had proved anything but.

Gloomily, I plodded on. In keeping with the depressing vista, it was nigh-on certain I would meet someone with a demeanour to match. I felt disappointed when it turned out to be a German. I'd met a couple in Slovenia a week or so ago, and the hospitality of Farmer Joseph and his honking pigs was still fresh in the memory. The afternoon had been another scorcher, so my new host and I had taken shelter in his garage.

Fifty-three-year-old Kurt looked every inch the builder: giant potbelly, baggy tracksuit bottoms, bulging biceps, white T-shirt caked in orange brick dust; and yet despite having downed two bottles of premium beer, he seemed amiable enough. With the handshakes and introductions over, I quickly steered the conversation to the whereabouts of Hrastovica's priest.

'You ask for the priest!' Kurt rocked back on his stool, shooting out a meaty hand to steady himself. A white-knuckled fist settled on the humming chest freezer.

'I want nothing to do with him! Nothing!'

Blimey. His cheeks have turned purple ... I was trapped in a garage with someone who was bigger, stronger, more pissed off (and more pissed, if I'm being frank) than I was. When I decided to walk to Jerusalem, I never signed up for this.

It would take a better German-speaker than I to establish why Kurt the builder had turned against the church. Despite the kind of iron concentration I only usually deploy when my life is in imminent danger, I only picked up garbled snippets. Formerly of Hamburg, it appeared that Kurt had been a frequent church-goer and made regular tithe payments as Catholics must in order to receive the sacraments. At some point he'd hurt his back and gone to the local priest for help. From the angry hand-waving I concluded that meeting hadn't gone too well.

I smiled at him. 'Well, I hope you get better soon. And thanks for the beer, I appreciate it.' I put the bottle on the ground and rose to leave.

Kurt's mouth twisted, like one who has just gulped a mouthful of vinegar. He looked away. *'Es war gar nichts.'* It was nothing.

The builder's rancour had dampened my spirits. With the shadows lengthening and the whereabouts of the priest unknown, I had no option but to bed down with whatever crawled, slithered or grazed in the surrounding fields. Morning reached new levels of awfulness. In the ghostly light of dawn I staggered out of my tent, hit a waist-high wall of dripping grass, then recoiled, cursing, legs and shorts totally drenched. I looked in my pocket mirror and found a bristled mountain man staring back. Bah. A public tap stood by the roadside. The muddy pool beneath was wriggling with about a million mosquito larvae. I found a sliver of soap retained for imminent border crossings and, scraping furiously with a three-month-old razor, made the best of it.

If there was any doubt I was marching into Bosnia it vanished at Hrvatska Kostajnica. This final outpost of Croatia begins on the heights above the River Una, and high above the far bank, on sweet green hills, soar the Muslim minarets: tall, white and pencil thin. Their spectacular copper cones glint in the sun like Apollo rockets waiting for a launch that will never come. As if on cue they began to sing:

'Allaaaaaah ~ uAkbar! Allaaa~AA~aa~A~a~A~aa~AAh ~ u ~ aakbar!'

For five minutes that seemed like fifty, I looked on in total wonder.

The hour had grown late. It seemed safer to spend one last night on Croatian soil. Kostajnica was small and crumbling, but it had all the pilgrim essentials: a post office to send packages home and at least one shop selling strange biscuits in unfamiliar packets. Accommodation was sorted in minutes. I finished my day in Hotel Central, feet up on the bed, watching impenetrable Croatian television. The screen flickered amiably. My mind was lost in copper-coned minarets.

In the morning I dropped off some maps at the post office then sauntered down to the riverbank. At the river I swung left and headed towards the bridge. Bosnia rose on my right: hilly, hazy, mysterious and splendidly green. It looked quite calm from a distance. No smoke. No gunshots. No shouting. Nothing to suggest any kind of trouble. I could see the bridge clearly now, a strip of flat concrete with railings laddering the edge and bobbing heads striding serenely across in twos and threes.

I walked on, wide-eyed like a child on his first day at school. The riverside rustled with blood-red poppies; bottle-green reeds broke the river's glassy surface. A two-towered fortress hugged the opposing bank. I looked at the pyramidal roofs battering the sky and the sloping stonework proudly jutting out toward the water's edge. War had taken place here once: medieval war. Old imperial hues rose above: the red, white and blue of Croatia's national flag flapping lazily in the breeze.

At the bridge I paused to compose myself. As I gazed down its length I ran Johanna's cross between my fingers and prayed for safe passage. What would I find at the end? There was no way of knowing, but if I was to reach Jerusalem the question demanded an answer. I glanced upward beyond the river. It was going to be a fine day once the sun burnt off the haze. It was going to be a *good* day.

And yet the unease remained. The sense of impending doom reminded me of Father Nikolaij's troubling question: 'What will you do if bad things happen?'

Three days into my Bosnian odyssey, I was going to find out.

Chapter Six

Bosnia Herzegovina

The Land of Beckoning Hands

Something bad did happen in Bosnia Herzegovina, but it was horrific luck, took a few days to erupt into monumental crisis and had nothing to do with those dark forests I'd been fretting about. It wasn't until late afternoon that I noticed the first sign of trouble. I sat on the motel bed and pulled off my socks. They were certainly the feet of a true pilgrim: pink scar tissue, blotchy red toes, a spectacular black toenail. The real menace lurked on the left foot, where two gigantic sores had begun to form on the heel. Fearing the worst, I threw together a makeshift ice pack using cubes drawn from the fridge.

I had good reason to be concerned. Long-distance walkers use all kinds of strategies to prevent blisters. Some folk switch their socks. Others recommend stopping every few hours to air the feet. In my case, I'd been using talcum powder to soak up sweat. Alas, my diligence wasn't enough. When I checked the next day the two blisters were on the verge of merging into something quite nasty. Seven months earlier a similar problem had forced me back to England. The feeling of déjà vu was palpable.

I marched on, trying to ignore the growing discomfort. I was limping through the outskirts of Busnovi when the storm hit. Oil-black clouds flashed bluish-white zigzags. Every thunderbolt sounded like a hundred cracking trees. Rain hammered my forehead; my T-shirt was a sopping rag, my spine a trickling river. This was farming country: crooked hay barns and chimneyed cottages, rickety fences snuggling right up to the road. All about lay endless watery green.

Suddenly, movement: the flutter of a hand on the left. I halted, blinked, took off my glasses and rubbed my eyes. I replaced them and tried to focus.

A white-painted porch beneath corrugated plastic.

Three patio chairs around a low table.

In the middle chair an arm waving.

Is this guy waving at me? I blinked again, trying to clear my eyes of water. The mysterious hand beckoned with more urgency. I looked up and down the puddled road.

There's no one else here you idiot!

At that moment it clicked. I'm never at my best in the middle of a monsoon, and I really wasn't expecting any hospitality. For the final time I tapped my chest. The watery phantom nodded; then I unclasped the gate and limped up the garden path.

I think terror was the first emotion. It's a frightening moment when you tug on a flap of loose skin and two inches of your body literally comes away in your hand. It's doubly frightening when you have thousands of kilometres to walk and you're stuck in a village miles from a hospital.

I leant over the stranger's bath for a closer look. The rain and constant chafing had caused the super-blister to split, leaving a mushy, gaping wound. Pink flesh shone beneath, gleaming like butcher's ham. The entire foot throbbed. *Okay, is this it? Am I simply going to give up?* No.

Then calm down and think.

Plaster seemed the immediate solution, as much as I could lay on. My rucksack sat dripping by the bath. I ripped open the cord and started to rummage for the first-aid kit. I cut off a gigantic strip with Father Nikolaij's warning screaming in both ears:

'But what will you do if bad things happen?'

As I gently smoothed down the edges, I was desperately trying to figure that one out.

With the rain slowly abating, back on the porch proper introductions now took place. Notwithstanding the pain and general angst, I carried on smiling in an effort to play the grateful guest. The beckoning hand belonged to Stanislav, an endlessly cheerful man with a crooked neck and arms like pipe-cleaners. His English was almost non-existent, so he gave me a bottle of beer and I consoled myself with frequent sips and polite conversation with his many friends.

I must have been nearing the end of my second bottle when Lana came striding up the path. Slender and olive-skinned, with huge owl-like eyes, the jet-black hair of a woman in her twenties clung to the shoulders of a blue denim jacket.

'It's Tony,' I grunted in response to the obvious question; then I let go of her hand and slumped back. I immediately sensed a sympathetic ear.

'Look,' she began, 'perhaps I can help. My mother's been a nurse at the hospital for years. I've seen many injuries, even gunshots.' She leant forward, cupping her knees with her hands. 'Can I see?'

'Sure . . . But I promise you, it's not pleasant.'

I leant over to loosen the laces, wincing as the heel slid out the back. Down came the sock. I felt her expectant gaze as I peeled back three inches of freshly laid plaster.

'Ouch!' Toying with the silver crucifix at her throat, she said, 'You're right. That looks quite bad.'

Stanislav threw a questioning look at Lana, who promptly said something back in their local language.

While they continued to talk I inched on the boot. My hands were visibly shaking, which rarely happens and never in the sight of total strangers. If that doesn't tell a story, then nothing will. As I looked up Lana was nodding in Stanislav's direction.

She turned to face me. 'Where are you staying tonight?'

I pointed uneasily to the road. 'Somewhere out there. I'm not really sure.'

I knew from last year's failure in Dordrecht that this type of injury needed days to heal, possibly weeks. In a large town the situation might have been manageable. I could have rested in a hotel, finding food would have been easy ... In Busnovi there was nothing—nothing but polka-dot cows mindlessly chewing grass and two Serbs I'd met barely half an hour ago.

I looked out beyond the picket fence to Bosnia's dripping green meadows. Could it all really end here in this speck of a village? I was halfway out of my chair and heading for my soggy rucksack when Stanislav waved me back.

Lana clapped her hands. I stared at her, wondering why she looked so pleased.

'I have some good news for you,' she said, with a smile that almost split her ears. 'Stanislav has agreed that you can spend the night at his house.'

And then.

'Tomorrow my husband will drive us to Prijedor. There is a hospital that can fix your foot. It's not great, not as good as what you have in England, but it will do. We can't let you walk on. After all,' and she swept her hand out toward the fence, 'where would you go?'

I'd just lost two essential inches of my left foot. I won't even try to describe the relief.

A pilgrim given a second lease of life is a wonderful thing to behold. He smiles, he laughs, he drinks a lot more beer than he really should. I was thinking of trying for a fourth bottle when Stanislav's wife appeared in the doorway. Maria was an ample woman, bustling and rarely still. Her cheeks were ruddy, she was puffing slightly and soapsuds were casting miniature rainbows on her yellow apron.

Lana caught her eye, they exchanged words, then Lana turned back to me and said, 'Maria asks where is the rest?'

'The rest? I'm not sure what you—'

'Your clothes. She asks where are your pants and socks, the wet ones you took off in the bathroom when you arrived.'

Ah, *those*.

I shook my head. 'You don't need to worry about that. I'll deal with them later when I get to Banja Luka.'

'No,' said Lana firmly, 'this woman will wash *all* your clothes.'

Truly no woman hath greater courage. I handed Maria a plastic bag, praying the stains weren't too brutal.

By the time morning came every thread was still damp. That hardly mattered as by then all thought had turned to mending my foot. Lana was as good as her word. Her husband pulled up shortly after breakfast driving what we in England politely call 'an old banger'. It rolled forward gamely, exploded huge clouds of exhaust and promised second gear on the slopes, but never quite delivered. For someone who had stubbornly refused lifts all over Europe the simple act of getting inside was more problematic than I thought. I had to force myself into the back.

The Prijedor hospital was much as expected, i.e. purely functional with lots of whitewash and long concrete passages; clouds of strong disinfectant assailed the nostrils. Face-down and white-knuckled on a trolley, I lost a few more inches of my precious left heel and hobbled off sporting a spectacular gauze strapping running halfway up my calf. The heel throbbed worse than ever. In between the gasps, I realised I'd had a lucky escape.

The closing moments at the cottage are the ones I remember best. Maria pushed to the front, puffing wildly and clutching a new pair of purple Y-fronts. If they carried a subliminal message about the washing, I was too amused to notice. She gave me a rib-crunching hug, lifting me onto my toes, then Lana stepped forward, bright and smiling.

'Lana, are you sure? I don't think I can accept this . . .' She was holding out a box of chocolate wafers, though what I was really objecting to was a twenty-euro note, probably a lot of money in these parts.

'Why?' Her face began to crease, and her owlish eyes became sad. 'Won't you need money?'

I didn't, but I was obviously giving offence, so took it quickly before we both became embarrassed.

Stanislav for his part had decided to focus on the practical. I popped open the umbrella, a fine black specimen worthy of any bowler-hatted civil servant. Given the circumstances of our first meeting, it seemed very appropriate. His next gift was undoubtedly unique in modern pilgrimage: a pair of fake crocodile-skin shoes. Nice, I thought. Slip-ons with an open heel. At least my gauze dressing won't chafe on the back.

I saw them for the final time at the gate. Lana stood there, tall and willowy, waving her hand in broad, stately sweeps; Maria biting her lips, hands planted on yellow-aproned hips; Stanislav standing between them in a sky-blue T-shirt, beer bottle raised shoulder high in solemn yet cheery salute. I waved back with only minor winces, then shuffled beyond their lingering gaze into the damp of another grim Bosnian morning.

As if on cue the heavens opened a few doors down. I popped open the umbrella and began to meander between the growing puddles. The sense of déjà vu came unbidden. Four months ago in Holland I'd been knocking timidly on doors. During a soggy evening in Dodewaard I'd nursed a small injury up the garden path of Frans and Heleen. I left the next morning praising God and euphorically clutching sandwiches. Whenever I found myself in difficulty something always seemed to turn up. Were these events nothing more than mere chance?

If there was the beginning of an answer, I like to think it shone through at these moments—in timeless truths hidden in tiny seconds. In a smile, a beckoning hand, in the wisdom of a heart that sees beyond itself. The world was full of Good Samaritans motivated by a higher purpose. In England I'd largely forgotten that. This was another extraordinary reminder. As for that nasty injury that could have set me back months or perhaps destroyed my chances of reaching Jerusalem forever. Was this the table the Father had prepared for me and for which I had laboured so long? Judge for yourself.

On the icy coast of Holland I'd only hoped.

In the village of Busnovi, I started to *believe*.

✳ ✳ ✳

That I should end up defending alleged war criminal Radovan Karadžić is not a political position I thought I'd ever take when I first planned a trip down Bosnia Herzegovina. Well, perhaps 'defending' would be a tad strong, but I didn't rush to condemn him, either.

Let's be clear. It wasn't that I didn't know anything about the leader of the Bosnian Serbs or the war in central Europe that had caused Yugoslavia to tear itself apart. During the nineties events in the Balkans were headline news in the United Kingdom. Each day fresh accusations were made: torture, rape, ethnic cleansing, genocide. With issues this important it wasn't long before British and European politicians began to take sides. Then American leaders waded in, ultimately setting the tone for a controversial NATO intervention. In a crude narrative seemingly constructed from the darker pages of US history, the view emerged that the Croats and Bosnians were the cowboys, and Serbs the Indians. I disagree. On my fourth day in Bosnia some of the Indians were starting to look like the good guys. Stanislav and his friends proved it. Gosh. Whatever next?

'*Zdravo!*' Two of Busnovi's finest citizens lifted small glasses in my direction. Four more seated heads immediately spun round.

I cut my stride and glanced at the flurry of beckoning hands. Beside a large steel barbecue griddle, six middle-aged blokes in various stages of hair loss were slumped around a table. A pear-shaped bottle wrapped in straw stood in the middle, regularly raised by those assembled.

An experienced pilgrim rarely passes up hospitality. Not wishing to miss out on all the good things that were surely imminent, I halted beside them, dropped my rucksack to the ground, and reached out to a thin man with more red hair than my sister and a black snake tattooed on his right forearm. As he slowly rose copious quantities of alcohol danced behind crazy darting eyes.

'So,' I said, 'your name's Dragon?'

Our swaying hands met halfway across the table.

'*Dragan*,' he said, abruptly releasing my grip and holding up a chastising finger.

I smiled. 'Dragan. Right, mate.'

He gave a crooked grin, fell back heavily and poured himself another drink. It was barely 10 a.m. I was seriously impressed.

For the others in the group it was a case of wash, rinse and repeat. One by one they staggered politely to their feet: three burly farmers in blue boilersuits, hands spotted with tractor oil; a bald guy sipping quietly in a red polo shirt. Big Bloke came last, a hefty six-footer in a cream T-shirt with a wrestler's forearms and a neck like a Spanish bull.

They didn't lose any time welcoming me into the fold. Little ribbed glasses were drained and swiftly refilled with a clear liquid that scorched the throat, setting the eyes streaming. In between sips I snacked on whatever was set before me. Since a bunch of Lana's chocolate wafers were still fizzing in my stomach (I'd only marched five hundred yards from Stanislav's house), the sudden addition of greasy pork made an unusually satisfying combination. Unfortunately, none of my hosts spoke a word of English, except for the smallest.

'I'm Dimitrije!' squeaked the voice. An elfin face looked up at me, hair cropped round and short like a church choirboy. 'I'm a nine-year-old boy, and I can speak to you the very good English!'

And he did: the *very* good English.

Dimitrije's timely arrival was the last piece of the linguistic puzzle. With our diminutive translator chomping at the bit, the questions flowed freely: name, rank, serial number, where did I live and what the hell was I doing tramping around Bosnia in a pair of fake crocodile-skin shoes? Dimitrije translated every sentence, eyes shining with pride. Suddenly, in a world of towering adults he was the centre of attention—and he loved it. When the questions eventually dropped off I decided to satisfy curiosity. I jabbed a finger at his chest.

'Dimitrije,' I said, 'who's that man on your T-shirt?'

'He looked down and began tugging at a bearded guy wearing a round felt hat. The face had an old-fashioned monocle in one eye and the stern appearance of a military commander who liked to be obeyed. My pilgrim sixth sense told me this was no Serbian Teletubby.

'Oh, that is Draža Mihailović. He's a very famous Serb leader.'

'Ahhh.' I nodded sagely and lifted my glass. 'I know, you mean like your Mr Karadžić.'

That little glass never reached my lips.

Six pairs of eyes swivelled in my direction. Red Polo Shirt sat bolt upright letting rip with a red-faced staccato burst.

'This man is now not happy,' squeaked Dimitrije. 'He says you have insulted the great heroes of our Mother Serbia!'

Eh? What? Before I could reply Big Bloke looked up and narrowed his eyes. He slammed his glass down on the table. Glasses shuddered. Drops of booze flew into the air. Something dark emerged through gritted teeth and Dimitrije duly translated.

'He says Karadžić is a great man, a strong man for Serbia!'

Blimey, I thought. These guys are tetchy.

'Yes,' I stammered, 'of course, of course . . .' What should I do to calm things down? I balled my fist and punched the air hoping Big Bloke wouldn't take it as a personal challenge. 'Karadžić is a strong man! Very strong man for Serbia!'

Red Polo Shirt grimaced. He exchanged a glance with Big Bloke who gave a grunt of approval and slumped backward as if stung by a tranquilliser dart. I let out a discreet sigh. Then I told myself to keep my mouth shut.

It wasn't enough to keep me out of trouble. Beware of little glasses offered by hands spotted with tractor oil. The first drink had left me merry, the fifth without any feeling below the waist. Big Bloke now had two heads and more flailing arms than the mythical Kraken. Even more disturbing, I was itching to punch his lights out.

A few sips later, the remainder of my liver became a suitable prop for the genius of Damien Hirst. Only a fresh tank of form-aldehyde was needed funded by an obscenely large cheque from Charles Saatchi. Mercifully, fate once more rode to the rescue. The café's owner (the grimacing Red Polo Shirt) had an empty cottage nearby. The last thing I can remember were two pairs of strong arms sweeping me up and dragging me off to somewhere warm and dark. As I left the scene in total disgrace Dimitrije's little elfin face floated beside me, '. . . church . . . celebration . . . Stratinska.' Ahhhh. I thought it was all just a dream.

* * *

The church celebration wasn't a dream, but given the throbbing headache I woke up with, there was part of me that hoped it might be. The cloud-cast day in May that saw me rushed into the gaping arms of the Serbian Orthodox Church began a few yards from Busnovi's favourite watering hole—the indomitable Café Piramida. Despite the gratitude I felt to the owner, I have to admit, I've greeted dawn in more salubrious surroundings. An old iron stove, a silver flue snaking up to the rafters, carpet strips nailed to the ceiling, a hand-carved chair—dark, dusty and seething with mice, the two-room cottage was a humble abode. Unsurprisingly, the toilet lurked outside. After snacking on some of Lana's leftover wafers, I staggered into a wooden shack and found the seat covered in the kind of splinters that dare a man to sit down. Blimey, I thought. That's just brilliant.

I didn't have long to swear. At 9 a.m. a group of burly men turned up and, under stern orders to help out, I was soon puffing wildly and lugging huge beer crates into car boots. The highlight of the frantic preparations was a glistening pig's carcass that had been roasted on the café's griddle. The magnificent steel skewer was as tall as I was. With a few more curses we manhandled the monstrosity onto a roof rack. Someone tightened a few leather straps. Red Polo Shirt fixed a couple of Serbian flags to the wing mirrors of the lead car. Then, with the radio blasting something suitably patriotic and a few more hearty cries of '*Zdravo!*', ten cars chock-full of thirsty Serbs headed off in noisy cavalcade.

Bosnia doesn't spend a lot of money on roads, so the journey isn't one my buttocks would like to repeat. Although the drive probably only lasted about thirty minutes, because of the broken macadam surface it seemed far longer. Enclosed by overhanging greenery we skirted the larger craters, were thrown helplessly to the side when we couldn't. Sunlight hazed the winding road. Nationalistic music blared fifty decibels above the legal limit. Two flags of a proud people fluttered. My co-travellers sat beside me, a group of ordinary, middle-aged men on a very ordinary trip. Their hospitality back at the café had been freely given, unexpected and really quite marvellous. As had Stanislav's the day before. The question deserved a proper answer. Were Bosnian Serbs really the bad guys the media made them out to be?

I had doubts long before we ever pulled up at Stratinska. There was a carnival atmosphere in the village that morning, reminding me not of the horrors of war, but instead of our own annual summer processions along the seafront. Once free of our cars, we stretched for a moment in the sun, strode onto dewy grass, and within seconds were engulfed in a seething crowd with rosy-cheeked children careering in every direction. Beside a domed marquee, bands of old women in black headscarves were gossiping while silver-haired men in olive blazers sipped beer, clinked brown bottles, slapped backs and shook hands enthusiastically. I got lost immediately, and it was only the sound of my nickname that enabled me to get my bearings.

'London!' I glanced to the left at the snake's nest of orange-red hair emerging from the throng.

It's funny how strangers bond if given the chance. At the café I'd fumbled Dragan's name, and after the hullabaloo about heroes of Mother Serbia, we'd barely spoken. The following morning had provided an opportunity to find out more about him. The short ride into Stratinska had provided another. He'd sketched an envelope in my diary, and from that I deduced he was a postman. The deduction was spot on. Dragan knew everyone, and that meant everyone wanted to know me.

'Hello, Hello, I'm Tony.' I smiled at blazers nine and ten, and began to shake hands.

For the rest of that day Dragan became my mentor in all things Serbian. There was much to learn, and he was eager for me to savour the best they had to offer.

'Beer?' he asked, as we dipped into the huge marquee.

I began to massage a throbbing temple. I still hadn't learnt my lesson from yesterday. Okay, Dragan, if you insist.

Bottles in hand, we ambled across the field toward Stratinska's church. It was a simple house of God: cellophane windows, layers of orange brick with cement oozing unevenly between the joints. Most of the artistry (and clearly most of the money) had been spent on the whitewashed bell tower where a traditional copper cupola bulged against the clouds. We halted outside to finish our beer. The raucous singing of the priests grew steadily louder, piquing my interest. For a second I glanced up at the red-blue-and-white flag; then, after getting rid of our empties, Dragan nudged me up the steps, and we pushed our way inside.

For a Protestant baptised into the no-frills Church of England the service at Stratinska was an intriguing novelty. I learnt three things vital to my salvation that morning:

1. Orthodox priests have insanely loud voices.
2. The blessing of Holy Mother Church does not come cheap; if you see a guy wandering around with a little black book, he's probably looking for you.
3. At the end of the service a sudden burst of gun fire is normal and not the sign of imminent NATO attack.

As the bullets rang out I wasn't the only one to duck. Yes, our Orthodox brothers in Republika Srpska are a colourful lot.

The service was well under way by the time we arrived. As there was no seating we had to stand shoulder to shoulder with a small army of wrinkly Babushka women clothed in drab headscarves and dark knitted tights. They may have been carrying the joy of Christ inside, but their faces were uniformly sombre. The three priests—two in black robes, one in scarlet—stood at the front. Behind them was a white-linen altar, glinting with silver candlesticks. One hour merged into two. Then incredibly became three. The stuffy air grew dense with cloying fumes. We shuffled on our feet, yet no one had the bad manners to leave. Resplendent in his flaming-red and gold threads, the bearded Episcopal led us forward to Communion with much chanting, hoarse singing and a vast amount of priestly hand-kissing.

When the time finally came to partake of the sacrament it was a blessing in more ways than one. Murmuring affably, the congregation tensed like a soccer crowd anticipating an imminent goal; then surged forward en masse, led by a group of withered Babushkas elbowing and pushing their way to the best spots at the front. At first I was dubious about participating, but Dragan would have none of it. Before I could protest, I was drawing bits of crusty bread from the basket and my beery lips were nailed to the Episcopal's wrinkled hand. As I left the scene a bespectacled nun in midnight black decided to douse me with several cupfuls of holy water. After three hours and twenty-three minutes my 'baptism' into the Serbian Orthodox Church was complete. Hallelujah!

Laughing and brushing our damp hair, we tumbled outside back into the chattering crowds. Dragan marched off toward the domed marquee, leaving me alone on a patch of trampled grass. The scene was much as before with plenty of backslapping and old men shaking hands. One group had linked arms and were dancing in a circle that moved in and out like an old-fashioned hokey cokey. I looked around trying to take in a sight I'd never see again. The gentle camaraderie of the moment reminded me of the street parties held during the Queen's 1977 Silver Jubilee.

Sadly, our community spirit had disappeared with the last of the crisps and tuna sandwiches. Most people back home were too affluent to need each other. No longer did my countrymen go to their neighbour to borrow a cup of sugar; instead they went to the supermarket and bought an entire bag. Had the British lost something important in the march toward greater prosperity? Did this matter? At that moment I was inclined to think it did.

Shortly after, Dragan reappeared clutching two beer bottles. He handed me one, and we stood there sipping, wondering what to do next. I was looking hopefully at a bench to rest my injured foot when he suddenly grabbed my arm and led me into a huddle of double-breasted suits.

'I'm a Member of Parliament,' said the tallest, smoothing down a pink silk tie, 'and you are?'

He extended his hand, and I gave it a polite shake. Black hair flooded with hair gel, charcoal-grey suit (immaculately tailored); there was no tractor oil on this gent's cuffs.

'I'm a pilgrim walking to Jerusalem,' I said chirpily, feeding him the rest of my improbable story in small, easy-to-swallow chunks.

I learnt one final thing that day, and it had nothing to do with God. In Bosnia the relationship between church and state is more than pure ceremony. Though Stratinska was nothing more than a speck on a map, this politician had shown up in his best suit to nibble on dry bread and get his head damp. Like the rest of us mere mortals he'd stood in a smoky fug for three long hours.

'Now tell me,' he continued, and his hand moved toward my chest. 'Why did you British drop bombs on us? Don't you like Serbs?'

I was facing more eyes than a strutting peacock. The air became tense. Dragan looked aghast. No one was smiling. When I got over the shock I realised it was a fair question. During the Yugoslav Wars it was NATO that dropped the bombs. The UK was part of NATO. I was a citizen of the UK. In his eyes I was guilty by association.

'It's complicated . . .' I stammered.

A masterful understatement.

'. . . but I would say . . .'

Yes!

'. . . that the Serbs are a wonderful, hospitable people.'

The tall politician smiled broadly and led me back inside the church to get a special blessing from the Episcopal. I was learning fast. In the Balkans it's wise to cultivate diplomacy.

✳ ✳ ✳

For two weeks that brought May to a close and ushered in a June both wet and tempestuous, I walked south toward the Bosnian capital Sarajevo embracing the many sights and sounds the country had to offer. More than the drenching storms, it was the shadow of war. Memorials to Bosnia's dead quickly began to line the roadside. Often I stopped to linger by those black marble plaques etched in silver or gold with the names and portraits of the fallen. Sometimes pots of flowers stood beneath, pansies dry and withered. Poignant though they were, nothing compared to that moment in Busnovi when one of my fellow drinkers had lifted his shirt. Dimitrije squeakily explained: 'They are cigarette burns made by Croat soldiers!' Little red circles, smooth in the centre, peppered the poor guy's chest. I looked at him dumbfounded. Just how do you commiserate with a victim of torture? There's not a lot you can say in that kind of situation, other than thank God you weren't the victim, and march on.

I made the most important town in the area on 1 June. I was still travelling through Republika Srpska, the part of the Bosnian federated state where most of the Serbs live. They have their own capital—the leafy Banja Luka—and I spent two days there finding sanctuary in the eaves of Hotel Ideja. I gladly paid for the privilege. Stanislav's crocodile slip-ons were gratefully received at the time, but weren't constructed for long-distance walking over heavily cratered roads. A fresh clutch of sore toes needed resting, and I was still worried about my throbbing heel. When not watching chess players in Gradski Park, I concentrated on the basics: buying rolls of plaster, changing bandages, adding fresh entries to my diary and gathering S-shaped bananas from small stores. As I peeled back one of those Frankenstein-esque fruits I privately wondered how many volts must be applied to produce such a blasphemy of nature. The answer escaped me, but I'm sure there's a branch of the EU eager to investigate.

With wide eyes, I carried my oddly shaped bananas deep into the interior. If there was a beauty to this part of the country, it was harsh and thoroughly uncompromising. The main road to Sarajevo cuts through miles of pristine canyon; sometimes sheer and suffocating, at others it broadens just enough for the next crumbling town—which isn't necessarily a blessing. The lone constant is the River Vrbas. Its Amazonian coils mark the route. Dripping with sweat, I huffed my way along the western bank, gasping in humid air, swatting angrily at circling flies, sipping gratefully beneath fiery suns, and on frequent breaks to smooth knotted muscles, gazing up at swathes of chaotic greenery clinging to granite lips hungry for fleeing skies. The placid river ran beside, a thread of algae-green mirroring perfectly all that lay above.

From a practical viewpoint it was a challenging walk. Camping is tricky when sandwiched between river and solid rock. Near Rekavice I was getting ready to send up another prayer when I caught a lucky break. A track leading down to the water's edge! Fantastic!

Amid waves of pea-green grass I pitched my tent and sat back to admire the pale mist blossoming along the granite ridges; it was an idyllic scene cut from any Welsh guidebook. Unfortunately, the similarity was more than superficial. True to valley life, the heavens swiftly opened. Each thunderclap was like a dozen Napoleonic cannons. The ground literally shook. Everything that could hop, crawl or flap wings made a beeline for my tent. Halfway through the tempest fourteen flies, a fleeing dormouse and a terrified toad were brutally evicted. The intruders should have known better. An Englishman's home is his castle, even if it is just a waterlogged bit of plastic.

I marched on for a few days, facing the storms and whatever the elements could conjure up. The town of Jajce was the next target, and it was here that I found a real castle. Sixty kilometres south of Banja Luka, at the top of a conical hill, stands a hefty skirt of sloping medieval stonework. Flaky houses circle beneath, roofs blown apart by Serbian mortar fire; a dirty-white caravan clings improbably to the hillside; the odd improvised minaret pokes up like a chimney stack . . . as Bosnian towns go, it's pretty grim. The one redeeming feature for any tourist has to be the fabulous waterfall. Three torrents of white water cascade with tropical seductiveness into a rocky pool. I've never been much good with a camera. I took the obligatory photos, though as was so often the case with the marvels of nature, they failed to do the scene justice.

I spent that night gratefully in three-star luxury; then, eager to speed up progress, went looking for a shortcut to Travnik. On the map there was a minor road passing through the village of Rika. It seemed like an excellent choice—until I began shopping in one of Jajce's floor-to-ceiling grocery shops. Tubes of mint-flavoured laxatives jostled against tins of beans, all in delightful chaos. Blue eyes met ancient grey; then the old woman tilted her head towards me as if sharing some terrible secret.

'This area is heavily wooded,' she whispered. (I'd laid the map on the counter so she could jab at it.) 'And many villages were destroyed in the war.'

Erm . . . heavily wooded. That didn't sound so good. Clutching another bunch of those strangely shaped bananas, I took her advice and trotted back to the main road.

Although almost certainly safer, it wasn't a decision without consequences. For someone used to a semi-comfortable life in England it can be a shock to see real poverty in the flesh. My opportunity to find enlightenment came just outside Jajce. I'd only been walking for fifteen minutes when I spotted groups of young women sitting in the lay-bys on plastic buckets, clutching the hands of toddlers. Each mother held a bowl of cherries for sale to passing trade. The day was frightfully hot, a real scorcher. I thought about making a purchase, but my heel still throbbed, and I was keen to get to the next town. After a moment of indecision I hurried by, thinking only of myself.

As God would have it, I didn't get very far before conscience returned to taunt. Further on, I came across an elderly couple standing alone in the sun. The man was at least sixty, the woman stooped and ancient. A black headscarf framed a kind, wrinkled face, and in her outstretched hands she held a wooden bowl. I glanced at the countryside, wondering where they'd come from. No houses were visible—not a single one. How far had they walked to get here? As I struggled to understand what I was witnessing, the words of Ecclesiastes 1:18 struck with hammer force:

For in much wisdom is much grief; and he who increases knowledge increases sorrow also.

There was nowhere for this old couple to sit and no shade. Yet here they stood, hoping to sell a handful of fruit for a few miserable pennies. Ignoring them was stupid and callous. Compared to these folk I was rich, perhaps obscenely so. I could easily have made their lives better, but in my selfishness I didn't even try.

By the time I fully understood my mistake there was nothing left to do except continue. I moved on a little wiser, and by the middle of June I'd left the Serb-dominated Republika Srpska behind and was deep into the Federation of Bosnia and Herzegovina—that part of this strange land where Muslims form a natural majority. It was around this time I abandoned the fields for a string of ageing hotels. Given my newfound wisdom it wasn't a brilliant choice. The plumbing was downright chaotic (red taps cold and blue taps hot!); staff were resentful and sullen. In all these crumbling establishments various types of omelette formed the entire breakfast menu, and none of it was particularly palatable. On the one occasion I dared to ask for something different the poor girl was left nonplussed. I let the disappointment go. The hotels provided hot showers and a decent bed, and if breakfast mattered, these things mattered more.

In between plates of greasy omelette, the road continued the established pattern. I don't know which is more iconic Bosnia: bare-chested boys in jeans threshing hay with scythes, or roof-less concrete cottages, charred black and lifeless. I saw both more than once. And for much of the time I was still navigating suffo-cating canyons. While dodging cars I gazed up at solid rock and hundred-foot-high wire nets pinning back crushing boulders. A short distance on, I stopped to ponder some black graffiti:

BAD BLUE BOYS WEST MOSTAR!

Were the Bad Blue Boys some paramilitary group left over from the war? Should I be worried? As I plodded sweatily through another airless fissure, T-shirt stiff with salt and socks drying on my rucksack, I had plenty of lonely hours to wonder.

It wasn't until I rejoined civilisation that I encountered further novelties. By now Christianity had long since faded leaving Islam to provoke the senses. Although that meant fewer church doors to knock on, there were some compensations. Once heard, the Muslim call to prayer—the beautiful adhan—is never quite for-gotten. Each dawn its mournful melody drew me back to con-sciousness and at night deep into cosy oblivion. I counted many mosques, and in larger towns copper-coned minarets were the norm. I quickly realised they were the same design, as if mass-produced and reassembled like an IKEA flatpack. Who knows? Perhaps they were. Elsewhere there was room for variation. The ribbed dome at Donji Vakuf was a splendid azure blue; and out in the country Allah was far less fussy, and it was common to see turret-like minarets bolted on to crooked cottages.

I powered on, pushing myself to the limit. Hassled by flies and drenched by storms, I ground out a succession of 30 km days, shaking dozens of beckoning hands, and pausing beside Islamic gravestones all white marble and shaped like the ace of spades. Even though my feet were taking a beating, I was astonished how I could recover in a single night, then do it all again.

The night before I entered Sarajevo I slumped on a bed and pulled out the maps. Like their owner, they'd taken a battering. Creased and dog-eared from frequent use, rain had exacted a heavy toll causing deep splits in the paper. No matter, I thought, a generous helping of duct tape would fix the problem. According to backpacker myth, duct tape could fix anything.

As rain hammered the window I let my finger trace the route. Sarajevo was the next stop, followed by Montenegro, a biggish town called Nikšić, the capital Podgorica, then down into horse-and-cart Albania. Did I have the strength to travel south all the way to Tirana? Probably not, though I wasn't unduly bothered about missing out on Albania's principal city. Just being able to ask the question seemed amazing.

Two thousand kilometres from my home in Britain, I realised my journey was about to grant me another incredible privilege. Tomorrow I would literally walk into one of the most historic cities on Earth. And how many of us will live to say that?

✳ ✳ ✳

My first memory of Bosnia's capital centred on the pale marble gravestones blizzarding the rightmost slopes; my second, on the muddy waters of the River Miljacka snaking beneath a series of white stone bridges. By the time I reached the corner of Mula Mustafe Bašeskije I was suffering sensory overload, bewildered by hawkish cries from shadowy doorways, a strange aroma of burning meat, the call to prayer twisting around fluted minarets, and long speculative stares from moustachioed old men sipping coffee. When my benefactor arrived, he came out of nowhere.

'Excuse me,' he said, blocking my path with an outstretched arm. 'Are you looking for a hostel?'

'Maybe ...' A glitzy Crimplene suit nearly always signifies a salesman. I came to a halt and found myself appraising a curly-haired fellow, about my height, with coffee-stained teeth.

'I know some rooms nearby. I work for the tourist board. Can I show you? It's not far.'

'You know what, mate, I think I'm probably going to be okay. I don't think I really need—'

'Ahhhhh, so my friend, you are English?'

I nodded cautiously at the finger pointed at my chest.

'I worked in England once, in London as a taxi driver. I know you English well.' He held up his left hand and with the fingers of the other began to count off the room's assets. 'The room has hot water, shower and TV with satellite, you will like it. I know you English. The English appreciate the finer things in life.'

Oh, yeah. We do. Powder-blue Ferrari Daytonas are quite nice ...

'Okay, mate, just tell me how much.'

A momentary pause, and then, 'For you, my friend, $10.'

The story of how $10 eventually ballooned into 30 is a salutary lesson for anyone hovering confused and uncertain in Sarajevo's historic Old Town. Poverty played its part. I later discovered unemployment is rife here, and many of the locals have nothing better to do than slump in cafés and watch for the approach of huge rucksacks. When they find one they make the most of it.

'Yes, that's right,' he twittered, 'this way please, this way,' and casting off considerable doubt, I grumpily followed on.

I didn't have far to walk to appreciate the finer things in life. The grandly named 'International Youth Hostel Marko Polo' turned out to be a woman's cramped apartment on Logavina, complete with a rich selection of floral dresses and miscellaneous ladieswear stuffed in the wardrobe. The room itself was a decent size, with a double bed, the much-vaunted satellite TV (which didn't work) and some hideous purple satin cushions that might have made great scene-setters in a porn movie.

'You like?' he asked, arms folded and daring me to say no.

I stood there, partially defeated by aching feet. The arrangement seemed incredibly dodgy, but after taking a good look around I figured it would probably be okay. Even so, each night I placed a heavy table against the bedroom door. Just to be safe.

I spent three nights in the city. I wish I'd had the good sense to stay longer. It's not often I fall in love, and rarer still I put pen to paper and start gushing like a starry-eyed teen. Sarajevo owned me from the moment I looked down upon its sprawling chaos. Everything about it appealed: the melodic call to prayer imbued with eastern mystery, the smell of charcoal-grilled meat drifting over swoop-necked copper pots in the Ottoman Bazaar, screeching orange trams careering beside imperial museums rooted in Hapsburg pomp and circumstance, the gypsum 'eyes' of the Latin Bridge casting an unblinking stare up and down the frothy waters of the River Miljacka. For every tourist the bridge is the place to be. Why? On 28 June 1914, a Serbian nationalist called Gavrilo Princip shot Archduke Ferdinand and in so doing sent four great empires spiralling to their death. The Austro-Hungarian Empire was one of them. The Latin Bridge was that place. To feel the moment, to test its weight with the beat of your own heart, that's the pull of the Old Town.

That there was more to see than I could cram into four days was no surprise. Sarajevo lives and breathes history, and if you're looking for God you'll find him in all his guises. Five hundred years ago Sephardi Jews arrived fleeing the horrors of the Spanish Inquisition. Popular legend says the newcomers named the city the 'European Jerusalem'. If so, it's a name well chosen. It's a rarity in Europe to find a mosque, a synagogue and a church standing in such close proximity.

I found the last of the three not far from the hostel. The Old Serb Church is a cramped little place, cool, dim and rather quiet, where rows of spindly, judicial-looking chairs flank bare lemon-painted walls. First impressions were of a strange court waiting to try a case. As I descended into the chamber, a young woman in a headscarf was leaning forward to kiss an icon. Afterwards, she reached into her purse and placed a handful of banknotes on the glass-topped surface. I assumed the priest came every now and then to gather donations. There was already quite a pile.

I stayed there about twenty minutes looking for God. The focal point of any Orthodox church is the iconostasis—a decorative screen separating the sanctuary from the nave. The partition in the Old Church is not the most spectacular in Christendom, but it's the only one I've ever seen. Rising from the floor to the ceiling is a wall of floral gold, interrupted at the centre by a pair of wooden doors, the structure in its entirety covered by religious icons rich in purple and red and pretty pink. The Blessed Virgin is the easiest motif to find. She sits on a throne—crown and halo, swathed in a crimson robe, and clutches a golden-gowned Jesus. As usual in this tradition the infant's face is decidedly adult-like, which to my mind always looks a trifle odd. I took a few photos, rummaged in my pockets, left a few notes as the previous worshipper had done. God floated about in a haze of dust motes. Did I still carry his favour? I didn't know. But I felt glad of the chance to pray among old stones.

On 15 June, with prayers said and not all yet answered, I left the European Jerusalem and struck south toward Montenegro. It wasn't a happy departure. New Sarajevo shapes the south and west, and thrown together by the socialist Yugoslavs infected by a desire to build nondescript apartment blocks, it's nothing like the picturesque Hapsburg and Ottoman parts. One gigantic road bisects the horizon, and everything that can toot a horn goes straight down. The rest is entirely mundane. Every intersection has a red-painted kiosk selling newspapers and sweets; and on the opposite corner a yawning policeman in a white crash helmet and jackboots. The pavements are unusually wide (almost like roads) and far too big to make any sense. My final act of defiance before fleeing the Old Town was to swap my ailing boots for a pair of thin-heeled trainers. I would soon regret the purchase.

Four days later, I was closing in on the border. My memories are of rising among pale mist and setting off to Srbinje at the ungodly hour of 5 a.m., licking spoons of honey handed to me by beekeepers sitting on grassy hillocks, and shivering in my tent not far from a charred cottage lashed by rain. After the skies cleared I crept out and filled a bottle with rainwater lying in a crease. At the first swallow I felt a certain pride in my ingenuity. The feeling didn't last. The rainwater carried specks of dirt and tasted like weak vinegar. No doubt Bear Grylls wouldn't have hesitated, but I was made of lesser stuff. And yet in the end I swallowed every drop, for like the buzzing flies of the meadow I was also maddened by thirst, and there was nothing else.

I spent the last hundred metres thinking about what I'd learnt from a country where I'd expected very little. History, with its wider perspective, may deliver a different verdict; but I found no good guys and no bad guys in Bosnia, no Muslims and no Serbs, no cowboys, no Indians, no war criminals and no saints. I found no one by virtue of their actions worthy of eternal damnation. Instead, I found the beckoning hands of ordinary people. People like Stanislav and his friend Lana, part of strong, close-knit communities willing to share and help others in need.

I'd misjudged the situation, and I knew it. For the twenty-four days I'd carried my cross through this welcoming country not a single man or woman had offered violence. And no one had frogmarched me into a forest. As I fell into the jaws of a mighty canyon, the sadness, then, grew not because I was leaving.

The sadness was I could ever have believed otherwise.

Chapter Seven

Montenegro

The Land of Heat and Rock

In keeping with the Internet age I began my tour of Montenegro on the World Wide Web. On a random travel blog I discovered the natives call their land *Crna Gora*, meaning 'black rock'. As descriptions go I would say it's lacking in a few places. Having spent eleven days there, sweating and grumbling my way down the length of the country, I now feel uniquely qualified to expand on the matter. As a dictionary definition I much prefer this:

> Montenegro   [mon-tuh-nee-groh]
> –noun
> A former republic of Yugoslavia: achieved independence in 2006. Mountainous and rugged with a capital R, this land of unending rock is the perfect place to maroon an ex-lover or anyone who thinks omelette makes a satisfying breakfast. In the high canyons scores of dark tunnels dominate—ideal locations to hit a car and enter the next world as a gooey mess on someone's windscreen wipers. Insanely hot in June. Water negligible. Suffering guaranteed.
> Capital: Podgorica (pop. 156,169).

Oh, yeah. Try to avoid the gargantuan snakes and those little black scorpions. They're not fun to play with. Now that's Montenegro, that's *Crna Gora*.

If you've been traipsing across Europe for three-and-a-half months, navigated six countries and lanced too many blisters to count, by the time you sober up and leave Café Piramida you'll end up at Šćepan Polje at the tip of the Tara and Piva Canyons. It's a simple village layout: chimneyed cottages, picket fences, golden grassland, smiling tourists in black wetsuits shouldering dripping canoes. I'd arrived just after 4 p.m. that day, and since I didn't fancy climbing a canyon in the dark, I decided to hang around and see if some kind of accommodation option would open up. Strangely, it was the village shop that eventually provided it. Behind barred windows the shelves were stacked to the rafters with old-fashioned cloth sacks and all kinds of strange brown wrappers; the big fridge was exceedingly well-stocked. I stumbled back outside rolling frosted cola cans against both cheeks. For a few seconds I was in heaven.

I'd barely ripped open the first can when the shopkeeper—an old woman in black tights—came charging out. Face scarlet, panting heavily and waving enormous arms, she cupped her hands and started hollering at the second floor of the neighbouring house.

'Ivana! Ivana! There is a reeech Engleeesh here! He is very stupid! Come out at once!'

Hey, steady on, love. Maybe I did overpay on the drinks . . .

'Come quickly Ivana! Give this reeech Engleeesh fool a room, and you will make the very big money!'

At this point I should state that my knowledge of the local language was rather slight. My most prized Serbo-Croat phrase was the immortal 'Do you sell white cotton underpants in packs of three?' I have to admit, so far it hadn't been very useful.

Regardless of what the shopkeeper actually said, the results speak for themselves. Instantly the upstairs window flew open. A puzzled face darted out. Our eyes met—a rapacious female lion appraising a nervous English zebra. The rapacious lion licked its lips and cocked a thumb to the rear. Thirty seconds later, I was at the top of the staircase wrestling a twenty-stone woman in dire need of very big money.

'You give me ten euro now!' she said, dragging me inside.

'Err . . . fine,' I mumbled, and let my body follow my wrist.

I don't think I'm stating anything new when I reveal it's in the nature of agricultural communities to rise early. At dawn any chance of a lie-in was eliminated by the unpleasant novelty of screaming cockerels. Covering my ears with two pillows failed to alleviate the situation. I packed quickly and nibbled on scraps of leftover cheese. Feeling it would be rude to just march out the door, I then went into the hall to look for Ivana.

A quick peek into some of the side rooms revealed the guest-house was cosily built. The largest room situated at the back was obviously the kitchen. (Either that or someone had an unnatural fetish for long steel spatulas.) The remaining space was turned over to relaxation, to comfy black armchairs, a cream-coloured sofa and the ubiquitous TV set blaring morning news. On pastel-blue walls oily icons of stern saints glared down accusingly at the poor sinners pulling up chairs for breakfast. I spotted Ivana standing by the stove, engulfed in clouds of steam.

She turned to me, her long black hair matted to her temples. 'Ahh . . . the Engleeesh is here.' The words came out in a venomous hiss. I froze in the doorway, wondering if we were going to wrestle again. 'Won't you join us?' said her broadening smile.

My gaze darted across the table: slices of juicy red melon, a bowl of green salad, a big jar of golden honey, hard-boiled eggs to come. To my delight there wasn't a trace of omelette in sight. Perhaps I'd misjudged the woman. I hadn't expected this.

An experienced pilgrim never passes up a free meal. I immediately sat down, smiled courteously, took spoonfuls of honey (but not too much) and prayed no one would notice the huge blobs I dropped on the tablecloth. Yeah. Some hope. Ivana's mother sat opposite mummified in ten yards of black cloth. A grumpy ninety-year-old Babushka with an unblinking eye resembling a milky-blue marble, she was commendably stiff-backed for one so ancient and never smiled once. Instead, I felt her one good eye tracking my every foray toward the honeypot. I swear she counted off every blob.

Several weeks of greasy Bosnian omelette had left me on the verge of murder. Hard-boiled eggs, however, were a different matter. Ivana circled the dining table, humming lightly, clutching a steaming pan. She stooped beside the old woman and began to lovingly stroke her head.

'Oh, Babushka!' she crooned in her ear. 'Babushka!'

A speckled-brown egg dropped with a crack onto the old dear's plate. The ancient mother remained strangely impassive. Clearly her mind was absorbed by the difficult process of egg dismemberment. I watched mesmerised as her one good eye began to rotate like a whizzing gyroscope. Bits of eggshell went flying in all directions. More than a few fell into her precious honey. As she started to devour her prize with toothless lips, the fourth member of our group spoke up.

Aleksandar shot me a glance. 'Do you like football?'

He picked up the remote and before I could get a word out started jabbing furiously at the TV.

I nodded at the grinning, track-suited football fanatic from Budva. 'Sure, why not.'

At 7 a.m. I may be a grumpy sod, but I'm easy to please.

Together we munched our way through the remaining dishes. Conversation was noticeably strained given that everyone at the table was extremely fluent in their own language, but not much else. Although willing to bridge the linguistic gap, Aleksandar seemed lost in the English Premier League.

'Ahhhh, Beckham ...' he declared with a sagely nod, when I pointed at Ivana's ancient mother.

The ancient mother tossed her head and snorted with disgust.

'Manchester United!' he insisted, when I asked him where he went to school.

Yeah, mate, not likely. For 99 per cent of men, plus virtually every schoolboy on Earth (and quite a few women), football is a uniquely unifying force with a culture and language of its own. However, as an effective means of communication it does have a few limitations.

An hour later, neither I nor the milky-eyed Babushka could eat any more. I shook hands with my hosts, shouldered my rucksack and walked down the outside staircase onto a circle of trampled grass. The village shop was already open, so I marched in and bought two half-litre bottles of water, thinking it would be more than enough to get me to the next well-stocked fridge. When I eventually emerged into the sunshine I noticed a strip of rising tarmac arched by lush green foliage. That mysterious tunnel of branches had to be the way forward. But where did it lead?

In the frighteningly hot hours that followed it was ancient geography that provided an answer. Two magnificent canyons guard the entrance to northern Montenegro, and outside the Balkans they're some of Europe's better kept secrets. Swinging far away to the southeast, the Tara Canyon is undoubtedly the more popular. At 1,300 metres deep its rushing river is a magnet for white-water junkies. Every year wet-suited tourists arrive in droves, drawn by cascading waterfalls tumbling into shingled pools. When the canoes finally stop there's plenty of entertainment for the adventurous. The adjacent Durmitor National Park has more than thirty peaks over 2,000 metres, and for blood-thirsty types even hunting is possible; there's ample opportunity to blast away at bears, wild boar and the much-maligned wolf.

Strangely for someone seeking profound spiritual enlightenment, the Mauser M98 bolt action rifle with Rigby-style cheek piece wasn't top priority when I packed my rucksack. Renouncing the opportunity to do battle with the local wildlife, I really can't say much more about the Tara. I can, however, offer words of reassurance for anyone travelling the neighbouring Piva. Having trekked along this V-shaped jungle as far as Plužine, I can reliably state there are no bears wandering the Piva Canyon.

This minor detail didn't spoil the view. If you can paint in the gliding pterodactyls with the power of your mind, the volcano-like rims and walls of trailing vines could have come straight out of *Jurassic Park*. On the fringes, giant fingers of grey rock poke upward in twos and threes. Trees shaped like cocktail umbrellas cling to sheer limestone in defiance of all reason. The canyon's pouting lips dwarf everything but the sky, and in between their gape lies a vast empty stillness just begging to be shattered.

'Helloooo!' I bellowed. 'Is anyone there?'

More than once I cupped my hands, then waited breathless for the reply.

Fun and games aside, I found the River Piva to be an alluring if not frustrating companion. Hopelessly distant and shining like blue glass, the remnant of this once mighty watercourse snaked around mounds of pretty rainbow shingle. I must have rubbed the sweat from my eyes a dozen times, thinking how wonderful it would be to ditch my clothes and float for a few minutes in that thin ribbon of aquamarine. To my considerable disappointment, I never did get the chance.

And then, in the afternoon, came that bridge . . .

When the east-west spanning bridge arrived it turned out to be an absolute shocker. Cross this tiny strip of concrete? Without a safety harness? I was aghast. White-knuckled and shaking, I peered over the barrier and down into the rocky depths. I'm famous for getting dizzy standing on a chair. Gripping that railing was either an act of supreme courage or complete stupidity.

I plodded on, oozing pints of sweat. Every few hundred metres there was another dark little tunnel hewn out of solid rock. You had to admire the engineering that made this improbable road possible—it couldn't have been easy. I strapped on my head torch and began to feel my way through the shadows. Cool air washed over reddened cheeks as feeble light bobbled along the ground. Dodging the occasional *plip, plip, plip* of falling water was not as important as sidestepping the traffic. Although cars were few in number, when they came they did so quickly. I was grateful for the shade but also relieved when I made it back into the sun.

Away from the gloom I saw plenty of wildlife. Bright-green lizards with almond eyes and sky-blue throats lay basking among tufts of withered grass. Aggressive flies seemed to be hiding in every bush. They were a terrible nuisance. Great clouds pursued me for a hundred metres or more, circling my sweaty head and buzzing with insane fury. My favourite animals were the delicate black-and-brown fritillary butterflies that floated around the gravel. What charming creatures they were! Like a latter-day St Francis of Assisi I held out my bare arms, feeling the skin tickle as dozens probed for life-giving moisture. If it's possible to feel kinship with an insect, I felt it then. The joy of a pilgrim is a strange thing.

Not long after I came across a dead snake, which wasn't a great surprise. Hot countries are famous for their creepy-crawlies, and in late June the southern Balkans are blistering. I looked down at its partially crushed body—a glistening, foot-long silver rope. One moment this poor beast had been quietly sunning itself on the road; the next, squashed flat. I was about to move off when something else caught my eye: black, shiny, about an inch long, with pincers outstretched. 'Wow! It's a scorpion!'

I couldn't pass this up. I sunk to my haunches, gripped by a childlike urge to prod it with a stick. But then my gaze fell on that crescent sting, and I had a disturbing vision of myself lying by the roadside mortally wounded by a thumb-sized bug. The desire to reach Jerusalem was greater. Butterflies, snakes, flies and pilgrims: we were all creatures of God trying to survive in the canyon. Even a deadly scorpion had a right to its place in the sun.

* * *

For two brutally hot days that were more Sahara than temperate Europe, I marched in a southeasterly direction, bypassing fields of hourglass haystacks, skirting blue-hazed valleys strung out with stone cottages, and most of the time meandering through a rocky mosaic of cratered greenery that is typical of limestone karst. It was hard walking throughout, particularly on the second day when I set my heart on reaching Nikšić and foolishly left myself 40 km to complete. I'm still not sure how I managed it. Perhaps stubborn stoicism is the answer, punctuated by frequent outbursts of desperate prayer, then elation when said prayers were seemingly answered. The E762 highway, which cuts down the backbone of Montenegro, is great for exploring if you're travelling in a well-provisioned car with ten gallons of water. If you're on foot, and lightly stocked, be prepared for something special. Be prepared to get very, very thirsty.

The morning naturally began where the previous evening left off. There's a little village called Plužine lying at the end of the Piva Canyon. Hilltop petrol station, eccentric hotel (no electricity until 8 p.m.), a single grocery store and a kiosk complete with imprisoned teenage girl yawning to stave off sleep: it would be fair to say there's not much going on. Breakfast, in true Balkans style, consisted of a greasy mushroom omelette served by scowling staff that seemed to resent my very existence. I ate it quietly and without fuss because I needed the calories. However, I don't think I'll ever be going back.

Once I took to the road I soon got into difficulty. I left the village around 9 a.m. loaded down with two litres of bottled water, a bottle of fizzy orange and several cans of cola. Despite running out of liquids the day before, I was convinced I'd over-stocked. Oh, yeah, if only . . . By midday my mouth had become a desert dry enough to rival any North African dust bowl, and about an hour after *that* I was ready to drink anything I could lay my hands on. Money wasn't a problem (I had loads); what I didn't have was anywhere to spend it. Out here in this rocky wilderness there were no air-conditioned supermarkets with piped music drifting across aisles the width of a motorway. On this stretch of tarmac I was on my own.

Or was I?

I felt a prayer building and in desperation let it out. 'Father, if it be your will let me find water soon.' My pitiful request floated upward to mingle with millions of others. In these situations my philosophy was and remains simple. A prayer is like a phone call to God. The phone always rings, but sometimes he chooses not to answer.

That God had lifted the receiver was not at first apparent to my gasping presence. As anyone from these parts can attest, Montenegrin motorists aren't known for their green credentials and have a nasty habit of tossing out their trash. Sun-bleached cola cans and fizzy drink bottles form the greater part of this detritus. Blown by the wind, they gather in the lay-bys forming huge, unattractive piles several inches deep. For the first time in my life I stopped and looked speculatively at a heap of rubbish. The question posed was obvious: would this English pilgrim be too proud to drink water that was weeks or even months old?

Nope. Not one bit.

In an instant I was on hands and knees, hurling bottles in all directions. The water sloshing around in the first seemed clear, but then I took a closer look and saw a group of tiny bugs doing the backstroke. I tossed it away and scrutinised another. Nope: that one had more swimmers than Bondi Beach. I'd more luck with the third. It was a hefty two litres, a quarter full, with no bugs. I spun the cap, took a small sip and swallowed cautiously. Normally warm water from a plastic bottle tastes horrendous. At that moment it tasted better than the finest champagne. I doubt even Moses parting the Red Sea could have been more ecstatic.

And I most likely would have stayed that way if it weren't for those pesky laws of physics. You know there's a problem brewing when a beetle scampers by and you think: 'Yes, maybe, with a little salt and a dash of tartar sauce.' If water is essential, then so is food. Every day a man of average build doing mostly nothing needs 2,500 calories to stay alive. A pilgrim sweating buckets with a big rucksack probably needs an extra 2,000—at least. For months I'd been living on scraps, eating where and whenever I could. As a weight loss programme my pilgrimage was delivering excellent results. As a healthy eating policy, it was a disaster.

Implausible though it might seem, the food crisis kicked off with an invasion of giant ants. I kid you not: never mess with Montenegrin ants. Never go anywhere near them. These vicious brutes laugh at cans of Nippon and can do a hundred press-ups with ease. Their astonishing gluttony is only matched by their Herculean strength. I watched, stupefied, as one individual tottered away with a lump of cheese the size of a double-decker bus. It disappeared into the long grass along with the rest. My rucksack, never well-stocked, had been picked clean. Eyes blazing, I fled my fly-ridden hillock and stormed off toward Nikšić.

A morning that awful just has to get better. Face like a fast-flowing river, I struggled on cursing my lack of survival skills. If I get out of this mess, I told myself, I will immediately write to the Discovery Channel and demand that Bear Grylls present a Montenegro *Born Survivor* Special. Even in this wilderness Bear would know where to find food. Bear always did. I could almost see him by the roadside plucking a tasty morsel from the rocky scrub: 'Now these little guys are packed with protein.'

Cue something gross, with lots of legs, struggling wildly and gazing with sheer terror at Bear's gaping mouth. Then there'd be a sudden crunch, Bear would perform his trademark grimace, swallow bravely and the camera would zoom in to see the last of the legs disappear down his throat. Afterward, the producers would pat themselves on the back as ratings soared, and all over the world millions would ask the same question: how on earth did he manage to eat *that*?

How, indeed. Twenty kilometres from Nikšić another desperate prayer went up.

And presto, another was answered.

They were scattered all across the roadside gravel—clumps of tiny red fruits hanging beneath delicate fronds of green. I knelt down for a closer look, pulled off a handful and at the first bite I knew immediately it was a strawberry. The only downside to this fortuitous discovery was it took ten fruits to make a mouthful and ten mouthfuls to make a decent meal. No matter,

I thought, as I gratefully filled a bag. At least I've avoided a Bear Grylls beetle snack. From somewhere in the heavens God returned the handset with a heavy spiritual clunk.

'And now,' he seemed to say with an irritated sigh, 'are you finally going to stop complaining? Did you really think I would not provide for you?'

I didn't doubt. Nor did I complain. In Bosnia Herzegovina I found the goodness of God in men. In Montenegro I found the goodness of God in God.

* * *

Lying approximately midway between the back end of the Piva Canyon and the Montenegrin capital Podgorica, the town of Nikšić is a useful stopover to shower off the sweat and grab a decent buffet breakfast in the company of Balkans businessmen, but it's not a place with great tourist appeal. I gathered up some fresh bandages and only stayed one night before moving on.

As I continued south there were many beautiful places to pitch camp that also offered a degree of privacy. A plethora of options existed off-road in those secretive forested craters that virtually demand exploration by anyone with a nose for adventure. At the close of that first afternoon I descended a dirt track scarred by tractor wheels, swung left into a corridor of deliciously green leaves, clambered over a pile of dead wood (presumably there to pen goats in), and discovered my own Garden of Eden complete with yellow plum tree deputising for the Tree of Life. It was an insects' paradise: ants grappling with hairy caterpillars, darting sky-blue dragonflies, dark furry bees tearing through the hot and sticky air. Above a purple sward drenched in golden sunlight saffron butterflies circled the skies—choirs of mute angels giving praise on a hundred tinsel wings. I fell in love with the scene immediately. I knew I wouldn't bother walking on.

Home for the night lay beneath the antler branches of a giant oak. After pushing in a few tent pegs and twanging a few guide ropes, the priority shifted to the second one I'd been struggling with—finding food. 'The wages of sin is death!' is one of the few things I can remember from my rare visits to Sunday school; and thirty-five years later, knee-high in grass, I never knew how true that might be until I went looking for bright yellow plums. The temptation was sweet, as it always is. Like the biblical Adam before me I reached up into the leaves. As I swallowed the first mouthful of juicy flesh there was a moment of sublime pleasure. Then a healthy dose of guilt snuffed it out.

What am I doing? These plums don't belong to me! Forty-three years of life had taught me that guilt was a message from conscience—and conscience was the domain of God. If I wanted to keep God's blessing, I needed to keep God's law. I withdrew my hand as if stung by a bee.

I should have known that wouldn't be the end of it. When a man in Eden bites into forbidden fruit there's always trouble. The tent was only ten metres away when I heard the first rustle. I spun around, eyes squinting, ears pricked like a dog.

Over there! It was a snake—a big one—forcing a rough S-shape through the grass.

Take it easy, I told myself. The snake's probably more afraid of you, than you are of it. It was a nice try, but the adrenalin had kicked in, and I just wasn't buying. I reckon I had good reason. It was the same kind of warped logic a parent uses to reassure a three-year-old child when they first spot something black and hairy hurtling towards them. Forty years on, I have a message for my parents. It doesn't work with spiders, and it doesn't work with snakes. In fact, it doesn't work at all. I broke cover and fled.

Bizarrely, a lifelong fascination with horror films held the key to what happened next. As any fan will testify, the best part of these old movies is where the unfortunate victim is dispatched. In a typical scene a terrified woman in stilettos trips and falls. Closing in with outstretched arms will be the dreaded mummy, a creature of frightening strength, clad head to toe in flapping bandages and moaning ecstatically as only the undead can. Real life, of course, is rarely so entertaining.

Nor is real danger.

Glancing back, I could see my own adversary was very much alive and slithering towards me with increasing interest. Though there were no cameras to record the drama, I was about to suffer my very own the-mummy's-gonna-get-ya! 'stiletto moment'. In sheer panic I tripped and fell face down into the grass.

Sadly, 3,000-year-old mummies tend toward extreme violence and the woman in stilettos usually dies horribly. The snake was clearly an avid filmgoer. True to plot, it slithered closer, sensing an easy meal. That was the final straw. All kinds of dark obscenities began to fill the air. How many times had I sat in front of the TV screaming 'Get up, you fool!' to the impending victim lying helpless on the ground?

I leant backward, pulling hard with both hands on the creeper wrapped tightly around my boot. With mounting menace the snake came on, flicking the air with its forked tongue. It wasn't supposed to end this way. I was a Christian walking to Jerusalem. I was a nice guy kind to babies and small animals. I wore size nine boots and had never donned stilettos in my life . . . One final yank did it. The vine dramatically gave way, leaving me in a heap, then I was on my feet and sprinting towards the tent.

Dawn broke around five. I lowered the zip a few inches and peered out into the purple meadow. There was no trace of the snake, no lingering print in the grass. I felt relieved. Nevertheless, I didn't want to tempt fate and hang about for round two.

I quickly sped through the usual drill: douse feet in talcum powder, clean face with baby wipe, smear face with blobs of sun cream, wrestle uncooperative sleeping bag into ill-fitting stuff sack. The latter was the curse of breaking camp. If you ever see a guy squirming on his knees with his arse waving in the air, have pity. For what must have been the better part of 45 km I then abandoned any regard for the sun and grimly set off towards Podgorica. Though temperatures don't peak till August, the sun in late June is fully capable of murder. By 8 a.m. I was staring bug-eyed at rippling tarmac; by ten my face was a coursing river.

Yet again, I ran out of precious water and had to scavenge for bottles in the lay-bys.

At least there was no chance of getting lost. After bailing out of Nikšić there's only one way to reach the Montenegrin capital, and that's on a southeasterly line straight down the throat of the Bjelopavlići Plain. The Prekornica Mountain Range ushers you in, a 3,000-foot flattish slab of sandy limestone, mottled green on the rise, charred black in places and in others exploding in striations of fiery orange. Deep fissures stripe the surface as if raked by the claw of some gigantic bear—it's not a welcoming sight. On the fringes, subsistence farmers do what they can to eke out a living. Dropping off the roadside is a maze of forested craters, purple-hazed meadows, lawns like putting greens and hourglass haystacks. Goat bells can be heard tinkling far below, but not much else.

It was a boring stretch of tarmac. A long-distance walker will be alone for 80 per cent of the time, so it's important to find ways of maintaining morale. Often I turned inward, thinking about my next email to friends and family. On other occasions I pictured my triumphant entry to the Holy City, falling to my knees in true Hollywood style, body wracked by heaving sobs. Who would play me better? De Niro, the great method actor? A swaggering Tom Cruise with a rucksack and banana grin? Haha! It was a pleasant way to soak up the time.

Very bad singing also played its part. With surprising gusto I returned to the hymns of my schooldays, filling jaded limbs and the silence of the road with the martial spirit of *The Battle Hymn of the Republic*. Consider this splendid verse:

> I have read a fiery gospel writ in burnished rows of steel:
> 'As ye deal with my contemners, so with you my grace shall deal;
> Let the Hero, born of woman, crush the serpent with his heel,
> Since God is marching onnnnnnn.'

I don't wish to exaggerate. But if fifty-nine repetitions of this stirring tune don't drive your parched lips on to the next heap of discarded water bottles, then nothing will. And never let anyone tell you that advanced dehydration can't boost creativity. Such was my enthusiasm for the song, in a fleeting moment of almost transcendental inspiration I conjured up a verse of my own:

There's a heaven in the distance, there's a heaven deep within,
As the words of Jesus heal me, so His words will purge my sin;
With faith I will crush the serpent, and no hardship end my grin,
This pilgrim marches onnnnnnn.

I doubt it will be added to the Church of England Hymnbook anytime soon, as they're quite picky about these things. But as a morale booster it kept me marching toward Podgorica's hotels.

I pressed on, hoping to find something of interest. It wasn't until the tail end of the morning that I chanced upon a sight that completely blew away the boredom and reminded me that there was more to Montenegro than the daily struggle for survival. Chiselled into a colossal wall of rock known as Ostroška Greda, Monastery Ostrog, situated about 20 km south of Nikšić, has the kind of striking visuals you'd expect to see in one of those fantastical *Indiana Jones* movies where Harrison Ford fights cartoon villains for possession of the Holy Grail. According to local guidebooks, reality is barely less exotic. The seventeenth-century monastery dedicated to St Basil boasts impressive views of the Bjelopavlići Plain plus a clutch of ghostly cave frescoes painted by the legendary iconographer Master Radul. Sporadic miracles and healings are also rumoured to occur, reinforcing the monastery's otherworldly image.

Unfortunately, the closest I got to this magnificent Balkans Shangri-La was the dry scrub bordering the E762, which is to say about 8 km away. Hand against dripping brow, I narrowed my gaze on rows of flaring arches. Strings of black dots on white paint suggested windows and cool corridors for sandaled feet. A billion tonnes of rock towered above, and a pencil-thin road snaked beneath. The adventurer in me demanded I make an immediate assault and request a bed; and I would have done, except a gruelling 16 km round trip with a flat 'No!' in between would have been one rejection too many. With half a day's walk already in my legs, I decided to pass. Days later, I was still regretting the decision.

Finally, the wider landscape levelled off. Signs of civilisation increased: gleaming red petrol stations guarded by silver pumps, a single black stallion galloping in a grassy corral, chimneyed farmsteads rising in patches of golden wheat swirling in a rare breeze. The heat was bat-shit crazy—'This one is for you, Jesus!' I snorted defiantly through gritted teeth. Suddenly, the plain widened again revealing handsome green fields tended by rows of elderly women doubled over like croquet hoops. I threw a handful of water onto my face and watched seven headscarves bob and duck. The moisture evaporated within seconds. These women had my sympathy and more than that, my respect.

If only I'd had the good sense to show the same respect to the Montenegrin sun. While purchasing a new sleeping bag in Munich I'd paid out a few extra euros for a hat by the German company Schöffel. Light and boringly practical, fashion-wise it was a complete faux pas (it's hard to feel at ease in a floppy green bonnet two sizes too big). Later on I pushed up the rim, turning the hat into a classic trilby and the wearer into a 1930's gangster. Mostly it languished in the depths of my rucksack with some rotting scraps. I was a fair-skinned Englishman used to summers like a nuclear winter. I figured I could do without it.

That was mistake number one.

Heatstroke struck with full force at the height of the afternoon. Nausea rushed over me in waves. What should I do? There was a public fountain across the road. I sprinted to the spot, hastily dumped my rucksack and spun the tap. Water gushed onto the concrete drain, splashing my shins. I leant forward with cupped hands, emptying great handfuls over face and neck. Blimey. The hose must be plugged straight into the Arctic . . . Each handful was like a slap in the face, but I instantly felt ten times better. A few yards from the fountain a dead tree offered the blessing of shade, and there I stayed, snoozing among some leggy wolf spiders hunting in the grass.

Mistake number two promptly followed: I got to my feet and, still hatless, embarked on a do-or-die 20 km march.

Perseverance is an admirable quality, but it shouldn't be confused with stubbornness, or indeed with outright stupidity. After barely half an hour, I powered on toward the capital with all the intelligence of a hamster galloping inside a treadmill. The result was inevitable. I'd barely eaten a decent meal in days. Getting enough fluids was still a major problem. By the time I staggered into the next petrol station, the world was spinning like a top and both hands were trembling.

Err . . . This isn't right!

Whiter than a clichéd sheet, I clung to the counter ignoring puzzled stares from the staff and frantically nibbling on chocolate bars. Soon the counter was obliterated by silver wrappers.

'My friend, are you well?' Two owlish eyes perched above a bushy moustache swivelled in my direction. It was the manager, a big chap with huge square shoulders, smiling pleasantly.

I nodded. 'I've had too much sun. I just need to rest here for a while, then I'll be all right.'

'Ah the sun, yes, you English are not used to it.'

'You're right, we're not. Hope it won't be this hot in Albania—'

'Albania?' His furry eyebrows shot up.

'Look, my friend,' and as he waved me forward with a finger his voice became low and conspiratorial, 'Albanians are very dangerous. I could tell you stories about such people, such terrible, terrible stories . . .'

And so he did: seven involving the illegal discharge of handguns, three the creative use of dynamite and half ending with the miraculous escape of the manager, much to the acclaim of family and friends. He made Albania sound like the Wild West, but twenty times worse. I was amazed he was still alive.

'. . . the Albanians are like the Jews, they always stick together. You must be very careful in that awful country.'

I let him prattle on. At that moment rebuilding my sugar levels and not vomiting on the floor were the only things that mattered. Albania might pose a few difficulties. But whatever came my way, I'd figure it out.

The nausea passed. Twenty minutes later, I was climbing the road to Podgorica, and four hours after *that* I finally shuffled into the outskirts. I made two appalling mistakes that day. The third never came: I kept my German-made trilby firmly on.

*** *** ***

The city that will very likely plunge Montenegro into the dubious arms of the European Union is the quintessential mix of old and new. 'Transition' is the capital's watchword, and having spent four days there cosseted in expensive hotels, I would suggest the process will be a long one. The streets have all the accoutrements of a typical Balkans metropolis: an Ottoman clock tower built when Charles II still ruled England, a clutch of Yugoslav-era Neo-Brutalist apartment bloks (yes, that's how they're spelt), a bunch of motorway-width pedestrian areas entirely devoid of pedestrians, aggressive Roma beggars cradling cutesy kids and, on the fringes where no one wants to look, the Vrela Ribnička refugee camp—home to several hundred Bosnians displaced by yet another Balkans war. What exists of economic progress resides mainly in the leafy city centre. I quickly spotted at least one blue-tinted tower erected by a cash-rich telecoms company, and I guess one shouldn't forget the scarlet brickwork of Republic Square, glowering hot and dusty like a French clay court. The transitional theme is best exemplified by the main church. All chalky white and gold-crossed domes, on the day I turned up at the grandly named 'Cathedral of the Resurrection of Christ' the front steps were littered with piles of timber. Perhaps I expected too much. It didn't look very grand to me.

On 23 June the walk I dedicated to Christ on the Bjelopavlići

Plain brought me to Podgorica, a few days' hike from the border with Albania. The journey into the city is not one I'm keen to repeat. Two 40 km marches in four days had left my feet on the verge of rebellion. I was out of bandages, plums, prayers, talcum powder and boots. My sawn-off toothbrush was a useless nylon stump. I needed to regroup and refit. But more than anything, I really needed to lie down.

I headed first to the air-conditioned rooms of Hotel Evropa lying a short walk from the city centre where 40 euros, if not a little pricey for the Balkans, seemed nevertheless well spent. I couldn't fault the buffet breakfast. Refreshingly omelette-free, the banquet-style sideboard was heaped with enough purple grapes to satisfy a Roman orgy. While scouting tables I spotted a snowy-haired gentleman in short white sleeves buttering a roll near the window. A straw hat lay beside his elbow. I hadn't spoken to a native English-speaker in nearly a month. Perhaps . . . ?

'Excuse me,' I said, fingers curling around the back of a gilt and velveteen chair. 'Do you mind if I join you?'

The old fellow immediately straightened up and dabbed his lips with a napkin. 'No, not at all.'

I smiled. 'Okay, I appreciate it.'

Leaving my keys on the table, I sauntered over to the buffet area, loaded up a plate with crusty rolls, added a few tin-foiled tubs of butter and a few more of honey, and as I returned to my seat said with a chummy voice, 'So, how long have you been in Podgorica? I've not seen much of the city yet, but this hotel seems pretty decent.'

'Oh, only a few days.'

'I've just come down from Nikšić. I've not met many English people in this part of the world.'

'I'm from Walsall originally, a retired teacher.' He stopped buttering and forced a well-mannered smile. 'And how about you?'

'Southend-on-Sea. I don't know whether you've ever been to Essex or whether you've heard of—'

'I can't say that I have.'

'It's not large, a seaside town like Blackpool if you've ever been there. We've got the usual stuff like amusement arcades, one-armed bandits, and there's an air show in May. Our biggest claim to fame is that we have the longest pier in the world. Hard to believe, but as a child I once walked thirty miles up and down it for charity.'

He grinned. 'You must like walking then.'

With an invitation like that the conversation could only head in one direction. After we'd fully broken the ice Brian proved engaging company and it was a pleasure to communicate without having to resort to sign language. I glanced down at the Panama hat; listened to his soft, well-educated tones. One hundred years ago he might have been a diplomat in a white sweat-stained suit swatting tarantulas for the British Empire. Instead, he was in his sixties, careering around the Balkans in stuffy little minibuses. Back home a life of meals on wheels probably awaited, but for now he'd escaped that awful slippered twilight.

He politely dabbed his mouth, placed the napkin on the table with an air of finality and glanced over my shoulder.

'Well, well, young man, judging from everything you've told me you will no doubt be interested to know I'm heading out to Kosovo later.'

'Really?' I lifted my cup, waiting for him to elaborate, then watched amused as he pulled a freshly buttered ham roll beneath the table. The rustle of a plastic bag revealed its destination. I pretended not to notice.

'Have you been there before? I mean, do you think Kosovo is safe for people like us, for tourists?'

His eyes darted behind me to the black-waistcoated waiter stifling a yawn by the curvaceous bar.

'Hard to say young man, deuce hard to say. But look, I'm taking the bus there right after breakfast.' Another furtive glance, then a sly wink, 'I'll let you know.'

Three crusty rolls and two apples later lunch was in the bag, so to speak. Smiling innocently, he rose from the table cradling the bag beneath his hat. With breathtaking audacity he even stopped to share a few words with the enemy.

'Hot, isn't it?' he said to the hapless waiter.

The young man twiddled his bowtie, nodding happily as he was paid to do.

A bit of first-hand intelligence on the Kosovo situation would no doubt have proved useful to someone in my position, but that was the last time I saw Brian from Walsall, and for that matter those generously laden breakfast tables. The Evropa was booked solid, and over the next three days I had to relocate to the city centre and shuffle between a succession of hotels. It was far from ideal: packing, unpacking, repacking. Washing well-used underwear was an added chore. I spent a lot of time scrubbing at immovable stains and forming a nice collection of scented soaps.

On the last night I shifted up a star to the Hotel Crna Gora, a grand place where all the staff are over seventy and wander about in shiny black waistcoats like ageing snooker players. I combed my hair extra nicely for this one; you know you're somewhere posh when the counter is solid mahogany and there are clocks on the wall spanning London, New York and Tokyo. Pity, then, that there was no air-conditioning. Podgorica in the summer regularly hits forty degrees, which is about fifteen more than any Englishman is used to. For the only time in my life I took a cold shower and whooped with joy.

I devoted the final afternoon to interrogating strangers in a mad search for new boots. It was my own silly fault. The thin-heeled trainers I'd bought in Sarajevo were great for navigating suburban streets, but on uneven roads they had an unenviable gift for generating quite spectacular blisters. More than the fear of rejection it was a fresh batch of foot sores that had stopped me from making an assault on Monastery Ostrog.

Even in the Balkans you can't buy much with a twenty-euro note. Before shopping could commence I made a pit stop at the Bank of Montenegro. I expected a damn good mugging. Commission rates for changing AMEX cheques are universally obscene.

I remain implacably convinced there should be an annual cull of bankers with the worst offenders force-fed omelette for an entire year. On this occasion I managed to get off lightly. Five times richer than I had been for weeks, I stepped out, smiling, into the sun. And *that* was when she stepped forward.

The beggar was at my side in seconds. I appraised her just as quickly: early twenties, skin like Brazilian coffee, black curls peeking under a drab white headscarf. Cradled under her right arm was a chubby girl with the same black curls in a chocolate-brown dress. You didn't need to be a rich Westerner clutching several hundred euros to know what happened next.

Our eyes met, and the mother held out her hand.

Okay, I thought, that's fine. I can spare some. As I dropped the coins into her palm my smile blossomed into something really quite wonderful. I was still enjoying those warm fuzzy feelings when the mother slipped the money into her daughter's fingers and without thanking me held out her hand and demanded a second donation.

My smile evaporated. 'I'm sorry, I've given you all my change. I have nothing else to give you.'

But the mother wouldn't be denied.

Wishing someone 'good day' is about the limit of my Slavic language skills. The stern-looking businessman in horn-rimmed glasses was far more eloquent. His blast of Serbo-Croat was unintelligible, but I'm pretty certain 'good day' wasn't included. The beggar's nose wrinkled in disgust. Clearly insulted, she hurried away clutching her daughter.

And so to the precious boots. The final act of the day was a frantic race against the clock. I made it to the shoe shop thirty minutes before closing time. The basement was a long-distance walker's paradise: black boots, brown boots, packs of laces in cellophane wrappers, the usual twirling stands. Everything smelt of leather and polish. The lanky assistant had a commendable work ethic. Six boxes later I went back to the very first pair, and he didn't complain once.

'Orthodox?' he asked, kneeling before me and untying a lace. He was eyeing Johanna's cross hanging from my wrist.

'Not exactly, mate.' I wondered how to put it, then said simply, 'I'm a Protestant in the Church of England.'

'Ahhh, Protestant . . .' As he rose, his voice trailed off in semi-confusion. No surprise there. Orthodoxy holds sway here and to a lesser extent the pope.

Grinning, he led me to the counter. *Ker-ching!* The till drawer shot open.

'Because you are Christian,' he said, 'I am pleased to give you a five-euro discount!'

I handed over the balance, grateful for the gesture. Shortly afterwards I left with a wooden medallion of St Luke swinging around my neck. 'For good luck!' he told me, as we both charged up the stairs.

I left Podgorica the next day in my shiny new boots. The two-day march to Albania provided just enough worn-out asphalt to begin the process of breaking them in. Serenaded by several thousand crickets, I skilfully escaped Podgorica's suburbs with their clattering Gypsy carriages, dropping off as I went my useless trainers by another charred, roofless cottage. Perhaps they lie there still—a bizarre milestone on the road to Jerusalem—though personally I doubt it. For the price I paid for them you could feed a starving Gypsy for months. When, on the second morning, I found myself on the heights above Lake Shkodër, all I could see was a vast finger of placid grey water and tracking the edge on the near bank, some fifty feet below, a narrow-gauge railway track laddering brown-tipped grass. Beyond the lake stood a trio of green, featureless humps. Was that Albania? I felt decidedly underwhelmed.

The final obstacle to progress emerged minutes before the border. Let all of Christendom know that not even wild horses could stop me—a wild boast that anywhere else would have been absurd. I must have been halfway down the lakeside road when a chestnut horse suddenly burst from the trees. Nostrils flaring and ears pinned back, it brazenly cantered past my shoulder in a flurry of hooves before veering off up a dusty track. Although only 8 a.m., the mind-numbing heat had lulled me almost to sleep. I've never had a wake-up call quite like it.

My expedition across Montenegro ended beside one of those dingy wooden huts that seem to house half of Europe's yawning border guards. As I offered up my passport I didn't feel a trace of regret. From Šćepan Polje in the north to the Albanian crossing at Hani i Hotit, I'd been forced to overcome an impressive list of opponents. The trip had produced all the usual suspects: blisters, hunger, thirst, biblical clouds of flies, but also a few new ones—snakes, aggressive beggars and a frightening dose of heatstroke. Without planning on it, I'd gazed into the mirror of Romans 5:3-4 and found someone new staring back:

Suffering leads to perseverance; perseverance, character; and character, hope.

And if that isn't the true definition of the hot and rocky land of Montenegro, then I don't know what is.

Chapter Eight

Albania

The Land Where Everyone Wants to Be Somewhere Else

Whether your information has been gained from the Internet or the hard yards of experience, I don't think anyone walking south would deny the countries of Europe line up in convenient groups of three. Orderly and prosperous, with their shared Germanic heritage the Netherlands, Germany and Austria form a natural cultural and ethnic block. Immediately following on are the former Yugoslav states of Slovenia, Croatia and Bosnia—a fractious trio united by shared language and, in recent memory at least, by the kind of conflict the previous three have been keen to avoid. If Montenegro begins the next group, heralding a gradual shift from the Slavic world into the Albanian, then it's in Albania itself the pilgrim road takes another turn. And the turn here in terms of reputation is rather sharp.

From the German waiter in Vellberg to the swashbuckling Montenegrin petrol attendant, the message was always the same. Drug use was rampant. Albanians settled disputes with guns and explosives. Every forest was thick with thieves. Even the advice of those who should have known better veered heavily toward the apocalyptic. According to the Foreign Office website, crime presented a 'serious problem' and a visit to the town of Kükes, bordering Kosovo, would be positively suicidal.

Yeah, right.

If Albania taught me anything it was this: if you want to know what a country is really like, don't expect your government to tell you. Don't expect your friends to tell you. Don't even expect a witty Bill Bryson travel novel to tell you. To find the *real* truth you have to climb out of your armchair and see for yourself. On 28 June, I did just that.

When you clamber out of a comfortable armchair in southern England you'll likely end up at places you never knew existed. So it was for me at a speck on the map called Hani i Hotit. Since Albania stands outside the Schengen Agreement this particular checkpoint is not one a Briton can just breeze past with a wave of the passport and a perfunctory nod. It's a real border with real guards and a real ten-euro entrance tax. After a moment's consideration I paid up, wondering why the 'tax' only applied to wealthier visitors, namely EU nationals. Was this my first taste of Albanian skulduggery? I did wonder.

With the formalities out of the way I settled into the serious business of walking. The options weren't hugely complex. There was only one obvious route on the map, and that involved travelling southward to Shkodër (the most populous northern city), then pinwheeling east toward the village of Vau i Dejës. From there I would march in a straight-ish line to the frontier town of Kukës, and thence to that place where lone pilgrims should never willingly venture, i.e. the Albanian-Serbian powder keg known as Kosovo. If I had any misgivings about the latter, I kept them hidden, even from myself.

The first target, and where I also hoped to find somewhere decent to sleep, was the town of Koplik, lying south and slightly east of Lake Shkodër. I won't fake courage to make myself look good—they were anxious times. My new boots were chafing, raising fears of fresh blisters. Thanks to the banks in Podgorica I had no local currency (not a single one could provide any lek, which probably says something about the Albanian economy). Dire warnings from seven countries were ringing in my ears.

Certain death seemed imminent among great herds of bleating goats jamming the hot and dusty roads.

Perhaps unsurprisingly, it was the animals that provided much of the initial fascination. I have no idea when a pair of oxen last took a summer stroll down Southend High Street, but it must have been well over three hundred years ago. By far the strangest sight for a confirmed town-dweller was a small girl, about four feet tall, in pink top and jeans, leading a pair of reddish-brown oxen by the harness. As their curling white horns plodded past my shoulder the beasts scrutinised me with their fly-blown eyes. They were magnificent creatures and appeared much larger in real life as animals always do.

Other impressions were of a landscape more alien than the moon: the red Albanian flag with its black double-headed eagle, old concrete bunkers exposing their iron ribs to the sun, mushrooming among grass, dry and withered. The valley's glittering soil was astonishingly poor, almost like sand. On one occasion I knelt down by the roadside and grabbed a handful letting the warm coarse grains drain between my fingers. Anyone making a living in this wilderness deserved respect; anyone actually living here deserved better. As I rose, another horse and cart clattered past in a flash of whirling spokes.

English eyes, wary and uncertain, met Albanian, impassive and fixed. I smiled politely, eager to make a good impression.

Zero response.

Most of the time I gave these guys a wide berth. Drivers were invariably male, with curly black hair, skin like prunes and cracking six-foot whips. To begin with I continued to beam heartily at every passing cart. Then I realised the good humour of a rich tourist might be unwelcome and gave up. The road was just as hostile. Swept by at least 3,000 plastic bottles, I found plenty of deep ruts ideal for snapping ankles. Somewhere in all this dust and clatter I stumbled across a concrete bridge spanning a dry riverbed overgrown with dandelions and tree saplings. Several decades of dilapidation had taken their toll. I swear I felt it move.

Thankfully, there was much more to see beyond the obvious decay. 'The poor give more than the rich,' goes the well-known saying, and in Albania it's true. Within minutes of crossing the border I knocked on a house for water and walked away with a gigantic two-litre bottle. My good fortune continued in the grocer's shop—a robust chunk of whitewashed concrete with all the charm of a bomb shelter. I ducked cautiously under the arch, fixing my eyes on an old woman with narrow shoulders and a yellow handkerchief knotted around her neck.

'Do you accept euros?' I asked hopefully.

A shaking head said no.

I would have left empty-handed, except the bemused shop-keeper simply flung open the chest freezer and handed me a free can of lemonade. I'd barely travelled another fifty metres when a red pickup truck screeched to a halt. A hand beckoned and I ran to the window. What's this? Could it be a lift? Nope. Seconds later, the grinning driver roared away leaving me clutching a bag of ready salted crisps. Three gifts in two hours . . . Hurrah! I never expected this!

It must have been near the end of the afternoon when I finally closed in on my first Albanian town. With 15 km of the parched Highland Region under my belt, I didn't have high hopes. It was a fair assessment. The consensus of several strangers was that 8,000 Muslims and 2,000 Catholics lived in Koplik; to which I can reliably add a pair of podgy cops wearing sky-blue shirts, too many skeletal dogs to mention and at least 23,000 pieces of wind-blown trash circling a dusty roundabout. The saving grace lurked a few hundred metres on beside a mushroom bunker choked with purple thistles—a strikingly lemon house of God. My eyes were moist with the joy of Christ as I approached the panelled doors. I felt gutted when I found them bolted.

The day could have ended there, but I'm stubborn around a church. Sensing that a warm bed might still be in the offing, I decided to linger in the hope the priest might show up. There was a timber yard directly opposite fragrant with sawdust and pine chips. I was squatting on a stack of four-by-two, sizing up the thistled bunker as a possible home, when:

'#@£#%#!'

An angry foreign expletive always demands attention. I swung round to face a young man: blue jeans, bronzed, bare-chested, black hair speckled with sawdust. After the accusing questions (Why are you sitting on my wood? Why are you in Albania? Blah, blah, blah) we both relaxed into our better selves.

Leaning forward to brush his hair free of sawdust, he straightened up with a gigantic yawn and, briefly scanning the passing traffic, grinned at me and said, 'Okay, Mister, but look, it is hot out here. Come sit in the shade, and we'll wait for the priest.'

I glanced behind him at the darkened hanger. It had to be better than this pile of splintered wood.

'We know where he lives. Trust me. When he comes back we will take you to him.'

I rose on creaky knees, dusting off my shorts. 'Are you sure? I mean, I don't want to interfere with your work . . .'

He swung a bronzed arm languidly towards the hanger. 'Of course I'm sure!'

I'm glad now that I don't run a business in Albania, and if I did, it would have nothing to do with selling timber. During the two hours we sat on our buckets, gulping water, not a single customer pulled up. The only visitor was a tall elderly gentleman with hair like cotton wool and a neck like a Galapagos tortoise. Impeccable in his white blazer, flaring white flannels and matching white shoes with fake gold buckles, at first he appraised me with mild disinterest. Then, learning I was English, surged forward to shake my hand.

'Aha! You are English, no?'

I'd never seen eyebrows rise that quickly. Startled by the vigorous hand pumping, I decided to take a step back.

'Yep, I'm waiting for the priest, Father Seli. This guy told me about him.' I pointed to my new friend, who merely nodded from his bucket.

'But of course, of course,' replied the old gentleman, smoothing down his gold cravat. 'Father Seli, yes, oh indeed yes. He will be here soon. You will see, you will see.'

Although Mr White refused to buy a single sliver of wood, he turned out to be amusing company. Every few seconds he'd snap his fingers, fix me with a triumphant grin, then toss out another line plucked from a dodgy English phrasebook. Such was the old fellow's excitement he didn't even wait for an answer:

'Can you direct me to the nearest train station, please?'

Pause.

'Is this ice cream twice the price it should be, please?'

Pause.

'I think you just ripped me off, please?'

Pause.

'Are you related to the Queen, please?'

Pause.

'Do you sell navy-blue garter socks, size nine-and-a-half, in cellophane packs of three, please?'

'Please. Excuse me, please. What is the time, please?'

Oh blimey, yes. What was the time? I smiled as politely as I could from my bucket praying for an end to this verbal torture. The respite lasted about twenty seconds.

Mr White looked down at his watch. 'Sir!' he said smartly, adjusting his gold cravat with a neat sideways twist. 'Would you care for a refreshing cup of tea?'

Erm . . . Now what? I looked up at his beaming face, wondering whether he was still locked in phrasebook mode. 'Do you have any here?' My voice wavered pathetically. Water is nice in hot weather, but you can't beat a good cuppa.

He shook his head and smiled ruefully. 'Aha! You English always drink tea at five o'clock. We know your ways!'

I had to laugh. Did they really teach that in Albanian schools?

He was the English teacher. Apparently, they did.

Father Artan Seli arrived shortly after, which brought proceedings nicely to a close. Flanked by two of his finest countrymen he could hardly have refused me shelter, and to his credit he didn't. Just before falling asleep on his sofa bed I realised something remarkable: I'd survived fourteen hours in Albania without being shot, blown up or trampled by an ox. For some unfathomable reason Albanians seemed to like me. Given all the dire warnings, it was a cracking end to the first day.

* * *

An enormous problem haunts the Albanian psyche, and if you can avoid being flattened by plodding oxen you eventually get to hear about it. Such is the profound importance of the issue that one enterprising individual even tried to bribe me with my favourite cola. 'Do you know how I can get into the UK without proper papers?' he asked. (Just for the record, I didn't.) The boldness of this gentlemen typified prevailing sentiment. Nearly everyone I met wanted to be somewhere else, with a particular longing for Greece and Italy. There was only one thing standing in their way: the dreaded and much lamented 'visa problem'.

When faced with a problem this huge you might reasonably expect that history has something to do with it. You'd be right. While the cost of European visas is indeed high for the average Albanian, to grasp why the issue has developed into a national obsession it's first necessary to understand why so many people wish to leave the country. The answer, according to all I met, lies in the country's communist past. I'll never be an expert in all the detail, but I'm rock-solid certain if it hadn't been for the eccentric leadership of Enver Hoxha there wouldn't be such a furore today. Certainly fewer of Albania's three million disgruntled citizens would wish to emigrate, which would do much to reduce the endless stream of complaints.

It wasn't that the Supreme Comrade didn't have enough time to perfect his communist paradise. Fanatical adherence to 'anti-revisionist Marxism-Leninism' has relatively little support these days, but in the dark hours of 1944 and for the next forty years Albania became its unlikely champion. The regime (despite a batty policy of making emigration illegal) wasn't without success. Throughout the Hoxha years female attendance at school rose dramatically. Employment opportunities for women increased, as did women's rights generally, and there was a dramatic rise in literacy. On the downside not even the Great Teacher could solve the country's economic woes. The nation's long march to the twenty-first century only began in 1985 with Hoxha's death. Actually, it's been more of a gasping stutter. The agricultural economy relies on scythes and nine-year-old girls pulling oxen. The chaotic cities mirror the countryside. Shuffling beggars are legion, power cuts frequent, toilets crouch-and-shoot, planning permission is considered optional and there's a quite spectacular lack of sewer lids. Most noticeable to outsiders are the concrete bunkers that mushroom in every town and field. Over 500,000 of the so-called 'Hoxha Bunkers' were built by heroic peasants to repel degenerate capitalist invaders fighting to get in. How ironic, then, that most Albanians are now fighting to get out.

It's surely a bitter quirk of fate that the only country Albanians don't need a visa for is Montenegro. Having just spent eleven days there, dripping sweat and draining discarded water bottles, I wasn't entirely convinced this concession was an act of kindness on the part of the Montenegrin Government. In any case, it hadn't dampened Albanian ire. My first taste of national outrage occurred halfway to Shkodër among four tanned faces chatting and drinking under a mountainous tree. They were all plump Muslim men with full righteous beards.

I loosened a few straps, dropped my rucksack to the ground and after a bit of rambling Jerusalem talk continued, 'and yes, I'm a Christian if that doesn't seem too obvious.'

The men slapped their hands on the table, laughing thickly in unison. Then the guy with the longest beard stood up.

'Friend,' he said, smiling, 'do not take any notice of them. That doesn't matter here.'

He walked around the table to where I was standing, pulled out an empty chair and gently urged my shoulders into the seat.

I was glad he did. Lunch was a fine spread: tall glasses of frothy beer, white china plates heaped with tomatoes, sliced cucumber, slices of juicy red melon. Weaned on the English national dish, I found the fried fish to be excellent. The meat fell away so easily from the bone it could have come straight from the net.

'The fish is delicious, no?' said the fellow next to me.

'It's brilliant!' I answered, and kept on cutting.

'The fish is from Lake Shkodër, just a few kilometres away,' another added with a hint of pride.

I turned to my right and nodded cheerfully.

The problem that haunts Albanian dreams didn't take long to join the party. It was just after someone had asked me whether I was trying to set a walking record (presumably of the Guinness variety) that the almighty grumble began.

'Visas to your England cost so much,' said Long Beard.

He looked across at me and began to rub his thumb and fore-finger together over imaginary banknotes. Knowing nods rippled around the table. Lush black beards were stroked in thought. As I listened to the disappointment in his voice I was surprised to found myself sharing it. The generosity of the Albanian people was starting to have an effect, and not just on my stomach.

'Yeah,' I told him, keeping my face grave, 'I've heard that, too. You know, I don't understand why our government makes this stuff so difficult.'

Actually, the UK work permit is the real problem. Anyone willing to risk a mugging in London's darker alleys needs at least £2,800 to apply. I don't know how many goatskins that translates into, but for most Albanians in the Highland Region it's about £2,750 too much.

I munched on happily right up to the first mention of Kosovo, or *Kosova* as the Albanians prefer to call it. Don't be fooled by the slight difference in spelling: there's a lot more to that political knot than a single letter. With an empty plate before me, I rose and started shaking hands.

'Friend,' said Long Beard, rising briskly and looking me straight in the eye. 'Don't forget to tell the truth about Albania. We are good people, friendly people. Don't forget what you have seen.'

Again, I felt it—the unmistakeable tug at the heart. 'I won't forget,' I told him. And as a weak smile broke across my face, 'I promise you, I won't forget.'

You've done it now, mate, I thought. Not only must you walk to Jerusalem, but you've embarked on a sworn mission to reha-bilitate the image of an entire nation. Could it be done? Was such a thing even possible?

Over the next few days, while turning down dozens of lifts, I found much in the Albanian character that encouraged me to try. Repressed for decades by their former communist government, the population of the arid north were like coiled springs, full of unfilled potential. I developed a picture of a hardy people with a passion for life, open to strangers, ambitious, and generous in a way that made a mockery of their humble means. Often I enjoyed so much hospitality I found it difficult to make my daily distance. And always the question around café tables was the same:

'Why on earth are you walking?'

'Why not?' I replied. 'If I was in a car or bus I'd pass through all your towns and villages in seconds. But if I'm walking I have more opportunities to meet people and exchange ideas. I also get to learn a lot more about each country. Think of it this way. It's all about opening yourself up to new experiences, and I don't think you can fully achieve that unless you're on foot.'

The explanation was very much the pilgrim, long-distance-walker mindset. I'm not sure everyone bought it, but most I met appeared to have a sense of the possibilities, and no one violently disagreed. In any case, such was my continuing popularity along the interminable E762, that it wasn't long before I was repeat-ing the argument. I must have been an hour away from Shkodër when I saw them: two slouched figures watching me from a six-foot-high bank of sandy earth glittering like sequins.

'Hey!' shouted the skinny boy. He shot to his feet and started crisscrossing both arms furiously.

Yep. They've seen me. I cut my stride and came to a cautious halt. The fat man glanced up, jowls burning red, thinning hair matted with sweat. He looked at me indifferently. The gangly teenager, by contrast, had already decided a fool plodding about with a massive rucksack was well worth investigating. He skidded down the bank, shooting earth in all directions. I watched him dust off his jeans, and after an exchange of names he shot back with, 'Where are you going, Mister?'

'Shkodër, straight down this road here for a few miles or so.'

'Do you know anything about building?'

'Yeah, a bit. What's up?'

'We are building a house over there.' He cocked a thumb over his shoulder towards a grey structure set back a few yards from the road. 'We have a big problem that needs fixing. Mister, would you like to see it?'

With seven European countries underfoot, wrestling with big problems had become something of a speciality. I told myself it was all part of the journey, and off we went.

We were an unlikely procession of fixers. Georges led the way, a paunchy, fifty-something builder, grimacing due to the 'big problem' and clutching a sizeable wrench like a man intent on murder. At his heels was Christian, a loping eighteen-year-old in an orange T-shirt helping dad build a house for his cousin. They'd been busy in the sun. We pulled up before two storeys of grey breeze block topped by cherry-red tiles. A mountain of yellow sand rose beside the doorless entrance.

'Follow me!' Christian ordered, as Georges wandered off to wreak havoc with the wrench. So I did. Everything seemed fine until we descended into the basement.

'A few months ago the water rose up to here,' he explained, drawing a hand across the wall. 'The whole garage was flooded.' He shrugged his boyish shoulders. 'We don't know what to do. Do you have any ideas?'

Umm . . . start again elsewhere? His hand had been at least five feet off the ground. The garage had become a swimming pool with enough water to give an Olympic swimmer a decent work-out. How was I supposed to fix this?

'Well?' he demanded.

Quite by chance, the essence of the problem wasn't completely unknown to me. In my early twenties I'd spent a year in my hometown working for a dampcourse company. It was boring work: drill holes into walls, inject silicone liquid, plug holes with cement. The method worked well against rising damp, but not rolling five-foot waves.

'You know what, mate, I'm not much of a builder really. I can't think of anything right now . . .'

I left the question unanswered, hoping he wouldn't press it. Luckily for English blushes, he didn't.

Unable to rectify matters, we sauntered around each room leaving our footprints in the dust. The second storey still had to be reached by ladder as there were no stairs yet in place. By the end of construction hopefully there would be; if the water rose any higher the future owner might appreciate the gesture.

As we tapped walls and tripped over screwdrivers, Christian spoke about his desire to study in Greece; Georges, about his former work as a labourer in the UK. It may have been cheeky of me, but I just had to ask.

'So, Georges, why exactly *did* you return to Albania?'

'Damn visa problem,' muttered Georges glumly, and wandered off to find his son.

＊ ＊ ＊

Beckoning legions of Kosovo Albanian holidaymakers and the occasional dishevelled Englishman desperate for a soft mattress, about two hundred Hoxha Bunkers south of Koplik lies Shkodër, a city of most extraordinary chaos. After spending several days wrestling with the indefatigable 'visa problem', I saw it for my-self. And I was not overly impressed.

I may be guilty of watching too many Westerns, but there's a wildness about Shkodër, a whiff of lawlessness that evokes the tin-starred sheriff dying heroically in a hail of bullets. Ex-pat Albanians may extol the 'great beauty' of their motherland on shaky YouTube videos, but nostalgia can be misleading. There's nothing beautiful about dingy garage-like shops, swirling trash, crumbling concrete the colour of rotting nectarines, aggressive beggars in every park, and all along the pavement street vendors by the score, sitting cross-legged among huge piles of second-hand shoes, used cigarette lighters and other crud, while hungry children in pink flip-flops look up with imploring eyes.

I only spent one night among the bedlam, and it proved more than enough to get a feel for the city. With no obvious tourist attractions to gawp at, it was time to stock up on essentials and crash out for a while on the softest mattress I could find. I wish now I'd paid out a few extra lek on somewhere upmarket, like the pretentiously named Hotel Colosseo. Believe me, if you're entering Shkodër from the north, don't take the first hotel you see. It's a grim little place just off the main road with iron bars on the windows and furnishings so Spartan even King Leonidas would object. Blankets are the kind good Marxists always sleep under, namely unyielding squares of Soviet weave with all the comfort of a Brillo pad. They tend to chafe a bit.

I may have been knackered, but I wasn't stupid enough to waste the remaining daylight. Before I stumbled across the blistered red *farmaci* sign the only Albanian word I knew was *faleminderit* (thank you). For a pilgrim short of plasters finding a pharmacy was indeed a fortuitous discovery. I must have trotted out with the shop's entire supply. What was the shopkeeper's response?

This was the land where everyone wants to be somewhere else: he threw up his hands like a lottery winner, then promptly booked a one-way ticket to Greece.

With my pockets considerably lighter I continued to wander, halting at random to peer in quizzically at unfamiliar windows. I don't recommend the practice outside Albanian banks. Like any good frontier town, Shkodër's have armed guards to discourage unhealthy criminal tendencies. Well ho-ho-ho to that. Mostly these guys exist to strut about in their crumpled uniforms, chat to friends while blatantly not doing their job and push dirty pilgrim trash towards the gutter. Any kind of protest would have been extremely foolish. As Clint Eastwood might have said (if I'd been his scriptwriter): 'There are two types of men in this world, those with guns and those without.' Yeah, quite. I took another grimace at those holsters and let the insult pass.

I found Shkodër's population an eclectic mix. Adult beggars outnumber everyone ten to one. Child beggars outnumber the adults. Hanging from trees like Sumatran panthers and generally creeping stealthily about, their favourite haunts are the city's greener bits of dust. One small boy in a white string vest was particularly persistent, and for several minutes we danced among the shrubbery in an annoying foxtrot until I finally paid up. Obvious tourists were scarce, though one accent I did hear was Italian—perhaps a legacy of Mussolini's 1939 invasion of Albania (the links between the two countries remain strong). Tanned young men with oily black hair and fashionable goatees, they were never without the coolest sunglasses.

'*Italiano?*' said a guy in a red T-shirt and calf-length shorts.

Damn! Those shades are cool! 'Sorry,' I said. 'Do you speak English?'

He seemed to be on the verge of saying something, then shook his head disappointedly, and the conversation fizzled out.

Despite some robust handling from the pushy bank guards, they did eventually let me in to offload a few AMEX cheques. I left flush with a bundle of sordid green notes and went hunting for a pair of shorts. I didn't stay flush for long. Probably the most expensive ever purchased in northern Albania, they were also the most unsuitable for long-distance walking. I could tolerate a waistband three sizes too big, but not those silly tassels dangling from the legs. Never mind, I thought, a few swift cuts from a Swiss Army knife will fix the problem.

The shopkeeper readily agreed, then took the rest of my cash, grinned broadly and booked a one-way ticket to Italy.

If I'd hoped for a good night's sleep beneath my Brillo pad blanket, I was disabused of the idea at 7 p.m. One of the more curious aspects of pilgrimage is the discovery of new, exciting talents. Incredible though it may seem, by simply carrying a very large rucksack, stuffing it full of junk and digging lots of holes with a small trowel, I'd unearthed a rare gift for choosing hotels where the noisiest parties were always imminent. Two hours after the walls began to tremble, pieces of plaster began to fall from the ceiling, and an hour after *that* the glass was literally dancing in the frame. Salvation only arrived at 2:30 a.m. after the third and final power cut. I know they'll never read this, but I'd like to thank the electricity company for pulling the plug.

For six days I turned my head east towards the border town of Kükes, navigating a diverse landscape of purple-thistled fields, waves of tinder grass littered with scores of Hoxha Bunkers, a beautiful topaz lake on a tiny chugging ferry squeezed between leering, green-granite cliffs and, during a particularly challenging forty-eight hours, a high mountain road zigzagging among the clouds where a wrong step meant instant death. As much as the mushrooming bunkers it was the goodness of the people that provided continuity. Every kilometre or so I'd spot another waving hand and drop gratefully into a chair. The feeling grew naturally, innocently, quietly. Despite all logic and every warning something amazing had happened.

I'd fallen in love with Albania.

It's true. I loved the people's open, generous nature. I loved big oxen plodding down sunny lanes, wrestling with like minds over the intractable 'visa problem' and the quaint idea that at five o'clock all Englishmen drink tea. Encouraged by a strong anti-establishment gene, I decided the chaotic undercurrents were particularly praiseworthy. There must be something good going on when no one bothers to seek planning permission, but simply points to a patch of dirt and says, 'Hey! This is the place for me!'

I was totally smitten, even to the point of believing that 500,000 lumps of useless crumbling concrete were a triumph of Albania's fighting spirit, rather than the ludicrous eyesore they undoubtedly were. No one could change my mind. Nothing could. I loved this country and its people, and I wanted to tell the world.

Blimey. I'm not entirely sure when Cupid let loose with his twanging bow, but with a love like that you can travel far, or at least 20 km down the road to Vau i Dejës. In the hot, hazy greys of a summer's dusk I dropped my rucksack to the ground and watched the townsfolk saunter by. I was standing under a tree, arms folded, eyes peeled for the village priest and looking my usual dishevelled self, when:

'Hello, mate!'

Mate? No one had called me that since leaving England! I squinted, eager to identify the mysterious voice. From the shadows appeared a stocky man, about my height, in polo top and jeans, with a razor haircut to rival my own. His Albanian name was Çesk, though 'It's Francis in your language,' he explained with a banana grin. 'So, mate, what brings you to Vau i Dejës?'

When I told him I thought his jaw was going to crack.

'Shkodër? Jerusalem? Wow! You must be thirsty then!'

I laughed, letting out some of the tension. There was only one place this could go.

He cocked a thumb over his shoulder. 'Fancy a drink?'

Silly question.

With Francis leading, we headed off down rough tracks bordered by the shadows of houses and illuminated above by soft yellow lights which, at the edge of eyesight, seemed to hang in the dark like globes. The café's functional interior was largely as expected: three round wooden tables, each with three chairs, and some cheap woven shades half pulled down.

I don't know if the drink he gave me had a name. But coupled with a good chat in English the frothy concoction of coffee and lemonade did much to lift flagging spirits. Kosovo, visa problems, Jerusalem, the real meaning of life (i.e. football): by the second glass the conversation had gone around the world and back. Not surprisingly, I had plenty of questions about Albania. This was my first time in the country, and as usual in foreign climes I was keen to get a feel for the place.

'Is it dangerous to live here? You know, I took advice as I went along, and none of it was good.'

'Mate,' he told me airily, 'I know where you're coming from. But look, nowhere is absolutely safe. I might be murdered, even here in my own village.'

Err, thanks for the brutal honesty . . . At least my prospects for finding shelter were reassuringly high.

'Tony, believe me, if our priest tells the congregation that an Englishman is here, then every person will raise their hand.'

Great, I thought, that's the accommodation sorted. Somewhere in all of this I gave a potted history of events so far, extolling the rich blessings of a spiritual life and forgetting the annoying parts, like sleeping bags that don't fit into their stuff sacks. I was getting ready to ask about his experiences in England when he snapped his fingers and broke into a grin. 'Hey, would you like to hear a story?'

I smiled at him. 'Sure, I'd love to hear one.'

Francis placed his glass on the table and settled back into his chair. 'This is an old tale my father told me when I was young.' His face became thoughtful for a few seconds, then, when he judged the moment right, he began:

'There was once a man who carried a wooden cross on his back. He was a determined kind of man. He took the cross with him everywhere, to the village, to the town and each day to the market. It was tiring work carrying such a heavy burden. As time went on the man became old, and his strength faded. To make things easier for himself he got into the habit of cutting of small pieces with a saw. For a while his cross would become lighter, and the man would feel happy. But he'd soon get tired again.

'Many years passed. Then, after a lifetime of struggle, the man died and he saw St Peter standing before the golden gates. He became full of joy, certain that he would be rewarded for his devotion. But as he looked down there was a problem. A deep abyss barred his way to Heaven. What could he do? Desperate to enter paradise, he dropped his cross for the final time and shoved it out, hoping it would bridge the gap. The man realised the truth and began to weep. His cross fell short by the exact amount he'd sawn off.'

When wisdom arrives in Solomon-esque parables it takes a while for the unconscious mind to decipher the meaning. If I'd known how significant those words were going to be, I might have taken more notice. As it was, I merely smiled politely and told him it all sounded jolly clever. By the time conversation had returned to Kosovo I thought this was going to be just another opportunity to air century-old Albanian grievances, but no.

'Listen, Tony, I've been thinking about your route. I've got an idea which will get you into Kosovo more quickly.'

'An idea?' I eyed him cautiously. I was planning to march down the main road to the border crossing near Kukës. That was the obvious and safest route.

'Now look, mate,' and he began to rock forward on his stool, 'just hear me out a minute. I have a friend who crosses the border on his way to work in Pristina. He takes the ferry from Koman to Fierzë and then travels to Kosovo from there. I reckon you could do the same and shorten your journey.' He settled back, hands forming a thoughtful triangle under his chin. 'This way will be much easier for you. What do you think?'

What I think is that Francis is an excellent salesman who could sell snow to an Eskimo. When he told me the convent at Fierzë was happy to put me up, I was sold. Only the distance to Koman threatened the plan.

'Okay,' I told him, 'sounds good. But what time does the ferry come? Remember, I'm on foot. I can only walk so quickly.'

'Oh,' he said, 'don't you worry about that.'

Nothing was going to stand in the way of this grand plan.

'The ferry doesn't arrive until ten. You'll do it easily.'

The sun rose at 5 a.m. I did the maths: 35 km in five hours on Albanian potholed roads. I was still exhausted from last night's noisy party. It would be asking a lot.

There's only one Catholic church in Vau i Dejës, and it was a generous host. After Francis departed, a church minder took me to a restaurant where I snacked on generous quantities of *qofte të fërguara* (fried meatballs served with rice). Seconds were offered, and I couldn't resist.

Opposite the church a charity called Caritas owned a corrugated outhouse. They were humble lodgings: cold stone floors, barred windows (de rigueur in Albania), a pair of iron bunk beds covered by coarse brown blankets. I was standing in the hallway looking at cobwebbed photos of children playing football when I heard the knock. With a hearty yank, I pulled open the reinforced door and found Francis peering in.

'All right, mate?' he said.

'Yeah, I think so. Everything's fine.'

'Good,' and he stepped in through the gap. 'By the way, I have some more information for you from Father Simone. There are four nuns at the convent. One Italian. One French.' He frowned for a moment as if thinking. 'Hmm. I'm guessing the one from India probably speaks English. Well anyway, I guess you'll find out soon enough.'

'Okay, I'll remember that. Anything else I should know?'

He shook his head. 'Don't worry, mate, it's all been arranged. When you get to Fierzë the nuns will give you further instructions. Do you have some paper?' He made a writing motion in the air. 'I could jot down some phrases for you.'

'Sure. I've got a diary in my rucksack.'

We strode back to the dorm. Francis sat on the bottom bunk, head bent forward, and I stood by the barred windows watching him scribble. Some folk have a strange sense of humour. I was praying they weren't Albanian obscenities.

He grinned mischievously and returning gaze to paper said,

'No, mate, nothing like that. Just a few phrases for you to use later.'

As he handed it back I glanced down at the unfamiliar scrawl:

Ku eshte trageti?　　English– where is the ferry?
where are the nuns? Albania-- Ku eshte shtepia e
murgeshave?

He was right: it was useful stuff. Though I wasn't entirely convinced about the Kosovo shortcut, a lot of well-meaning people were doing their best to help me. Francis was one of them. This wasn't the moment to voice doubts.

'Okay, mate,' he said, placing hands on knees and pushing himself to his feet. He shook my hand. 'Good luck with everything, and I really hope you make it.'

'Yeah, you too, and please give my thanks to Father Simone. I really appreciate his help.'

I saw him out the door, then glanced at the watch. Damn. It's already gone eleven. I took a quick shower, fluffed up a pillow and clambered under one of those coarse-looking blankets. All I had to do was walk thirty-five kilometres in five hours. Around the table it all sounded so simple . . .

That the journey proved to be anything but is a testament to the harsh realities of Balkans travel. The road to Koman is an awful stretch of tarmac: potholed, fissured, a ruinous surface for sore feet still adjusting to new boots. Battalions of spiky fir trees cling uneasily to the steep banks, sweeping downward to meet a pool of inky black water lapping against foamy green hills. Every half hour you catch the sound. From the rear a solitary car approaches, crunching loose stones. It swerves around you and moves on. Laboured gasps recycle the unnatural stillness. Something clinks about in your rucksack. A tin cup, maybe?

I'm not prone to defeatism. I honestly gave it my all, and then some. After rising above the dam I started briskly, sidestepping the largest fissures, jogging in bursts, thinking I might make it. That was my mistake—giving myself false hope. When the end came nearly six hours later I was running flat out. Reaching this wretched ferry had assumed the significance of Jerusalem itself. I glanced at the watch in panic, then again in disbelief.

Oh God, where–is–this–place?

My Albanian love affair ended abruptly at 10:45 a.m. on a mound of dirt. Koman, if it really existed, was nowhere in sight. I wriggled out of my rucksack, tossed it aside and crashed to the ground, head in hands.

There's a great deal of wisdom to be found in parables. As a Christian I should have known that. The story Francis had recounted only a few hours ago, so innocent in delivery, so simple in plot and which at the time had seemed nothing more than a mild entertainment, now thundered toward me like a freight train.

Wait a minute, I thought. Why I am getting on a damn ferry anyway? I'm supposed to be walking to Jerusalem!

The feathered branches rustled secretively seeking the pleasure of the winds. 'Think!' they urged. 'Think back!' Slowly the gist of Francis' story returned. I pictured the man taking a saw to his cross, easing his burden as I was by taking a shortcut into Kosovo. Was this terrible road a punishment for shortening my cross? If so, without God's blessing how could I succeed?

The question was also the answer as only God can be. The truth blazed brighter than a thousand suns. It wasn't blessings or good roads I needed, but the words of Philippians 4:13:

I can do all things through him who strengthens me.

Sitting on a patch of dirt feeling sorry for oneself is rarely conducive to success. I glanced wistfully at my watch, dusted off my shorts and with renewed determination, marched on.

I did eventually live to see Koman, though I was thoroughly knackered and neither pleased nor surprised to learn I'd missed what I believed to be the only ferry. Fortunately, a second boat departed in the early evening—a pint-sized vessel that sank as low in the water as it could without pulling everyone down into the depths. We were a mixed bunch of adventurers. A rowdy group of Hells Angels had gathered on the bow, all black leather and savage, flowing hair. Soon crumpled beer cans began to pepper aquamarine water. Fearful I might join the debris, I stayed on the roof deck among a crowd of Kosovo Albanians returning from a holiday by Lake Shkodër. The language barrier prevented conversation, bar one: Rina Bo, a twenty-two-year-old student with hazel eyes like saucers. She lived in Pristina, the largest city in Kosovo and de facto capital. 'We're very tired and it's a long way home,' she told me. I smiled glumly. I knew the feeling.

Fifteen hours after leaving Vau i Dejës I finally arrived in total darkness outside the convent in Fierzë. A few hearty knocks at the gated entrance revealed that everyone had gone to bed. The grand plan to get me into Kosovo was unravelling faster than an ageing sweater.

Blast! I thought. Will there be no end to this dreadful day?

With characteristic stubbornness I ran to the houses opposite and started banging on doors. The first two refused to answer; then an elderly woman appeared, yawning in a knee-length coat. She clearly wanted to be somewhere else, i.e. in bed, in Italy, in Greece, or any place where there weren't stupid English. This wasn't a moment for faint hearts. I pulled out my diary and began to massacre one of the phrases Francis had given me.

'*Ku eshte shtepia e murgeshave?*'

The old woman gasped, clutching at her throat.

It was the moment that turned the tide.

After that there was no stopping her. The old woman inflated her lungs and bellowed to someone a few doors down—who promptly shouted to someone else. Darkened windows flared orange. The call went up in Albanian all over the village, 'There is an English here! There is an English here! We must find the key!' That was enough to bring them all out. People streamed out of their doors drawn by the huge commotion. Shadowy figures started running about like headless chickens. A braying donkey came trotting down the hill. Everything with legs and lungs wanted to join the search.

Eventually, the miracle was wrought: from the gloom a pony-tailed girl appeared, allowing me to gratefully slip through the convent gate. Scenting victory, I mounted the stone steps and announced my dishevelled presence to the nuns of Fierzë with a firm and slightly desperate knock. *Rap. Rap. Rap.* Thirty-second pause. Oak swung open on well-oiled hinges, and in the gap appeared a dimpled Asian face circled by rays of golden light.

'Welcome!' said the tiny figure dressed in a nun's white habit. 'We have been expecting you!'

Hey. Now that's more like it.

For all the new foot sores acquired in getting there, I didn't stay long at the convent. Even now I'm still kicking myself for not trying to wangle another night. The nuns were quite simply brilliant, fussing over their hungry English charge like hens over a newborn chick.

'Tony, tonight you will sleep in a nice bed,' Sister Mary told me mumsily.

The hostile Koman road had been a unique blend of physical and spiritual torture. I let soft words heal ebbing wounds.

I was especially grateful for the blessing of a hot meal. Dinner was a tasty stew washed down by red wine; breakfast, crowned at 6 a.m. by a wonderfully tangy marmalade. The hospitality of the Catholic Church in Albania couldn't be faulted. Grotesquely rich in comparison, I can think of several German and Croatian churches that should hang their heads in shame.

I saw the nuns for the final time where the road forks right toward Kukës. They were in their black Land Rover and heading left into Kosovo on a shopping trip to Pristina. God bless Sister Mary; she was still trying to coax me into their car.

'Are you sure?' Her voice was heavy with disappointment. 'We do have plenty of room,' and she tilted her head toward the rear seat.

Our eyes met again. I shook my head. 'I know, and thanks for all you've done, but I've been thinking a lot about this passport business. I really need to get to Kukës, so I can get it stamped. You do understand? You do understand I can't join you?'

It was a point worth making. To the best of my knowledge there were no border controls on the road to Pristina. Without a Kosovo entry stamp I might face awkward questions when I finally left the country.

Her smile weakened and she began to wind down the window. 'Okay then,' she said with a sigh, 'safe journey.'

Sister Christiana gunned the engine; then the three of them sped away, leaving me sweating in the early morning sun. On the map an inch-long red squiggle awaited. Beyond that lay the frontier town of Kukës, and farther still the international border crossing with Kosovo at Vrbnica. With so much invested in this project there was no way I was going to risk trouble with passport stamps. I had to go through Kukës.

I realise now the nuns got the better deal. The journey from Fierzë to Qafë Mali was a hell in high mountains regularly endured by sure-footed Albanians returning to their villages, but I suspect rather less by foreigners, and not at all by innocent natives of English seaside towns.

For anyone stupid enough to follow in my footsteps, the pain begins a short distance from the edge of the village. Miles of twisting road spiral up, over and around the colossal dam. Ankle-snapping fissures rend the broken tarmac. Sheer rock faces mean there's hardly anywhere to camp, so after twelve hours of toil a night-time adventure is entirely possible for anyone with the guts to wander around a cliff in the dark. And the heat's choking. In July it's more brutal than a *Death Wish* movie. Imagine the hottest beach you've ever been on, add a few degrees more, then picture yourself lugging a 30 lb pack up a 1,500-foot corkscrew. Does that sound like fun? Great.

Because that's the easy part.

When the corkscrew ends, the fun really begins—except it's not that funny scrambling along a narrow ledge on blistered, weeping stumps. Clinging tenaciously to the mountainside, the road zigzags like the red squiggle on the map. Though the right side is generally safe, the left is straitjacket crazy. Don't get too close unless you intend calling upon the Lord to prevent certain death. If you can stay alive for long enough, you'd probably like some refreshment. Well, forget that. There isn't any. There's nothing remotely drinkable except the occasional rock-strewn gully fed by bubbling streams. Your only reward, as you stand dripping in sweat, will be the view: a panorama of endless hump-back hills, pencil-thin dirt tracks suffocated in bluish haze, and far below Lake Koman, a ribbon of shimmering topaz. Enjoy.

Eight years on from those rarefied heights, I think the jury's still out on whether the view was worth the trouble. I spent the first night gratefully, but very improbably, in a hotel clinging to the edge of a cliff; the next, (and the only time outside) cocooned in three feet of golden leaf litter. I took the third more comfortably and rather more safely on a mattress in Shemeri—a remote village with a stubby bolt-on minaret and a two-table café on a breezy hill. Within minutes of collapsing onto a chair I'd gained a free meal plus promised mattress. My new benefactor used to work in London as a builder and loved the British. He lived in Tirana and only visited his brother once a year. This was that day. It was either very good luck or an astonishing synchronicity.

There's not much to do in the land where everyone wants to be somewhere else. When morning arrived I woke to find the main street full of boisterous boys with tussled hair and deep Mediterranean tans. They wandered up and down, some with hands in pockets, others pushing their friends, kicking stones, waiting for something, for *anything* to happen. At precisely 8:33 a.m., it did: a thirsty English pilgrim went in search of a drink.

I'm not sure even Tom Cruise could have pulled in a bigger crowd. When I entered the village shop it was completely empty bar one grinning handlebar moustache with dollar-sign eyes. Within seconds the place was packed more tightly than Nelson's Column on New Year's Eve.

'Mister! Mister!' they cried. 'What is your name?'

'Mister! Why are you in Albania?'

Movie stars rarely visit Shemeri. Nor for that matter does anyone else. Startled by my newfound celebrity, I spent the next fifteen minutes fielding questions from fifteen-year-old boys. My dishevelled presence had been enough to fill an entire store in less than thirty seconds. Amazing.

I was still learning, even in those final days. Several more lies and distortions went the way of the dodo, including much of the nonsense spouted by the Foreign Office. 'It's far too dangerous to visit Kukës,' they said pompously. Really? At dusk on 5 July I walked straight in. At daybreak I swallowed an omelette breakfast and walked straight out. In between, I spent a pleasant night in the glitzy Hotel Amerika, sipping cola from orange-and-white banded straws, watching the locals watching me, and typing up email number eleven to scattered well-wishers. On leaving the town I decided to stock up on some bottles of orange juice from another of those bunker-style shops. No one interfered. No one attacked me. No one did anything.

When, a few hours later, I arrived at my ninth international border, grey shadows were already deepening in the fields. I felt the sadness rise in the chest in a heavy, suffocating kind of way, for I still had a special fondness for all things Albanian. The brutal Koman road hadn't destroyed the feeling, nor could it. Out of great poverty much had been given and with much gratitude received. The love held.

Up ahead, a single guard in khaki green stood idly at a drop-down barrier with hands clasped behind his back. In that final step to whatever lay beyond I once more recalled the words of all I'd met:

'Don't forget to tell the truth about Albania. We are good people, friendly people. Don't forget what you have seen.'

They were right. The advice on Albania had been absurdly wrong.

I knew. I climbed out of my armchair. I'd been there.

Chapter Nine

Kosovo

The Land Divided

In the first week of July, when the distinctive Hoxha Bunkers had disappeared from view and the brilliant Albanian hospitality became no more than scattered entries in a burgeoning diary, I journeyed east into one of the more troubled parts of Europe. Sandwiched between Albania to the west and Macedonia to the south, is tiny Kosovo, a poor land yet greatly coveted by Serbs and Albanians alike. From a pilgrim's perspective, arrival at the innocuous-looking border is not necessarily a cause for celebration. The Balkans are steeped in nationalist sentiment, and once you factor in the white heat of religion, you quickly realise the warring parties don't have much interest in compromise.

The Serbian claim is built on Christ and old battles from medieval history. Minarets dominate the towns and cities in Kosovo, but there are Orthodox churches throughout the region, with their distinctive cupolas shining splendidly in the sun. Gračanica and Dečani are fine examples, though I wasn't privileged to see them myself. The historical aspects relate to the famous battle of 1389. One of the most revered sights in Kosovo is a patch of dirt 5 km northwest of Pristina. It was here that Prince Lazar met a large Ottoman Army at the Battle of Kosovo Field. Lazar's small force was virtually annihilated, turning the dying prince into a hero and the event into a potent symbol of national pride. Six centuries later, it can still get Serbs out onto the streets.

That Albanians feel just as strongly about Kosovo cannot be disputed. They've lived here for centuries, fighting allcomers for their rights. The early years of the twentieth century were some of the most violent. In 1910 an armed revolt broke out against Ottoman rule. Then a second, two years later. In an attempt to end the bloodletting even the ostrich-plumed sultan turned up. Peace did eventually return and concessions were granted, but in the grand sweep of things they barely mattered. The pattern in Kosovo had been set: a small people fighting bravely against a larger, more powerful oppressor. This image would persist.

Unfortunately for the Serbs, who seem forever doomed to be cast as the bad guys of the Balkans, the image persisted until spring 1999. Once the international community had made up its mind, the result of the Kosovo War of Independence was never in doubt. The militarily superior Serbs not only faced armed rebellion from the Albanian Kosovo majority, but also the formidable air power of NATO. When diplomacy failed (as it quite often does), along came the American laser-guided bombs. The Serbian Army never stood a chance.

Since then, force has given way to democracy through the lofty principle of self-determination. Today, Kosovo is independent of Serbia because 92 per cent of residents (i.e. every Albanian there is) say so. Only a day after leaving Kukës I arrived here myself, mulling the history and geography of what I feared would be a difficult walk. At Vrbnica it was the usual setup: wooden hut, plus drop-down barrier, plus border guard of questionable temperament. All I had to do was avoid politics and say something bland about the weather. Heavens, Albanians were in the majority here. I'd have to be stupid to even mention Serbia . . .

'Serbian dinars are not popular here,' growled the voice.

Bah. The guard was an evil-looking bloke, gaunt in the face, shorter than I was by a good six inches, with black appraising eyes. He looked up at me stonily, as if I'd castrated his dog.

'They're not?' and I heard my voice trail off. I had nearly 6,000 to spend.

'Of course not!' he said, eyes sparking. A hand swung out from behind his back, and he jabbed stiffly at the ground. 'Don't you know this is Kosovo?'

I nodded sheepishly and started to shuffle about.

'Everyone here uses euros. Not the Serbian dinar.' The guard narrowed his eyes. 'You should remember that.'

'Yeah, all right, mate. I think I got it.' I forced a tepid smile, hoping to lighten the mood. Not only were my Serbian dinars as useful as a chocolate teapot, but the mere sight of them was likely to antagonise 92 per cent of everyone I met. Worse still, I was down to my last few dollars and had absolutely no euros.

Marvellous.

With stamped passport in hand, I went looking for friendly faces in the village of Vrbnica. I never made it. As I fled the scene I'd forgotten the first rule of any pilgrimage: just when you think things can't get any worse, they do.

On a long-distance walk there's always a point where idealism meets the limits of what the human condition can tolerate. It's an ugly word, *compromise*, and I found out all about it an hour after leaving the checkpoint. The Hotel Univers is a bluish tower of corporate-looking glass. It's also extremely well sighted to catch the border trade. In the dwindling daylight of 6 July it caught a tired pilgrim with 6,000 useless Serbian dinars. I felt great until I started guzzling water from the bathroom tap. After that: disaster. At two in the morning I was obliged to yield to the inevitable, gripping the toilet pan with frightening force and retching violently. I hardly slept at all.

Morning brought more of the same—a lot more. Soon I was head-down in the toilet trapped in that grisly netherworld between life and death. The smell was rank. If there was any doubt about what to do next, it came to me just before breakfast in a river of fast-flowing diarrhoea. Without any euros I couldn't stay in the hotel. Nor could I simply buy food and camp in the adjacent fields until the illness passed. I didn't seem to have any choice. For the first time since leaving England I would have to do the unthinkable.

I would have to take a lift.

It was an unwelcome change in plan. When you've made a commitment to yourself and promised dozens of people that you're going to walk all the way to Jerusalem, this isn't the decision you want to make. Just the thought of it made me feel like a cheat.

And yet, the notion of slotting myself into a car wasn't completely alien. I'd taken a ride in Bosnia when Lana's husband had driven me from Stanislav's house to the hospital in Prijedor. I'd needed treatment for my damaged heel, and I was glad of their help. But then, the situation had been very different. I was going backward, *away from Jerusalem*, and I felt no guilt. This compromise was different—it stung the soul. If I made too many I might lose God's blessing. The whole journey might start to unravel. I could never allow that to happen.

Distasteful though it was to the iron-willed saint in me, the unthinkable wasn't without a touch of humour. Having refused scores of lifts in eight countries, I discovered hitchhiking is not as simple as it looks. After fifteen minutes I was still frantically cocking thumbs; I had to laugh at the irony. I was beginning to think it might never happen when a black Skoda pulled over, belching exhaust. Sickly beggars can't be choosers. The student eyes seemed friendly, so I squeezed into the back and cradling rucksack on lap we revved off towards Prizren.

Twenty kilometres whizz by at 50 kmh. Everything seemed a dreamy blur: the cloud-swept greens of the countryside, little shops with strange signs in peeling red paint; amid the roar of traffic, water-stained tower blocks poked their grubby fingers up into the purple ocean of a burning sky. In the final minutes we skimmed the UN base skulking on the outskirts like an old Legionnaire fort ready to repel the revolting Berber. Behind twelve-foot-high fences topped by rolling barbed wire the brave peacemakers cowered. I found their confidence in the process less than reassuring. Shortly afterwards I clambered out, totally bewildered. What did God think of me now?

Is everything all right between us? I asked anxiously.

Yes, came back the reply. Don't worry. Everything's all right.

The answer was gentle, the response of a parent to a child. It was okay to be weak. It was okay to be human. I was imperfect, and my pilgrimage would be, too.

* * *

The kind of illness that makes you want to go to bed for a week does not, alas, confer a cloak of invisibility. If you're a nervous Englishman hoping to make an inconspicuous entry into Prizren, the busy taxi rank on the corner of Adem Jashari Road is the last place you should consider. No sooner had I tightened the final rucksack strap, than I was caught in an impromptu scrum. The chorus was nothing if not enthusiastic.

'My friend!' yelled a smiling face, slapping the door of his car.

'You need a taxi?' someone shouted through cupped hands. 'I drive you to Macedonia and back!'

A fat bloke in shorts shrieked, 'Here in Kosovo we love Tony Blair! You join me now!' and began sprinting towards the exchange office in an obvious bid to cut me off. I'd just started to pick up speed myself when:

'Hey! You English!'

I slowed and turned ninety degrees to the left. About ten feet away a car window rolled down. A tousled head sporting a thin black moustache popped out. 'Psst,' it said, waving me forward, 'forget those others, they will rip you off. They are very bad guys, very bad'—the face wrinkled with mock disgust—'they are not like me. Are you really British?'

I nodded for the briefest of seconds. The safety of the exchange office was almost within reach.

'Then you must join me. We love the British! We love Tony Blair! We love . . .'

And so the we-love-Blair mantra went on. Unable to remember what Blair had said about Kosovo, my ignorance was clearly immaterial. What mattered here is that Blair had been British Prime Minister, Great Britain was part of NATO and NATO planes had conveniently bombed the Serbs into utter oblivion. No wonder these Albanians were happy.

The need for foreign currency often leads one into less than salubrious surroundings. The Prizren exchange office fully met expectations: a waist-high counter peppered with cigarette burns, an electronic board studded with small red bulbs flashing dollar and euro rates. Seated behind, swivelling on squeaky stools, were two grinning sharks in white T-shirts masquerading as human beings. The ambience was of a seedy betting shop where fag ends litter the floor and all the punters have lost their life savings. I should have listened to my intuition and got the hell out.

'Welcome, my friend!' said the smaller shark with a smile oozing insincerity. 'You have come to the right place! We are ready to give you the very good deal!'

Thus, at 9 a.m., did I meet my first Kosovo crook.

Boy, the little shark was right. There was a very good deal on offer that day, and it was very good for the exchange office. After the special 'low, low rate' of commission was applied, I left with 20 per cent less than expected. It could have been worse. In a moment of near insanity I considered offering my Serbian dinars, then felt courage wane as the bigger shark got off his stool. His head practically touched the ceiling. There was a 92 per cent chance he was Albanian. I gulped hard and decided against.

Naturally, they were all waiting for me outside. Potbellied taxi drivers have huge families to feed, and if you've just left an exchange office they expect you to feed them. The rumour on the street was that a rich English was in town, and he surely wanted to go for a drive at the special 'low, low rate'. I think every tourist will agree when I state taxi drivers are genetically unable to take no for an answer. It took all my remaining strength to fight my way across the street.

As a veteran traveller supremely versed in the worst aspects of hotel life I wasn't expecting much from Hotel Tirana. The lobby was happy to oblige. Plush one hundred years ago when most townspeople still wore turbans, the threadbare carpet boasting complex Arabian squiggles in astonishing blues and greens now resembled a frighteningly cheap off-cut. Turning pages behind the counter of this magnificent abode stood a sunken-cheeked, narrow-shouldered ninety-year-old in a crumpled brown shirt reading a newspaper. I coughed, and he looked up sleepily, eyes flickering like a candle.

'Excuse me,' I said, pushing out the words with as much cheer as near death can muster.

'Yes?' The flicker suddenly intensified. 'Can I help you?'

'I'm looking for a single room for the night. Do you have any vacancies?'

'Hmm. British?' He closed the newspaper and fixed me with tortoise eyes.

'Yes,' supremely cautiously, 'I'm British.'

'You!' A bony finger pointed at me accusingly.

Err . . . Yes?

'You are . . .'

Err . . . Yes?!

'The brother of Tony Blair!' and the old guy burst out laughing. After he'd stopped shaking (which was at least a full minute), I placed my passport on the counter and he countered the obvious question with, 'One person, one night is thirty euros.'

I sniffed, feeling undecided and thoroughly ill.

'Look, why do you wait?' he asked. 'This is the finest hotel in all Prizren. Come—' And he beckoned me closer with a finger, 'listen to me, listen to me for I am going to help you. Right now we do a special deal for all our good British friends.'

Interesting. Could it possibly be?

'I will give you the low, low rate.'

Ha-ha-ha. Of course, it had to be. Feeling the vomit suddenly rise, I slapped the money on the counter and sprinted upstairs.

Kneeling face down in a toilet is not the most obvious place to find deep wisdom, but there's no knowing when providence will strike. In barely thirty minutes I'd sussed the Kosovo mentality: anyone mentioning a 'low, low rate' was probably a crook, Blair was a quasi-God-like figure and the British were all damn good blokes. Okay. I guess Albanians liked Americans, too. After all, they did drop most of the bombs.

I ended up staying three nights in Prizren. As befits my snivelling condition, I did little during the first forty-eight hours. I rose listlessly, showered lazily, found limited distraction in the bizarre world of Albanian TV. At breakfast I battled with hard-boiled eggs seemingly made out of reconstituted concrete. The comparison isn't as ridiculous as it sounds. History has it that when the builders of the Sinan Pasha Mosque ran out of cement they chose to improvise with a mix of eggshells and matted goat hair. That was five centuries ago. Since then, the demand for imperial mosques has dropped off, and the builders' turban-less descendants have found new employment in hotel catering. The Hotel Tirana is delighted to continue the tradition.

In other respects I found the city had plenty to offer. The main public space—Shadervan Square—boasts a pillar fountain with the intriguing legend that 'anyone who drinks this water shall never leave.' (I did, and I did, so legend busted). The very agreeable call to prayer is reassuring in its constancy, and there's an ample supply of chalky Ottoman mosques to photograph. Food is also absurdly cheap, which means there's no need to buy jumbo packs. If you want two yoghurts in a bunch of six, you can just snap them off. That said, I'm not convinced every purchase is a bargain. I squeezed a random tube of toothpaste and out oozed a sickly green gunge that might have graced the melting reactors of Chernobyl. Interesting, I thought. Would the contents of Ukrainian-branded *Best White Smile!* glow in the dark?

I'll never know. I was too scared to turn the light off.

Then, on the third day, a miracle of Lourdes-like proportions occurred: I finally got better.

It takes a special kind of determination to pay a guy to drive you to Albania just so you can spend the next three hours walking back. But that's exactly what I did. I'd latched onto the plan during my chaotic arrival. With so many taxi drivers itching to drive me around in big circles at huge expense, why not let one take me to Hotel Univers? Then I could walk back into Prizren, thus making up the distance on foot. The iron-willed saint in me, never happy with the forced compromise, let out an ear-splitting cheer. The walk to Jerusalem was back on track.

In a tune popularised by old music halls you had to be either bonkers or English to run about in painfully hot weather. I've come to share that view, not least because barely twelve hours after recovering from gastro-enteritis I was stiffening my British upper lip to do precisely that. Just after breakfast I strode out of the bathroom, face heavily oiled with sun cream. The tube was manufactured by the same company that made the dodgy toothpaste. I don't usually bother, but on this occasion I decided to scan the accompanying leaflet:

> Apply with the greatest liberality to all the affected areas . . .
> Only the very best ingredients used . . . Very soon you will
> be protected from hot sun . . . Allergic reaction possible:
> nausea, diarrhoea, flatulence, impotence, stroke, catatonic
> seizures and death. In the case of unconsciousness seek
> urgent medical advice. Not tested on rabbits. Do not ingest.

Crikey. I replaced the leaflet into the box, hands shaking uncontrollably. I was wearing an entire tube of this junk. Would the obnoxious green gunge spewing from a tube of Titan Strength *Deep Sun Kiss 4!* glow in the dark?

I have no idea. Once again, I was too afraid to find out.

The remainder of that morning went largely to plan. I had little trouble getting a taxi ride back to the Albanian border, and I never expected otherwise. The lucky driver eventually tasked with the mission was reading a newspaper stretched out across the roof of a black Volkswagen. The scent of an easy fare soon caught his attention.

'British?' The guy studying me was roughly my age with thinning, salt-and-pepper hair. Beads of sweat covered his brow. It was only 8 a.m., and already the heat was building.

I grinned. 'Yeah, I'm British. Do you know the Hotel Univers, the one near the Albanian border?'

'The hotel?' He shot me a wry smile as if feigning insult. 'Of course! One of the best hotels in all Kosovo! Get in, my friend, get in!' In a thrice he folded his newspaper, flung open the door and scurried around to the driver's side. 'For our British friends all things are possible. Here we love Tony Blair!'

'Great, but how much will it cost?'

'Ah, let me think. Hmm, yes, the Hotel Univers. It is very far, so very far to the border . . .'

The driver's face softened, acquiring an angelic quality. His voice became gentle, as one might when talking to a child. Never before or since have I beheld a picture of greater sincerity . . .

'Twelve euros,' he said.

Thus, did I meet my third and greatest Kosovo crook.

You had to admire the guy's audacity. Even for a taxi driver's code of ethics the price was insane. Later, in Macedonia, someone would offer to drive me 20 km to Skopje for a paltry 2 euros. Here I was being charged six times more for the same distance. Sensing my uncertainty, he rushed in to clinch the deal.

'After you come back we can drink coffee together!' Which roughly translated means: 'After I have mercilessly overcharged you, I can take the rest of the day off. No—let's make that an entire week.'

Gotcha.

I spent the next three hours walking slowly back into Prizren. In spite of my illness, or perhaps because of it and all the time I'd wasted lying in bed, I returned to the taxi rank with plenty of energy and enthusiasm for sightseeing. From Adem Jashari Road I looked up at the trees high above the seething River Bistrica.

A large silver cupola glinted in the sun. Was it an abandoned monastery? Was it the ruins of a mosque? The sight intrigued me. After buying another bottle of water I crossed the stone bridge, eager to see more.

As I started to climb it was the absence of people I noticed first, that and the abandoned homes. Charred timbers at forty-five-degree angles, splashes of yellow and purple paint, odd bits of prefabricated concrete woven into loose cement: an image came to mind of a magpie's nest constructed from random objects. Further up the path I encountered stern notices pinned to jagged fencing—German, Serbian, Albanian—then suddenly a flash of flamingo pink incongruous among the trees. I stood motionless for several minutes, staring into the gutted ruins of a child's playroom. Only three years earlier Christians had been running for their lives. Christians like me. On a pleasant summer's day, echoing with birdsong, such an event barely seemed possible.

The summit came quickly. After navigating a sharp right-hand bend, I pulled up before a tall gate crisscrossed with barbed wire. I peered behind, spotting a jeep bearing the white letters KFOR. I recognised this insignia immediately. Kosovo Force was the NATO-led command tasked by the UN with preventing ethnic unrest. For a professional outfit they had a mixed reputation. During the Albanian riots of 2004 several units returned to their barracks leaving the mob to run unchecked. Afterwards, nineteen people lay dead, hundreds more injured; thousands of Serbs were chased from these hills, never to return. As I turned away from the mottled brown stonework, etched with the cross of Christ, I now understood that the roofless Church of the Holy Saviour was nothing more than a military observation post.

Yet despite the scars of conflict there *was* a different picture for those willing to look. Among the boiling backstreets around Shadervan Square I discovered a small but determined Christian presence. First, the silvery cupolas of the Cathedral of St George bubbling up behind a six-foot wall enclosing gurgling cement mixers; then at high convent windows a pair of rosy-cheeked nuns in their familiar black habits, white sleeves bunched at the elbows, scrubbing with impressive vigour. And rising from the north, tall gold lettering splintered the fading sunshine. It spoke of a building far grander than the iron-barred outhouse that had been my home in Vau i Dejës, for the Catholic charity Caritas had not deserted the people. Might Christians again call Prizren home? Could Serbs and Albanians ever be reconciled?

None in Heaven could answer.

Yet hope still flickered under Prizren skies. And on the cusp of evening I left my brothers and sisters behind to the sound of cement mixers churning in the breeze.

* * *

Cured of the mysterious nausea that threatened to rob Jerusalem of my increasingly dishevelled presence, I didn't linger among the chalky mosques of Prizren. Only four days after arriving I headed south through the Zhupa Valley towards the village of Brezovica. It was a grand time to be a nature lover. While a true wilderness is a rarity in Europe, we do have them. At the valley's end lie the fabulous Sharr Mountains, a wall of trees rippling out towards the northwestern fringes of Macedonia. I'd been nailed to dreary tarmac since 8 a.m. and gasping up steep hills for the last hour. Should I risk it? Dare I step inside this great forest?

I did, though stepping out proved more problematic. I fed a grey squirrel a piece of bread, and when it scampered up into the canopy I was instantly reminded of the wilder parts of Germany I'd braved during those frozen weeks of March. I glanced down at a pair of stag beetles locking horns on a log flume. Purple earthworms oozed from every mossy bank. The dirt was awash with gold-veined leaves, and the scent of wriggling earth was rapturous. I picked up a sturdy branch, about shoulder high, finding real pleasure in a friend to lean on. The pleasure quickly dissipated. Unlike German forests, there are no orderly lines of red blobs to follow. In fact, inside the Sharr there are no trail markers at all.

'Blast these wretched nettles!' Mid-afternoon I crashed back out onto the road, neck swelling with mosquito bites. And where the hell was Brezovica?

I peered at the road sign, noting the embossed deer, fluttering birds of prey, wild boar and . . . was that really a bear? I decided to play it safe, avoiding the forest (other than for impromptu toilet breaks) and sticking to the boring but predictable tarmac. To get through those long hours I resorted to my usual devices. I hummed hymns while thinking of interesting things to write in my next email to friends and family. I looked up at southern skies, trying to imagine what Jerusalem might look like. That troubled city was still many moons away. I figured there would be plenty of time to work out where I stood on the big issues of Middle Eastern politics.

The Arab raised his eyebrows. 'Jerusalem, you say?'

He was a substantial figure: beige trousers bulging at the waist, a broad face, tanned, with jowls like a bulldog. Sweat blossomed under the arms of his pink open-necked shirt. We stood beside his car clutching polystyrene cups filled with orange juice.

I sipped again, and said, 'Yeah, that's the plan. If all goes well I'm thinking I might reach the city in November.'

'You must walk very quickly.'

'I can do thirty kilometres a day, sometimes more. In fact—'

'Palestine is the most wonderful of countries. Have you been there before?'

'Oh. Nope, but I'm looking forward to it.'

He suddenly scowled. 'Then when you arrive you must be very careful of the Jews.'

And *that* was the moment when the klaxon sounded. It was a shame because up to then the encounter had followed all the familiar lines: spot waving hand, stop, smile, accept proffered hospitality, answer the usual questions while studiously avoiding any subject that might give offence. During four-and-a-half months of travel there had been little deviation.

'We Christians and Muslims are brothers,' said the Arab. He

pointed in turn at our chests. 'But the Jews . . . Tell me, friend. Why does America support the Jews? Why does America hate Iran? Iran is a great country.'

'That's a good question. I don't really know.'

'You don't know? You don't know? Let me tell you, friend, let me tell you something. If someone broke in, broke into your house, wouldn't you try to evict them?'

'Yes, I would.'

'So,' he said, and shook a finger in my face, 'who can blame the Palestinians for wanting their land back? Who can blame them? Tell me that.'

'Yeah, I see your point. But I don't think there's an easy—'

'Let me tell you something, my friend. Right now I know two hundred young men, all they want to do is kill Jews. The minds of our young have been poisoned by war. It's not good for them,' he muttered, 'not good at all.'

Israel was still several thousand kilometres away, and yet the strength of feeling, the anger . . . Just what kind of storm was I walking into? The thought raised doubts, and doubts aren't good for confidence. I pushed them aside, cursing myself for stopping.

He took the cup from my fingers, eyes sad and empty. 'Walk another six kilometres, and you'll see Brezovica.'

We shook hands. Then I turned and began to joylessly plod up the snaking hill. The road to Brezovica has more hairpins than the Monaco Grand Prix, and it's never very encouraging when you spend as much time going backward as forward. I saw few signs of life, but those I did appeared in a variety of guises. Groups of fat polka-dot cows stood in green pasture mindlessly chewing grass. Toothless farmers in baggy pantaloons blinked with utter astonishment as I marched straight past. On a rare drop I was buzzed by black-and-yellow spandex gliding effortlessly by in a blur of spokes. I'd lost the lung capacity to form an effective curse hours ago. I looked on with undisguised envy.

In addition to the unexpected lecture on the Arab-Israeli conflict, I also discovered something else. Kosovars have a terrible sense of distance. Twelve kilometres after leaving the Arab I'd lost count of the number of cries 'But it's only six kilometres to Brezovica!' I began to pant heavily, feeling patience tear. As I dropped through ranks of willow trees what I remember most are the crazy road signs. Kosovo is the only country in Europe where I saw speed limits for tanks. A few signs even carried a picture of a lion. Yes: a lion, a male lion, *with a mane.* I was gobsmacked. These Sharr Mountains were more dangerous than I thought. Could there really be lions in Kosovo?

Not likely. During an extended breather I remembered the lion symbol marked one of the military routes used by KFOR. Get a grip! I told myself. This isn't Africa!

I made Brezovica shortly before dusk. Despite superhuman effort expended over ten hours, there wasn't a lot to see among those agricultural breeze block houses. Popular during the free-spending eighties with the Bulgarian hordes, by all accounts the northern slopes of the Sharr Mountains make fine skiing and this entire area had even been considered as a possible venue for the 1984 Winter Olympics. Then along came the Kosovo War, and the economy took the mother of all nose dives. Apparently, here and in neighbouring Štrpce the beleaguered Serbs form a rare majority. I'm not sure it's much consolation.

Today in Brezovica a little grocer's shop sells strange yoghurts and bashed-in tomatoes. The ski slopes are largely abandoned, the majority of townsfolk are unemployed and the three hotels have become very effective dust traps. The whole place is in dire need of a foreign investor with exceedingly deep pockets. On the edge of a crimson dusk, sparkling with golden stars, I staggered into the cavernous lobby of Hotel Narcis. With nearly 45 km behind me, I reached into my very deepest pocket. It was shallower than I hoped, but on this night it would be enough.

I left the hotel early, and for an entire day and the cooler hours of the next marched steadily toward Macedonia. Once you lace up a pair of boots and start walking there's no knowing how you're going to feel. I was surprised I could still lift a foot. Just how *did* I keep going? It was a question I often asked myself, finding answers mostly in stubbornness, faith, fanatical will-power, and during the more testing moments—some ferociously bad singing. Eight months ago a 40 km hike would have left me dead by the roadside. I was no longer the puny innocent who had faltered outside Dordrecht.

I had it easy that first day, for which I thank geography. After departing the hotel I began to descend almost immediately, and although every step pulled hard on the knees, I felt glad to be finally heading down. It was a quaint agricultural landscape not like anything I'd seen before. Red-and-gold chickens strutted and pecked; crystal water gurgled along furrowed fields; blue skies, soft like crumbling chalk, were dotted yellow by ripening corn; birds sung sweetly like choirboys to a tune; and everywhere the labours of farmers were marked by the rising haystack, hour-glasses all, each a perfect timepiece burning beneath the sun.

A charming summer's walk in mid-July? Yes, for the most part. But it also delivered an unwanted obstacle. It says something about my commitment to reaching Jerusalem on foot, that when a policeman waved me over my main concern was I'd be forced to take a ride in his jeep and have to waste valuable time walking back. When he told me 'last month three foreigners went missing in Albania', the news barely registered. I'd just come from there. No problem.

'Then you are very fortunate to be alive. Were you hitchhiking in Albania?'

From the sky-blue shirt, the machine-stitched insignia on the shoulder and the distinctive blue UN beret, I knew this was no ordinary cop. Suspicious grey eyes raked my face.

'Hitchhiking?' I said with a touch of defiance.

'I think you are a hitchhiker. Hitchhiking is very dangerous in Kosovo.'

'But I'm not hitchhiking, I'm walking.'

'So where did you cross the border?'

'The border? I think it ... no wait, I think it was UNMIK—'

'No,' he said bluntly, 'UNMIK is what *we* are called.'

I slapped my head. 'Damn, yeah, that's right. I'm sorry. I've just remembered, it was somewhere back there at Vrbnica.'

'Hmm, Vrbnica ...' The cop began to drum his fingers on the side door. *Thrum. Thrum. Thrum.* 'And where are you going to?' *Thrum. Thrum.*

'I'm on my way to Macedonia, and after that I'm heading into Greece.'

He nodded without emotion and turned away to gaze at the magnificent willows overhanging the road. 'You must look for the crossing called General Jankovic. You will see it soon.'

'Okay, I will certainly do that. Thanks for the advice and now I'll just—'

'Wait a moment.'

Blast! Now what?

He turned back to face me, stretched out a hand, and beckoning with his fingertips said, 'Let me see your passport. Give it to me.'

I pulled the document from my shorts. He began to turn the pages, studying each inky smudge like a schoolboy examining a prized stamp collection. I was starting to think I might be going for a pointless ride after all when:

'Do not worry,' he said, and suddenly his demeanour softened, 'I do not stop you because you have done anything wrong.'

Great. Now you tell me ...

The cop pulled a pen from his shirt pocket and began writing on a scrap of paper. He shoved it through the window and, with a voice pregnant with impending catastrophe, said, 'If anything strange happens, if anyone stops you, do not hesitate to ring this number.'

He dropped his eyes to the paper, and I glanced down at the string of digits. Since I didn't carry a telephone the information was virtually useless.

'Okay, I will. And thanks again for your help.' I forced another smile, hoping to be rid of him. He was on the verge of speaking again when I gave him what he really wanted to hear. 'And yes, I'm going to be out of Kosovo very soon.'

He clipped the pen back into his pocket and sighed heavily. 'I think that's best.'

A short while later he roared away, and I was left alone by the roadside trying to work out whether I should have been grateful for his intervention. After all, in Albania three foreigners *had* gone missing. On the other hand, I found it hard to reconcile his concerns with my own first-hand experience. I'd just come from there and seven more countries besides. Nothing terrible had happened, and I'd received an unprecedented amount of good fortune. So far the old Bible saying had held up: 'If God is for us, who can be against us?'

For the better part of that day I continued to sift the available evidence. Despite Albanian advice to the contrary, their Kosovo cousins were every bit as hospitable as their brethren. By far the largest number of Good Samaritans stood ankle-deep in pine chips at the timber yard near Doganovic. They were a friendly crew: six youngsters with easy grins and sawdust dandruff. Our lunch was potatoes, chicken, tomatoes and boiling tea as black as boot polish. Forget boring food. The real business of the day involved swigging a fiery liquid in little glasses.

'Another! Another!' they cried in unison, slamming glasses on the table.

I clutched my chest. 'What? You want me to drink *another?*'

Luckily, my un-blokeish timidity didn't affect their enthusiasm for the other rite of improbable meetings: the cheesy group photo. Somewhere in southern Kosovo I live on, immortalised by a 176 × 208 pixelated left ear. A mobile phone can work wonders, though I suggest not in a wildly swaying hand.

The camaraderie was more civilised as I approached Kačanik. Having taken up residence in a motel-cum-restaurant where a constant flow of electricity was dangerously lacking, I decided to risk a mixed grill on the verandah overlooking the rear yard. The skies were foaming black, building into storm. Winds whipped at the table napkins bringing the scent of rain. After enjoying a good fry-up, I was about to leave when my waiter reappeared, a short white-smocked chap with permanent dimples.

'My sister works in London as a cleaner,' he explained. 'She would want me to help you!'

I looked down at the pancakes drenched in syrup, feeling the telltale lump grow in my throat. Though already full, I ate them anyway. The pancakes were a gift, and I was far too polite to do anything else.

Just before midday I slipped quietly into Macedonia at General Jankovic. There were no film crews to capture the moment, no reporters with fluffy microphones keen to record pilgrim words. When the triumph faded I was left staring south into a mass of darkening trees. As for what lay behind, who could say? Was it Serbia, Kosovo, or Kosova? I still had no idea what to call this divided land. Hostility between Serbs and Albanians had been obvious, particularly on the forested slopes above Prizren. The charred houses, the roofless churches, that flash of pink paint—a child's playroom destroyed among the boughs. Something was needed to break the cycle. What then, was the lesson of Kosovo?

Perhaps the poet George Roemisch nailed it when he wrote 'Forgiveness is the fragrance of the violet which still clings fast to the heel that crushed it.' Many years ago I remember chancing on a story about a British soldier returning home after being held captive by the Japanese. As he stood on the great ship, hatred for his captors threatened to consume him like acid devouring limestone. Giving way to these emotions would have been easy, some might even say natural. Yet this soldier chose differently. Long before the ship docked he realised his feelings were leading him to self-destruction. For him, there was only one solution: in order to find peace, he would first have to forgive.

This man obtained the peace he sought. He had no real choice. When the fires of hatred burn out forgiveness is all that remains among the ashes. As I took my leave of Kosovo I felt the question had to be asked. Would God offer any less for a struggling pilgrim who had weakened and taken a lift into Prizren?

You, Lord, are good, and ready to forgive; abundant in loving kindness to all those who call on you.

The nineteen words of Psalm 86:5 promised forgiveness—for everyone. The answer from the Divine could not be otherwise.

From the shores and windmills of Holland the Creator of all things had stood by me. Evidenced by the goodwill of the people, I hoped and believed he stood by me still. Now, behind a wall of advancing trees, the lush vineyards and stony hills of Macedonia awaited, another poor country, another remnant of Tito's failed communist experiment. New obstacles lay beyond the horizon, fresh challenges for the body and spirit in a land still struggling to shake off its Yugoslavian yoke.

In the ensuing red tape the Kosovo border guard had the last word. The guy that had the privilege of stamping me out wore a green uniform and an officer's peaked cap. He must have been important—he had an entire room to himself.

'Ahhh, British,' he said, running an inky finger over the passport's little maroon jacket and gazing at it with barely concealed rapture. He glanced up from his stool, hand motionless over the page, ready to deliver the fateful stamp. 'My friend, please tell me. Where are you going?'

'I'm headed towards Skopje.' On this strange road that had become my life there was nowhere left to go.

'Ahhh, yes . . . the beautiful Skopje.' He closed the document and held out his hand. 'Skopje is very, very good. Now, let me tell you something, friend . . .'

I swear he plucked the words straight off my lips.

'In Kosovo we love Tony Blair!'

I smiled at him pityingly. Okay, I'm out of here.

Chapter Ten

The Former Yugoslav Republic of

Macedonia

The Land with No Name

It's strange how national rivalries and antipathies change as you descend through Europe. As you wander south the history kicks in with varying degrees of vehemence: Holland's subjugation by Hitler's Germany, Germany's complex love-hate relationship with Austria, and in the embers of the First World War, a nasty argument between Austria and Slovenia over borders. By the time you stagger into Croatia, it seems to be the whole of the Balkans against the Serbs. Such had been the continuing animosity pointing in this direction I was caught off-guard when the pattern suddenly changed. At the tail end of the wonderful Sharr Mountains lies Macedonia. The Macedonians don't look to Serbia for quarrel—they look south to Greece.

Nations are rightly proud of their heroes. The Greeks have theirs and are particularly protective of Alexander the Great. It's surely understandable given Alexander's singular achievements. In 336 BC a young Macedonian rose to power and through his energy and leadership carved out an enormous empire extending from Europe to India. Two thousand years have passed, yet few stories can surpass it: the gleaming bronze armour, the hedgehog phalanx, the heroic battles won against enormous odds. Then the untimely death of the young conqueror securing a legend that is truly worthy of the word 'great'. Who would not be proud of such a heritage? Whose blood could remain unstirred by such an inspiring figure?

Well, definitely not that of the Greeks. In 2006 their Macedonian neighbours decided to rename Skopje Airport in honour of Alexander the Great. The ceremonial ribbon had barely hit the runway before Athenians took to the streets, letting off firecrackers and waving flags. I don't doubt the long-running name dispute helped fuel the response. In 1991 the Macedonians won independence from Yugoslavia, and after innocently taking the name 'Republic of Macedonia', all hell broke loose. The Greek Government objected to everything: the Vergina sunburst flag; the term 'Macedonia', which their foreign minister claimed was inextricably linked to Greece. Eventually, the UN waded in with their usual exuberance. The chastised Macedonians altered their flag to include fewer sunrays and as a compromise adopted the current ponderous title.

As a Briton with scant knowledge of southern Europe, none of this was apparent to me at the time. In what turned out to be one of the hottest summers ever, I was too busy guzzling the last of my water in fragrant forest just beyond the immigration hut. Slowly I edged my way down a cycle path overgrown with thorns. Birds twittered gaily and insects buzzed. Unseen meadow sweetened the haze, painting images drawn from a lifetime of experience; I pictured purple cornflowers shifting on a breeze among feathered wheat. The yellow plums lining the path were deliciously sweet—a real treat. I'd already collected several dozen before I walked out to face the sun.

And boy, what an incredible sun it was.

The Balkans set new records that year. On 24 July the village of Demir Kapija posted a whopping 45.7 degrees. On the day I crossed the border the temperature couldn't have been much less. Under an extremely rare tree, I pulled my bonnet down and began to smear my face with great blobs of *Deep Sun Kiss 4!* A steady stream of juggernauts thundered past heading for Skopje. About fifty metres away three boys were clambering onto a bus shelter. Were they yelling insults or encouragement? I had no idea, but they were throwing plenty of rocks.

While it would be a recurring theme, I had little time to contemplate the aggressive nature of modern Macedonian youth. During those first few steps I was too busy gasping with thirst beside vast plains of tinder straw. At a four-way junction I spotted a pair of windmilling arms in a green fluorescent jacket. A traffic cop maybe? I jogged to the spot, hoping to find water.

'Wait!' yelled the giant cop. A bicep began to flex as he waved forward a gleaming cab.

I stood patiently head in line with his shoulder. The guy had a neck the size of a truck tyre and shoulders like an ox—clearly outstanding phalanx material . . .

'So,' he said, and turned to face me, 'you want water?'

'Yeah, I'm looking for some. Is there any near here? Or maybe somewhere to buy—'

He shook his head with two mighty twists and, as the smirk spread across his face, said, 'You must forget about water, there is no water here. And no, err . . . how you say—'

'Shops?'

He nodded. 'For shops, for water, for food, you must go to Skopje, and it's a long way.'

'So, how far do I have to walk?'

'Hmm, let me see,' and after several strokes of a hairless chin he replied, 'I would say about ten kilometres.'

That awful revelation might have killed the conversation stone dead, except I needed an extended breather and Zoran was the first Macedonian I'd ever met. Apparently, life post-Alexander was pretty grim.

'Things are not good in Macedonia. There's not much money and few jobs. Also, there is a big problem here with the mafia.'

'Really?'

'Oh, sure . . . we have big problems in Tetovo, Kumanovo, I

think all those cities. But you go elsewhere, you go to Skopje, yes?' As another tanker swung left, revving and hissing violently, he glanced down at me with a questioning look.

'Yeah, I think I'll stay there for a few days. I don't know where exactly. You know, probably in the youth hostel if there's space. I'll work it out when I get there.'

'Okay, but in Skopje you must be very careful.' He grinned, none too pleasantly. 'Someone like me might attack you.'

I looked again at those bulging biceps and took a discreet step back. I was a man of peace. Violence was abhorrent as well as futile.

God must have been watching closely that afternoon because I soon had an opportunity to test those noble sentiments. The heat had been brutal, so around five I'd taken refuge in a random motel. It was typical budget fodder: bathroom mirror smudged with fingerprints, white subway tiling creeping with mildew, a TV remote control with a sticky key. The air conditioning unit stank of stale cigarette smoke. Tired and irritable, I crashed into bed around eight. Blessed sleep came quickly.

It must have been an hour later when eyelids flickered open. I lay among the sheets, listening intently in the darkness.

Jangling keys outside the door.

A key forced into the lock.

Terror.

I jumped out of bed, heart thumping wildly. I held my breath. The sinister sounds persisted. Who could it be? If it was the hotel staff, why hadn't they knocked? They always had before.

Perhaps it's not someone from the hotel.

Then who?

Cue a heavy silence, pregnant with every kind of imagined horror (mostly starring the dreaded Macedonian mafia). I stayed under the sheets, hoping the intruder would go away. Disappearing footsteps seemed to suggest it. Then, much to my dismay, they returned a minute later with a second bunch of keys.

Almost immediately gruff voices began to filter up from the

courtyard. Now what? I sprinted to the window and threw back the drapes. Brawny truckers in string vests were laughing loudly and dragging large wooden crates along the ground—perfect for kidnapping rich pilgrims. Were they late guests checking in? Possibly, but I didn't like the look of it.

It was the third key rammed in the lock that enabled anger to overcome fear. I was tired, hungry and pissed off. I'd also paid a generous bill for what I assumed would be a good night's rest. Eyes blazing, I pulled on some shorts, stuck a tent peg in my pocket and flung open the door.

In the gap stood the receptionist, a teenage boy with a mop of black ram's hair. He looked at me, startled. 'I . . . err . . . another guest has arrived. They need the satellite box.'

'What? Now? Oh, fine,' I said, 'come in if you must.'

With thumbs in belt, he swaggered into the room, unplugged a few leads beside the TV, dragged the satellite box out into the corridor trailing yards of coaxial cable. The fact that I'd already paid for the use of the equipment didn't seem to bother him.

It took a while to get back to sleep. Robbery, I concluded, had been the intent. Surprised by my presence, the shifty-eyed teenager had smirked and deployed a prepared excuse. It seemed to fit all the facts. The last thing I can remember before drifting off was Zoran's roadside warning.

'In Skopje you must be very careful. Someone like me might attack you.'

Indeed, Zoran, they might even try to ransack your room. On such a mighty journey there was no such thing as 'safe', only the endless road that called me south and various degrees of danger.

✱ ✱ ✱

When Anjezë Gonxhe Bojaxhiu became Mother Theresa and began her march to sainthood in the slums of Calcutta, few outside Macedonia knew she was born in Skopje. Unless you've done some serious Balkans backpacking that's not really surprising. The capital cities of the former Yugoslavia still possess a certain mystique, and it's a rare individual that can boast all seven. On 13 July I had more to brag about than most. I'd bagged five.

I spent three days there dodging child muggers in string vests. Wrestling with a boy over a ten-euro note is not a very dignified thing to do in the grounds of a church, but in Skopje it can be something of a necessity. As always, finding a place to sleep was the first dilemma. Seeing as it topped the Google search results, I opted for the hostel on Ognjan Prica, a ramshackle villa hiding under shady conifers where beaded hair is rampant and spaced-out looks scarily common. Arty types claim they run it. I could see why. The ambience was an unnerving cross between a sixth form art exhibition gone hideously wrong and a smoky London crack den. I went there hoping to meet interesting people. By golly, I met plenty.

'Hey, dude! Hey you, sweet dude! Don't you just love it?'

Out from the trees a strange figure floated towards me clad in an ankle-length rainbow robe. Crikey. Who's this? I took a small step back. I'm not fond of heavily beaded hair invading my personal space.

'What's that, mate?' I asked him.

Blue eyes peered at me through a cloud of illegal smoke. 'Look, dude, look over there!'

I followed the direction of the swaying finger: a one-wheeled bicycle wedged in a conifer tree. High art to be sure.

'It's lovely,' I lied, realising he was clearly out of his. Shortly after, Rainbow Man wandered off to pester someone else, and I was able to lug my giant kit inside.

The dorms were the usual deal: bunks, rucksacks, lots of drying towels and stale air that reeked of unwashed socks. The pick of the guests was probably a Somali called Idris with too much knowledge of self-propelled grenades to be entirely innocent. There were girls as well: two gigglers in the next room. They hailed from Poland and endlessly pranced about in very small sequined tank tops. Apparently, their sole aim in life was to wear the least possible without being arrested. On both counts they enjoyed enormous success. I had to wait until late afternoon to meet the most annoying resident. Dave from Cambridge was the fellow's name. He had all the advantages of life: a full head of blond curls, a sunbed tan, a PhD in Classics and a smile normally only seen in toothpaste commercials. I had nine 'O' levels and a growing bald patch. He got under my skin immediately.

'Hi!' he said, grinning breathlessly, 'I'm Dave!' and, carving out a space on my bunk (mainly by shoving my precious £185 tent to the floor), proceeded to give me every detail of his epic trip.

I shot him a fake smile. It didn't take long to figure out Dave was one of those insufferable know-it-all globetrotters who have pretty much been everywhere. Any experienced backpacker will recognise the type: they're on first-name terms with the barman in twenty countries and know the price of a yak-hair shirt in Kathmandu. Most infuriating of all, they've just returned from wherever you're heading, and they make it sound so blasé. Since leaving England I'd walked through nine countries—a decent tally that some considered worthy of note. Did Dave agree?

'To be perfectly frank with you, I didn't find the Austrian Alps that fantastic, but it was several years ago.' He leant forward and began to unlace a boot. 'Look, I don't know. Maybe I'll give them another go some day. After all, there's always another peak to climb.'

'Huh, so you consider yourself well-travelled, then?'

A smug smile played across his lips. 'Well, you know, Tony,' and grunting slightly he pulled off the other boot, 'I'm certainly not one to boast.'

Ha-ha. Not much.

'What about Ljubljana?' I asked him.

'Seen it.'

'Zagreb?'

'Done it.'

'And Podgorica?'

Now it was his turn to be snide. 'It's the capital of Monte-negro, isn't it?'

Blast! Desperate to end that smug grin, I summoned up the most exotic place I could think of: Montenegro's spectacular Piva Canyon.

'Oh, I went there in '98 with some old pals from university. You did take the raft back down the Tara, didn't you? Only a fool would miss that.'

Like I said, 'insufferable' is a good way to describe these travel supermen. There are others.

Having determined in a matter of minutes that Dave was far more worldly than I, we rapidly returned to his favourite subject: himself. It was less than riveting. I didn't really need to know about his diarrhoea in the desert or that time a Bactrian camel called Custer spat in his face. 'I never saw it coming,' he confided in a moment of rare weakness. Naturally, I had to endure his holiday snaps—all 229 of them.

'Is there one of you and the camel?' I asked him.

He switched off the camera abruptly. 'Err, nope,' and his smile wavered.

Shame. I might have paid to see that. At least our limited time together wasn't completely wasted. In wilder moments I'd been considering ditching Johanna's route through Turkey (and with it the doubtful ferry to Haifa), and taking my pilgrimage down into Syria and Jordan. I would only walk to Jerusalem once, so I figured why not? Getting hold of a Syrian visa appeared to be the main stumbling block, but even here Dave had the answer.

'You don't need to worry about that.' He pushed himself to his feet, picked up his boots, crossed the floor to his own bunk in three quick strides. I looked at him quizzically, and he said, 'You can easily get one at the border.'

'Are you sure? The Foreign Office website says a UK citizen should apply—'

'Oh, for goodness' sake, Tony, forget all that nonsense. Look,' he said, pausing only to sweep a few blond curls from his eyes, 'you might have to slip the border guards a few extra dollars, but I've been there, mate. I'm telling you, I've done it.'

Of course you have. And presumably you've got the T-shirt. (Annoyingly, he did deliver the punchline.)

'Believe me,' Dave insisted, dismissing me with a swift about-turn and easing himself languidly into his bunk. He crossed both feet and began to twiddle his toes. 'It won't be a problem.'

I thanked him pleasantly through gritted teeth. By all accounts this travel superman had been brazenly slipping US dollars all over the Middle East. Obnoxiously perfect as he was, Dave knew the score.

Apart from a Spaniard rumoured to be stuck in the toilet (don't ask me how), I'd met everyone by the time I left the dorms. With so much international sweat on my hands, I felt almost cosmopolitan. The kitchen was the next stop: two tiers of owl-printed cupboards rising beside a long, heavily notched oak table. A trio of mustard-coloured mugs stood on the aluminium drainer. The receptionist was lurking behind the fridge, a huge Jamaican with Mike Tyson arms, beaded dreadlocks and crazy smiles. Physically his head was lodged somewhere near the milk. Mentally he'd just fired his booster rocket and was cruising the asteroid belt. He might have been an artist, too, but I didn't dare ask.

Just then, Dave sauntered in. Scooping up a random mug of dubious hygiene, he spun a tap and began to fill the kettle.

'Sorry, Tony, drink?'

'You know what, mate, I had trouble finding water yesterday, and I'm still parched. I wouldn't mind one.'

'Sure, that's no problem. So, what would you like?' He began to rub his hands together enthusiastically. 'Tea, coffee, orange juice? We've got the lot.'

'Since you ask . . .' I pointed at the heavily beaded hair rising from behind the fridge. 'I'll have whatever he's drinking.'

The huge Jamaican grinned, but his eyes were busy exploring Neptune.

'Actually, Dave, on second thoughts . . .' I was far too righteous to get that intoxicated.

There was a sudden change of guard on the second day. Just

after breakfast Dave set off in a rush; then the Polish girls followed, giggling and wafting clouds of deodorant. With the girls
gone the kitchen lost the famed 'woman's touch' and everything
descended into chaos. At least they could be trusted to put the
butter back in the fridge. Flipping hell! The smell was nearly as
bad as my socks! I was still reeling from the stench when a tall guy
in denim shorts wandered in shouldering a khaki knapsack. I'd
seen fatter legs on a flamingo. Was this the missing Spaniard let
loose from the toilet?

The stranger offered his hand and said curtly, 'Ivo Novák, from
Prague.' Above a wispy goatee, eyes like black opals perused the
scene. 'And you are?' he asked.

'Tony,' I beamed, 'from the beautiful, powder-white beaches
of Southend-on-Sea.'

A Spaniard? Hell, no. This was a creature far more exotic. I'd
just bagged my first Czech.

Back in the dorm, hostel decorum dictated we observe the
usual courtesies. I fed him bits of my life in bite-sized chunks;
he returned with several of his own: twenty-nine years old, unmarried, lived in Prague, a student of architecture on a blitz tour
of the Balkans. Rather improbably he claimed relation to one of
the kings of Bohemia. I do admit to momentarily indulging the
imagination.

Yes, I thought, that aquiline nose, those high cheekbones, the
disdainful gaze, the unmistakable voice of command; I could just
see him sitting in a castle lording it over grovelling peasants.

All was going brilliantly until Ivo started checking his bunk.
He let out a snort of disgust.

'What's up, mate?' I looked up from my map, and as I did so
he said, 'I can't tolerate this, I just can't.' He was kneeling beside
his bed, frowning hard and peering intently at his blanket. 'This
would never happen in my country.' He turned to me, and a
princely finger beckoned. 'Come over here and see.'

I jumped up and crossed the floor, wondering what had set him
off. As I looked down at the cloth I noticed a small hole near the

edge, perhaps a cigarette burn, nothing more and certainly not enough to complain about.

'This is outrageous,' he said, rising to his feet and shaking his head. Placing hands on hips, he shot me a defiant stare. 'I can't sleep in this. In fact, I absolutely refuse to. I'm going to get the manager right now.'

So he did, who was none other than that strange fellow in a rainbow robe I'd seen hanging around the garden on day one. The conversation was pure farce.

'Hey, dude. What's the problem?' Rainbow Man floated in, all summer-of-love smiles. He was clutching a trowel, of all things.

Ivo glared at him and pointed down at his bunk. 'This blanket,' he said, trembling, 'this obscenity is the problem!'

Wow, what anger. I took two discreet steps back.

Rainbow Man glanced down at the offending article. He sniffed glumly. 'Look, chill out, dude, all of us are doing our best here. There's no need to lose your zing and get all—'

'What? What did you just say to me?'

Ivo's face darkened. He'd just spent seven hours on a hot, stuffy train. His blanket had a hole in it, and now some freak in a rainbow robe had dared to criticise his zing. He was furious.

'Then,' he sneered, wagging a princely finger at the poor guy's reddening face, 'your best clearly isn't good enough. I want a fresh blanket brought to me, and I want it now!'

It was a total mismatch. Rainbow Man was a man of peace. His ideal day involved tending hothouse plants of a dubious nature and placing bicycles in trees. He shrank back, totally beaten.

'Okay, dude,' he mumbled, waving Ivo quiet with a shushing motion. 'Just lower your voice, and I'll go get one. Jeez . . .'

He shrugged unhappily and floated back out into the corridor, muttering quietly to himself. To the best of my knowledge they never spoke again. I don't think Ivo could have cared less.

The pace picked up again after lunch. There was a big city to explore, so we piled out into the sun, two wide-eyed tourists clutching cameras. Ivo led the way, eating up the pavement with his flamingo legs. 'My God, we really must look at this,' and off he stormed toward another domed hammam.

I languished half a yard behind, sipping madly on my precious water bottle and grunting approval at anything remotely interesting—which wasn't much. I'm not a great art lover myself. For me a pot is just a pot, and a coin bearing the head of Caesar is as useful as a pilgrim with no walking boots. The 'Czech Prince' saw things differently. Only in Skopje for the day, he wanted to see as much as possible, and that meant seeing *everything*.

'Extraordinary!' he said. 'Just look at this magnificent second-century Macedonian statue.' (Actually, it was more of an order.) 'See the curve of the neck, the exquisite detail on the toga . . .'

I followed the direction of the princely finger. It was another old marble statue with a missing arm. I smiled grumpily and collapsed on a bench.

I was soon back on my feet, struggling to maintain pace with those loping legs. Ivo's appetite for art was insatiable. Not even the management of the national museum could slow him down. Arriving at reception, we discovered the lights had been turned off to save electricity. Ivo would have none of it. I don't know what the Macedonian is for 'I'm descended from a Czech prince and you're going to turn on all the lights NOW!', but whatever came out of his mouth did the trick. The look on the manager's face was priceless.

'I am deeply displeased,' Ivo declared, suddenly launching into the Queen's English. The manager flushed, humbled by the royal stare. To remedy the situation, a pimpled teenage minder was hastily dragged out of a cloakroom, told to bow deferentially to the esteemed guests (which he did with hilarious regularity), and for the rest of the day followed us about, flipping huge banks of light switches. The electricity bill must have been enormous. By late afternoon we'd scrutinised every pot, every vase, every icon and every hammered Roman coin the city had to offer.

But alas, not every castle.

The princely finger pointed upward. 'Ahhh, Tony, let's see

what's over there.' A sandy turret was teasing a gently rising hill. Inwardly, I groaned.

As luck would have it, I was glad I made the ascent. You never know what a climb will bring, and on a hot day in July it brought an impressive array of square-toothed battlements. For the best part of 1,500 years there's been something military standing on top of this hill. The current Kale Fortress—so named after the Turkish 'kale', meaning 'castle'—is just the last in a long line of fortifications dating back to Roman times. The view was suitably commanding. Beneath orange-streaked skies I let my gaze roam the glittering domes of Orthodoxy, sweeping down into the impersonal grids and haughty oblongs of a modern city. The ancient military planners were no fools. A century ago I could easily imagine Ottoman Janissaries doing much the same.

It was probably an hour later when we turned back. To reach the River Vardar we had to navigate the archaic Turkish Bazaar, and here the closed streets are quite unlike the rest of Skopje. In a thrice I was back in Sarajevo, where old men in pill-shaped hats gather in twos and threes, people-watching outside coffee joints. The bazaar's tightly packed shops offered everything from greasy kebabs to hand-embroidered leather moccasins.

Ivo jabbed his finger disdainfully at three wrinkled faces sitting on stools and playing with red-backed cards. 'You will see a lot of this in Turkey.'

I grunted and trudged on. My brain was still suffering from pot overload—and I don't mean the kind you inhale.

We continued our plodding descent. The stone bridge, built by Sultan Mehmed II, is an impressive Ottoman relic and an obvious tourist draw. Though executions were once common, these days it's more peaceful, populated by hopeful traders selling fake-branded sunglasses. Despite their beckoning smiles, I avoided temptation. At the bridge Ivo wandered off to fix a visa problem, and I gathered up some much-needed groceries from the many fruit vendors. Amid the background noise I happened to glance up at the Millennium Cross rising fuzzily from the summit of Mt Vodno. Since 2002 this sixty-six-metre statement of Christ's supremacy has totally dominated the city.

'I wonder what Muslims think about that?' Ivo had remarked caustically only a few hours ago.

The criticism in his voice gave pause for thought. In neighbouring Kosovo a crude mix of nationalism and religion had turned Christian and Muslim into mortal enemies. Could that awful fate happen here?

For the only time in Skopje I stopped to consider what I'd seen. I looked up at the cross and wondered, too.

✳ ✳ ✳

For three burning days fused into memory and blurred like molten glass, I shouldered my rucksack deep into the Macedonian interior, taking shelter in the modest towns and humble villages that grace the southern road. In nearly every case I found much more than just another bed. Katlanovska Banja provided a smoky hilltop chapel where chirping blue tits nested among the eaves; the forest outside Veles, the miracle of a real wolf glaring with yellow eyes among the trees. Shy and not the least bit fierce, it instantly turned and fled at my approach.

The landscape was an eclectic mix: one moment, sharp stony hills speckled green and tinkling with goat bells; the next, grapevines sweeping across dusty orange hills in rows of white-tipped sticks. I met very few people, but all hearts were friendly. On one occasion a vineyard worker spotted me, ran off and came back with a huge bunch of grapes. The fruits were delicious and did much to moisten the throat. Elsewhere I dawdled through leering canyons, grey as slate, circled by flapping hawks, where silence was louder than any thunder. I saw no one in these valleys save for a few Good Samaritans drilling the road. I can still see the potbellied foreman in his portable cabin, kicking back on his chair and declaring, 'It's forty-two degrees in the shade and fifty on the tarmac!' I don't think he was far off. I eventually picked up the threads of civilisation at Gradsko: two lines of smouldering iron track laddering pasture so dry a single match would have devastated acres. I gulped great mouthfuls of super-heated air, praying no one would be so stupid. No one was. The Macedonian hands handing me water knew their country well—they knew better.

Though entirely devoid of any touristic merit, the little town of Gradsko does have its uses. While traversing the main street I licked a pair of cracked lips, looking for signs of impending hospitality. I was about to abandon the search when I spotted a baldheaded guy waving beneath a grapevine trellis. I slowed and came to a cautious halt outside a big-windowed restaurant.

'*Bitte!*' he said, pointing to a chair. '*Setzen Sie sich!*'

A portly man in blue denim shorts with indecently hairy legs stood looking at me. He was hosing down the patio to cool the air, a common practice in these parts. Despite modest linguistic skills, I knew an invitation to sit down when I heard one. I threw off my rucksack, grateful for the shade.

I wasn't surprised to find another German in the Balkans. I'd encountered several in Slovenia and a couple in Croatia. These hairy legs belonged to a fifty-year-old émigré from Cologne, and in spite of the more unlikely aspects of our meeting, I'm glad I stopped; two free glasses of cola are always welcome. I was less sure about the direction of the conversation. Strangely unmoved by my massive walk to Jerusalem, Karl's main concern was that I was forty-three years old and still unmarried—a mortal sin in his eyes. Apparently, my marriage prospects were as bleak as Gradsko's economy. Was that bad? A dozy dog came sniffing the air, looking for scraps. It keeled over, never to rise again. Yep: pretty bad.

I was hoping for better things inside the restaurant. For days I'd been getting by on donated grapes and clumps of roadside pears; I needed feeding up. Karl owned this crimson-papered, L-shaped eatery. Knives and forks glittered on lacy white table-cloths. In the heel of the L a flat-screen TV hung precariously, threatening to drop and permanently ruin someone's lunch. I sat a safe distance opposite, waiting for something to happen. About twenty-five minutes later, something did.

Karl's son, Goran, was a typical sixteen-year-old obsessed with football, computer games and girls (though not necessarily in that order). Tall and muscular with a boxer's nose, he wore a navy-blue football shirt stencilled in white numerals with the number twelve. I watched him swagger across the floor, a brash young Macedonian, a Macedonian with *attitude*.

'Do you want to listen to some music?' He hovered over me, clutching the remote like a club.

I paused to think.

'Well? Do you want to listen to some music or not?'

And he's impatient, too.

I sniffed pleasantly, hoping for food, which twenty minutes after being ordered was conspicuous by its absence. 'Sure,' I said mildly, 'why not.'

Goran shot me a triumphant grin. He wanted to show off, and we both knew it. While Karl's wife, Elena, hummed and clattered plates in the kitchen, I waited patiently as Goran fiddled with the remote. The screen sputtered into life immediately settling on a pretty blond pop star with fake eyelashes and an unnaturally large chest. Like most female pop stars wishing to sell records, she was cavorting in a most suggestive manner. I had little doubt her strategy was succeeding.

Goran's face began to flush. He jabbed at the screen. 'Do you see this?' he cried. 'Do you see this?'

'Yes, mate. I see it.' It was hard not to.

'Typical Balkans music,' he said with an enormous sigh. 'And I do not like it.'

This statement surprised me, particularly as we were glued to the same channel for some time. After thirty minutes the screen flickered again. The roar of the crowd and frenetic commentary were unmistakable. There was no way I could leave the table without declaring my football credentials. In the fiercely tribal world of teenage males that would have been unforgivable.

'I've never been one to support a club, but I do support England in the World Cup and the European Cup.' I pushed my empty plate across the table, fervently hoping for dessert and preferably several slices of red melon. I caught his eye. 'What about your country? Does Macedonia have a good football team?'

Goran shook his head. 'Our team has never been in the big finals. The Macedonian league is very poor. At least, compared to the English.'

A sober point and well put, though 'poor' is not a word that could ever be applied to the Premier League. The fact that England regularly crash out of the World Cup because no one can take a penalty is no bar to an obscene seven-figure salary.

I spent the rest of that afternoon dozing in my room. (Karl had finally forgiven me for being unmarried and decided to offer me a place to sleep.) In the evening, Goran continued my Macedonian education in the upstairs lounge. His brother quickly joined us, a tubby teenager crammed unconvincingly into a cherry-red football strip.

'Dim the lights!' Goran ordered, so I did, and we crowded around the computer. Little did I realise, but the highlight of an 80 km march from Skopje was imminent. We'd argued over pop music, and we'd determined that neither Macedonia nor England could win the World Cup. (The latter was felt to be particularly unlikely.) Now it was time to sample the final element of the Macedonian teen diet: the gratuitously violent computer game.

For those unfamiliar with *Street Fighter II* let me enlighten you. *Street Fighter* is a classic arcade game from the nineties. It's a game of mindless violence where players use special moves like *Psycho Fire* and *Dragon Punch* to bludgeon each other to death. That's it. There's nothing else to know.

Suddenly, English honour was at stake. I picked up a control pad and settled down for battle. In a thrice I was sixteen again, blocking, punching and dropkicking with un-Christian macho ferocity. I'm not sure Jesus would have approved ... After getting my head kicked in for the tenth time, I lost my cool.

'Damn it! There's something wrong with my controls!'

Goran roared with laughter; I'd been given the pad with the sticky key.

A lull in the action brought the evening's entertainment to a fitting close. Cushions started to whizz through the air, crashing into Elena's precious vases as the boisterous teens decided open warfare was far more satisfying. I ducked behind the sofa, praying she wouldn't blame me for the damage. These Macedonians, I thought, they just can't stop fighting.

Alexander the Great would have been so proud.

'The signs, Tony, always look for the signs.'

On the road to Jerusalem nine months had passed since my meeting in Holland with Johanna van Fessem. On a sun-warmed stone in the heart of Macedonia I sat down to reminisce. I still recalled many of the details: Johanna talking quietly about 'staying open to the experience', her cross of plaited string handed to me over a table swamped with maps. I'd smiled politely, not comprehending her cryptic talk. I was a novice on the verge of a magnificent adventure; I didn't know any better. Since then, I'd discovered the splendid truth. There was more to pilgrimage than lancing blisters. Greater than the physical journey was the inner, and the inner journey was marked by gifts of the heart.

Through those eleven days of summer I received many such gifts. If good fortune can be measured in bunches of grapes, I'd been blessed. All told I must have gobbled several kilos. I found more hospitality on a hill at Negotino. Some students relaxing in their garden offered me ice-cold beer, and nothing topped it until I turned up at the village of Demir Kapija—made famous that year for its stultifying heat. In search of an elusive priest I bumped into Palija Jovance pushing a bicycle with a flat tyre. Minutes later, I was eating heartily under another grapevine trellis. His only regret was that his house was too small to put me up. I left feeling elated. Surely God himself was leading me on?

Two days after departing Gradsko I was still toying with the question. Sprawling below hazy green mountains and busy with the sound of chugging tractors, the little village of Korešnica is not an obvious place to be rampant with gifts of the heart. First impressions weren't very encouraging. The church looked like a disused greenhouse, and the priest was inconveniently away on business. Ever hopeful, I marched straight to the village shop. Five gruff agricultural types sat on stools, chewing straw and swilling beer. Did anyone have a field where I could camp?

A large man with shoulders like an ox looked up and with a smirk said, 'You can camp on the football field.'

The thought was written all over their faces. An Englishman? Here? What the hell for?

Despite their incredulity, I discovered something of supreme importance that afternoon. If you want a decent night's sleep never camp on a football pitch. In Macedonia cottages have eyes and most of them are wearing football shirts. I was flat on my back listening to neighing horses when they approached. The sound of young male voices couldn't be ignored, not this close to my tent. I hastily pulled on some boots and scrambled out.

I was right about the company: six boys of various heights and ages. The largest was built like a middleweight boxer with blond close-cropped hair—a kind of Goran mark II. I eyed them warily, wondering how this would play out. There was a tense pause, then the large boy spoke up.

'Mister, do you like football?'

Yes, but not after a 30 km march.

I stood my ground, face impassive and fervently hoping they would retreat. The boys lingered, shooting each other whispers through cupped hands, before looking back at me.

Damn. What should I do now? I could hardly refuse. My feet were sore and brutally tender. On the other hand, I was camping on *their* football pitch. Their quiet perseverance paid off. 'I'm going to pay for this tomorrow,' I muttered, and off we went.

With the large boy leading the way, we sauntered across the

field. Joe was his name, and he seemed to be the dominant personality in the group. At the centre spot he ordered one of the younger boys to fetch the football, then amid much excitement we divided into two teams of three. While picked last, I didn't have long to blush. I was still stupidly waiting for the 'official' start when a freckled kid in blue shorts gave the ball a massive hoof, and everyone charged off in the same direction. By rights I should have ended my day snoozing in a tent.

I'm glad I didn't.

For the next two hours I ran, I passed, I chipped—I swerved like a middle-aged Bobby Charlton, but with slightly more hair. Burning up five hundred calories had never been so much fun.

'The English! The English!' screamed our ten-year-old goalkeeper, frantically jabbing his finger in my direction.

I waved my arms enthusiastically, eager to show willing. The contest was getting serious. Joe's blood was up. Our goalkeeper's blood was up. Even my own heart rate had topped 100 beats a minute, and that hadn't happened since the freak Montenegrin snake attack. With the ball at my feet, I thundered down the left touchline as fast as size nine hiking boots would allow, which wasn't very fast. Sadly, I was as effective as an England striker in a World Cup shootout; the ball skidded off my boot and ballooned over the crossbar. Joe scowled. I hung my English head in shame. Clearly the seven-figure salary was as far away as ever.

We played for a while longer, then at half-time a fight broke out. I'd half expected that. Football has a way of turning even respectable bank managers into mindless louts. A small Turkish boy playing with no boots started arguing with Joe, and we all stood about while they rolled around on the grass in a juvenile struggle for dominance. Soon tufts began flying in all directions. A few may have been hair, such was the ferocity of the struggle. Intervention from a mildly concerned adult (i.e. myself) would have been suicidal. Eager to see another dawn, I let them get on with it.

Eventually, the new pecking order was established, or rather the old confirmed. Joe remained top dog courtesy of being two feet taller than his adversary. Still, the Turk put up a good fight and had the respect of the others. The two boys embraced each other like long-lost cousins, and all hostility vanished in a flash. When they'd stopped hugging it was time for refreshment.

Joe picked up the ball. He turned to me and said, 'Do you like ice cream?'

A few of the smaller boys shot me envious looks. I guess they wanted ice cream, too, and wondered why they weren't getting any. I glanced at their faces, unsure whether to accept, then figured Joe might get upset if I refused. I smiled at him. 'Sure, that would be great.'

Joe grinned, pulled some notes from his pocket and our goalkeeper sprinted off to the village shop. Ice cream was followed by a slightly molten chocolate bar and ice-cold cola in plastic cups. We were still practising our passing skills an hour after dusk. I hadn't had so much fun in years.

There was an unexpected turn to the day's events. It must have been an hour later when they returned. I unzipped the tent, using my pocket torch to pick out their excited faces. Some younger boys had joined the original group and a couple of teenage girls had arrived to meet the mysterious 'Ingleesh'. I started, realising the children were clutching gifts. Up they proudly stepped, tiny hands presenting offerings like visiting nobles before a king. One held a bag of homemade biscuits dusted with icing sugar; another, a bottle of fizzy orange. Joe stood there grinning, holding a melon. It was an absolute monster and far too heavy to carry. Instead, we carved it up and ate great slices with sticky fingers. When the melon was gone I shook hands solemnly with each child in turn, then they melted away like ghosts towards flecks of yellow lantern light.

I had much to consider in the darkness. My tent was filled with assorted gifts that would keep me going for days. The friendship of the children had caught me off-guard, reopening old moral questions long thought settled. In comparison to these people

I was rich, perhaps obscenely so. Was I really worthy of their help? Should I have accepted their gifts, the gifts of children?

We know that all things work together for the good of those who love God, to those who are called according to his purpose.

After reading my New Testament I turned away from the words of Romans 8:28 finding reassurance in strange dreams.

'Were you not the one I called to Jerusalem? Is your cause not worthy of help from men, but children also?'

My dream-self clearly had great wisdom, for it decided no answer was necessary. Not so at dawn when I was again reminded of the children's generosity. I packed each gift carefully, almost tenderly, not daring to break even a single biscuit. And at the rising of that sun came deep gratitude for gifts from tiny hands.

And crushing humility came with it.

* * *

I spent another three days marching toward the Greek border. If it hadn't become clear by now that Johanna's signs were an essential part of pilgrimage, I still had a tad less than seventy-two hours to see the light. Heartened by the generosity of the children, I embraced humility for the final time at Valandovo. It's a typical Macedonian town: hillsides are unnaturally green, pavements are a nest of hard-baked rutted tracks, electricity is sporadic and grapes dangle voluptuously from every trellis. In keeping with local geography the Monastery of St George rests at the top of a very high stony hill. I shouldn't have bothered. Sitting cross-legged by the door, in a huddle of grey rags, was the most inhospitable bag of bones in the southern Balkans.

The whiskered deacon folded his arms and broke into perfect German. *'Diese Zimmer sind für unsere Freunde.'*

These rooms were for his friends. I wasn't one of them. Case closed.

Thankfully, the notion of Christian fellowship in Valandovo wasn't completely dead. With considerable relief I was taken in by forty-five-year-old Petar surviving on 200 euros a month in the western foothills. Petar's son, Jove, was the family's main English-speaker. A spiky-haired young man wearing a gold crucifix, he spent his time waiting tables on the high street for 3 euros a day—a pitiful sum by Western European standards. At first he told me he wanted to study tourism in Greece. Minutes later, he was chatting about university in Croatia. In truth, he just wanted out of Macedonia.

'Can you help me find a job in England?' His voice carried a hint of desperation.

I sat on the family's patio munching an extra large meat and ketchup pie—a pie he'd just bought. How much of today's wages was I eating?

I dropped my eyes to the table. 'It will be difficult. I honestly can't do anything until I've returned to England, but I'll try once I get back.' I straightened up and met his gaze. 'Look, why don't you give me your email address, then we can keep in touch?'

He brightened noticeably, leading me to question the wisdom of raising his hopes. Setting up home in a foreign land is no mean feat, especially for one so young. When the moment to depart eventually came, I left the house weighed down with two litres of ice-cold water, a litre of orange juice, several pomegranates and a generous quantity of the family's bread and salami. I don't know how much of their 200-euro budget I was walking away with, but another lump in my throat made me wonder.

I spent that night at Gevgelija in a cheap hotel. Then, in the afternoon, another Good Samaritan helped me refill my water bottle from a disused factory and find the minor road leading to the border. Hemmed in by fencing on the left and four lanes of the E75 motorway on the right, I allowed myself to be funnelled toward country number eleven.

I paused and gazed deep into the south. The ancient horizon of Persian humiliation at Marathon, of three hundred Spartans who died beneath Xerxes' arrows, and all the wonders of Hellenic antiquity that a bespectacled schoolboy had only read about in books, rippled outward in sheets of dreamy cloud-swept blue. Despite the unfavourable odds I'd trodden a path all the way to Greece. I looked down at dusty boots with awe.

Thus, at 10 a.m. on 22 July, what began in the Slovenian village of Podkoren finally came to an end; my journey through the former Yugoslavia and Albania was over. Had I chosen well? I was inclined to think so. Although poor in means, the people of these lands had been rich in all the ways that mattered. Every country had produced Good Samaritans. I would never forget Rok and Irena in Slovenia, Farmer Joseph in Croatia, or Ivana and Aleksandar in their little guesthouse at the entrance to the Piva Canyon. Help in Bosnia had been almost miraculous. When an ugly foot wound threatened disaster a stranger had given me shelter and arranged medical treatment at their expense. If gifts were coins, then I'd amassed a real pilgrim's treasure.

The European Union edged closer in brash blue signs painted with cars and lorries. I glanced about, trying to get a feel for the moment. I'd spent the last four-and-a-half months whining to God about water, food and every little thing. With ten countries safely behind me, how could I have doubted? I'd found reassurance everywhere: in the wild plums I gathered from the trees, in the strawberries on the ground, in the mountain streams of Albania that sustained me when nothing else could. Still greater gifts had been gifts of the heart. Daily I received them, in tiny villages and towns, in the hills and the fields, and on scores of hot dusty roads. In a hundred improbable encounters I'd seen the face of God written on the face of men, and on women and children, too, for all had given freely and asked for nothing in return.

The feeling sprung from the soul: did you really think I would forsake you? You who have toiled for so long in my name?

The question needed no answer. I was alone and yet not alone. I was friendless and yet had the greatest friend of all.

And so, giving thanks for the good things that had come my way, I took what remained of my strength into Greece. Several million steps lay underfoot, three thousand kilometres still in the distance. The way would be hard, the path long, the road difficult and uncertain. In the last few metres I threw up a prayer.

It's going to be hard crossing Greece, I thought.

I know, he replied, but we can make it.

He was right: we could. Under azure skies, I gave thanks to God my friend.

I gave thanks for helping hands.

And I walked on.

Chapter Eleven

Greece

The Land of Heroes

Maintained at a steady temperature of 20.73 degrees inside the British Museum's Duveen Gallery, the famous sculptures chiselled out of the Parthenon by Lord Elgin have a lot to answer for. Jack's exile to my junk email folder turned out to be one of them. A few days before entering Greece I received another dire warning. It was the eighth on the same subject. I groaned and began to speed-read his ponderous prose:

> Watch your step, mate ... Nana Mouskouri's coming out of retirement ... new campaign launched today ... it's in all the papers ... Oh, yeah, Bill's still asking about that tenner you owe from last Christmas ...

Hmm. He would have to mention that. I soldiered on.

> Elgin Marbles belong to Greece ... British Museum denounced ... big demonstration in Athens ... Union Jack set on fire ...

Bah; if the Greeks wanted trouble, I was ready. Churchill could not have put it better: 'We shall fight them on the beaches, we shall fight them in the olive groves . . .' The marbles undoubtedly belonged to Britain, and even if they *were* an ancient monument of priceless value looted without due authority, I'm quite sure it was an innocent mistake. We Britons are honourable people (used car salesmen and most politicians obviously excluded). So Nana was breathing fire. So what? I could put up with anything, just as long as she didn't sing.

Dishonourable though it may be for one seeking deep spiritual truths, I began my first day in the land of heroes wrestling with a child over a strawberry cornet—hot weather always seems to bring out the worst in people. I had two fingers and a thumb on the slippery wrapper when a small boy wearing spectacles made the same desperate lunge. 'Give me that!' he shouted. I'd like to say I nobly surrendered the prize, but the truth is my grip loosened at the critical moment, leaving my hand grasping at thin air. The boy's face was pure triumph. Mine was the epitome of Greek tragedy. I don't think I've ever been more disappointed.

For that final week of July Thessaloniki was the next big target. From Evzonoi's criminally understocked chest freezers I struck south, taking the minor road shadowing the motorway. With ten countries to the rear I was feeling mildly heroic. The euphoria was short-lived. Wannabe heroes don't last long in Greece. They either fall like Spartans peppered by Persian arrows or die of thirst on the outskirts of Mikro Dasos. I collapsed under a rainbow parasol and ordered the biggest cola on the menu.

'What?' she said. 'Jerusalem?' The waitress gasped and clutched at the silver crucifix at her throat. I nodded at the slender figure in black hovering beside the table. 'But,' she added, 'I've always wanted to go there!'

Yeah. That makes two of us.

Maria was this gorgeous woman's name, and with her olive skin and jet-black hair pulled up in the classic Greek style, she did a fine impression of the Goddess Athena. I swiftly dealt with all the usual pilgrim questions (How far do you walk each day? How heavy is your rucksack?). I was heading for Polykastro next.

'Wait a second! Yes, wait! I think there is someone there who can help you!'

I blinked, unsure what was coming.

'He is one of our most famous priests, a man well known for helping the homeless.' Her cheeks began to flush, and I thought she was going to giggle. 'We call him the Grandfather of Love.'

Wow, the Grandfather of Love. Now there's a name you don't hear every day . . . I stifled a chuckle and threw her a questioning look. 'Do you know where this guy lives? I might look him up and see if he can offer me a room.'

'I don't know for sure, but if you ask around, someone will. Everyone in the town knows him.'

We grinned at each other like two silly teenagers. I drained my glass, placed it on the table and rose to leave.

'Oh, no,' said Maria, shaking her head and holding up both hands. 'There is no need to pay.'

'Are you sure?' I already had the coins on the table.

Without answering she shook her head again and dashed back into the café. Thirty seconds later, I left clutching two half-litre bottles of mineral water. The powerful sun of the southern Balkans had given me an extraordinary new appreciation of H_2O. I thanked her profusely and marched on.

I made Polykastro sometime mid-afternoon. Having lived the experience, I can tell you it's a brave man that wanders around northern Greece mumbling strange sentences about love. The first passer-by was male, bald, unshaven and fat. He was also surprisingly friendly.

'So, my English friend, you are perhaps wanting some love?'

The bald lover winked at me, and I realised we were on the wrong track.

As the afternoon continued to fade, only elderly women with bowlegs plagued the streets. Of course! I thought, with desperate cunning. Who would know better where to find a grandfather than a *grandmother*? It made perfect sense at the time. Up sauntered victim number five, dressed in widow's black.

'Excuse me, madam.' A pair of sleepy eyes looked up. 'Do you know where I can find the Grandfather of Love?'

Ha-ha. Not likely. I watched aghast as another grandmother of Greece shrugged her shoulders. Perhaps with hindsight that was just as well. Back home I could already imagine Jack's response.

'So, mate, where did you stay in Polykastro?'

'Oh, nowhere that special. Actually, I spent the night with the Grandfather of Love.'

'You did what!'

I don't often claim the gift of prophecy, but the ensuing conversation would surely be unprintable for a Christian, family-orientated audience.

Would it really?

Trust me: it would be.

I never did find the mysterious grandfather. Instead, I stayed over at Hotel Vienna and when dawn returned, hot and dusty, continued to march in parallel with the railway track. I'd only been walking for two hours when I scribbled down one of the more profound truths of my journey: 'I suspect my pilgrimage will move at a slower pace.' It was a masterful understatement. Shortly after, the tone became thus: 'Knackered! Going nowhere fast! Covered 7 km in 4 hours!!!' (Note the triple exclamation marks—a sure sign of impending doom.) Stripped of all heroic pretensions, I collapsed under a rare tree and refused to emerge for three hours. I hadn't walked this slowly since kindergarten.

I didn't have long to wait before any lingering comedy reverted to Greek tragedy. I slumped on the grass, boots off, socks drying on branches, right foot cooling off in a plastic bag sloshing with water: a heavenly experience and one to savour for as long as possible. I was munching a cheese sandwich with one hand, and rummaging through a second bag with the other, when I felt my stomach tighten. I checked once. Then I checked again. Nope. There was no trace of the map—nothing except a bottle of water and a partially squashed nectarine. Only twenty-four hours after crossing the border I'd lost my directions to Thessaloniki.

Fantastic.

Thankfully, the loss of such an important item wasn't a complete disaster. I've got a prodigious memory for detail, and in any case, if you keep walking south a city of 320,000 Greeks is hard to miss. I packed up my gear and marched on. Great swathes of tinder grassland stood one match away from inferno. In a nod to agriculture, patches of yellow corn speckled the dreamy haze. Huge farm hoses hissed and jerked, squirting water in all directions like a demented cobra spitting venom. The impulse was almost primordial. I charged headlong into the field, letting cold spray rip across face and chest. And the discarded melons were another boon. A popular crop on the plains, the roadside was dotted with little mottled footballs. I don't usually eat things that have fallen off trucks, but they were far too delicious to waste.

It was just after another bout of scavenging that I came across an unusual sight. The pretty white plaster shrines are a regular feature of northern Greece. I saw my first example at the turn-off to Akropotamos—a miniature Orthodox church, about a foot square, pastel blue, standing on a pedestal and stencilled with a smattering of Greek. I peered inside, finding a small oil burner, unlit, and a bottle of pale-green oil. The ubiquitous icon stood to the left: Madonna and Child on a glossy postcard, curling slightly at the edges. The shrine's owner must have been devout; even a silver censer dangled from the ceiling. I crossed myself respectfully and returned to the road. Through the missionary efforts of St Paul, the Greeks had been among the first converts to Christianity. His legacy had withstood twenty devastating centuries. Has any man done more in the service of Christ?

For three days I staggered up and down shimmering slip roads, searching for things to drink and daring the heat to overwhelm me. In hard-won yards the villages retreated: Aspros, Axiochori, Akropotamos—sleepy little hamlets where silver-haired men in crumpled shirts gather in cafés to play cards and drink beer. I was guzzling eight litres of fluids a day, so often joined them. I found the road signs incomprehensible, a mix of alphas and thetas, and symbols I last saw in maths class thirty years ago. As I was still doggedly tracking the railway, I didn't worry too much about getting lost. My main grumble was the lack of church support. Orthodox doors were usually locked and there wasn't a smiling priest in sight. To communicate with the non-English-speaking locals (which was basically everyone), I whipped out my diary and drew a stick figure wearing a mitre. Unsurprisingly, no one knew where this strange anorexic character lived.

I had to wait to the third day before these disappointments eased. The traffic started to pick up on the adjacent motorway, and I sensed the draw of a big city. With civilisation so close, this was surely the last chance to indulge. I'd just given up hope when I spotted a familiar round shape nestling among the grass. A flatbed truck rattling past captured the moment. I glanced up, mouth dribbling with juice, eyes feral with hunger, surrounded by odd chunks of melon in various states of consumption. I was still waving my penknife about. I could almost read their minds.

Gaping male driver: 'Good God! Who's that fool scavenging by the roadside?'

Cheery female passenger: 'Don't worry, dear. It's just another starving pilgrim walking to Jerusalem.'

Gaping male driver: 'Ahhh, that figures. Best avoid eye contact. Those blighters are dangerous.'

* * *

If you navigate the border at Evzonoi and follow the long railway south, you eventually end up at Greece's second-largest city named after Alexander the Great's half sister. After three days sucking the life out of old melon skins, you'll be well rewarded. Thessaloniki is much like Skopje, but with fewer beggars, more churches, the novelty of a real Roman arch (well, a third of one), and what I strongly maintain is the considerable benefit of the Aegean Sea lapping just yards from a windy quayside Starbucks.

It seemed like an ideal time to take a break. I stayed put in the city almost to week's end, sightseeing and quietly rehydrating on cartons of strawberry slush. With its shorts-and-T-shirt atmosphere, the seafront is the place to be. Sapphire swells splinter the Aegean into a million shifting diamonds, snow-white tenements blizzard the coastline, green lawns bordered by orange chrysanthemums project a general Mediterranean lushness. Orthodox Christianity fills the gaps. Churches range from smoky chapels the size of a telephone box to the olive-green dome of Hagia Sophia—a Byzantine giant rising from Babylonian gardens in smouldering orange paint. A photo can hardly capture the grandeur, but all tourists try. After traversing the arid plains of the north, the pull of the sea was irresistible. On the very first day I struggled towards the quayside, bypassing swivelling postcard stands and yards of taped-off pavement. The centre was a mass of flailing trowels. Were they workmen relaying the road? It's hard to tell in Greece; the area looked like a huge archaeological dig. If they find anything at all it's normally old (i.e. Roman) and very likely to be declared a UNESCO World Heritage Site.

Which nicely brings discussion to the hideous hostel situation. The only budget accommodation I managed to track down was an ancient apartment block on Alexandrou Svolou. I spent two ghastly nights there sweating buckets in forty-degree heat, and imprisoned three floors up, without air-conditioning, not even wild horses could drag me back. Something unpleasant was invariably floating in the toilet, and since there were no lockers, anyone leaving the hostel had to place blind faith in their fellow residents not to rob them blind. For someone used to drawing from the deep well of human kindness, my faith wasn't that strong: passport, cash and camera automatically went with me.

An elderly Turk with a tiny moustache ran the place. Each day at precisely 11 a.m. this archaic remnant of the defunct Ottoman Empire turned up in a black waistcoat and a crisp white shirt. After giving a polite nod to the waiting guests, he'd tune in to Radio Istanbul (or something deeply evocative of swerving belly dancers) then, with onyx prayer beads in one hand, proceed to take money with the other. It was all a far cry from past imperial splendours. Less than a hundred years ago he might have been on the Bosphorus conversing with turbaned Janissaries. Now the old fellow's empire consisted of twenty fetid bunk beds. He seemed happy, though. So I figured the money must be good.

The hostel residents were the usual colourful mix. In my dorm we gained a pair of gay guys from Italy who insisted on strutting about bare-chested in clingy shorts. I remember well the first chap: a tall guy with black curls drowning in hair gel.

'Hi! I'm Carlos from Milano!' Crikey, I could almost see myself reflected in the chest wax. 'I'm gay, by the way,' and he shot me a questioning look. 'Actually, did I mention that?'

He had—about five times. I stayed good-humoured, figuring it was some kind of gay pride thing. The most irritating presence turned out to be a scrawny Dutchman from Amsterdam. His foot odour was so biologically deadly that even scientists at Porton Down might have balked. I felt a particular kind of joy when he announced his attention to shower. 'At last, Porton's had a wash!' trumpeted my diary. Unfortunately, the night-time temperature had risen to an astonishing thirty-five degrees, so the olfactory respite was purely temporary. Our final guests were a pair of blond Polish teens. They spent most of the time on their bunks clutching each other tightly with Hansel-and-Gretel lost-in-the-forest eyes.

'We are so worried about thieves taking our rucksacks,' they confided.

'Just do what I do,' I told them.

They looked up hopefully. 'What's that?'

'Pray.'

The girl's face cracked and she immediately turned away, sobbing quietly into her boyfriend's shoulder. As a partial attempt at humour, I had to admit it wasn't overly successful. Later that evening we caught up again on the lobby's stone verandah. Red-faced motorists with large bellies were shouting and brawling in the streets below. It was a corker of a battle. I hadn't seen this much action since the Tyson–Holyfield fight.

'My money's on the one in the red!' I said to them.

A large bloke in a striped green shirt staggered back, crashing into a barrow of melons. Hansel and Gretel merely smiled wanly. What's wrong with them? I thought. They don't drink to excess. They don't snore. They don't try to bag the only radiator with their fetid towels. They even wash their feet on a regular basis. I began to wonder whether these pink-cheeked innocents were really cut out for international backpacking.

I spent the next morning photographing every church I could find, then when evening came reluctantly returned to my dorm. Forward planning is not as exciting as running around a foreign city, but it's an essential activity that has to be tackled at some point. I unfolded my latest acquisition—a map of Turkey—and spread it across the blanket. Naturally, the unneeded parts had already been trimmed off. Travelling light was the iron rule.

'Sure,' he grunted cheerfully, 'I'll have a look.'

The voice rose from the opposite bunk. Tall and lanky, with the kind of tan only available under a burning Anatolian sun, the latest addition to our community was a twenty-three-year-old Turk from Bursa on a whirlwind tour of Europe. He'd ditched his job for snowdrifts in northern Sweden and troublesome girlfriend for hot adventures in southern Sicily. Fifty days later, he had no regrets. Travel's a drug, and I knew a fellow addict when I saw one. Mehmet sauntered over, pulling at his shorts.

'So,' I asked him, 'what do you think about all this? Are there any places I should avoid?'

He sniffed glumly and wiped the sleep from his eyes. 'Okay,' he said, waving me quiet, 'just give me a second to think.'

I stood beside him, arms folded, watching his eyes crawl across the paper, weighing the endless possibilities.

'Well, everything here is safe,' he said eventually, jabbing the map in various places. 'Over here though'—and with a tight smile he swept his hand rightward—'for someone like you, over here is not safe.'

The map was disconcertingly large, at least six feet across. I leant forward for a closer look: Istanbul, formerly Constanti-nople and capital of the Byzantine Empire; Ankara, the modern-day capital in the north; dozens of large cities and scores of modest towns. The safe areas were western and central Turkey; 'not safe' was the border with Iran and everywhere nearby for at least 100 km. The country that gave us the *fatwa* had never been on my itinerary. I felt relieved.

'Okay, but what about these guys over here?' I jabbed at the southern cities bordering the eastern Mediterranean.

'Adana, Iskenderun, Antakya, yeah, sure'—he swept his hand casually down the map—'these are safe for tourists, no problem. Iskenderun is a great place. My family have a house down there. I hate Adana, though,' and his grin became a grimace, 'it's always so hot in summer. It must be the hottest city in Turkey.'

I nodded absentmindedly and continued to gaze in awe at the enormous map.

'Are you travelling to Syria?' he asked, breaking my reverie.

'I don't really know yet. I'm starting to think about it, but I don't have a visa, and when I did some research on the Internet there seemed to be huge problems getting hold of one.'

It was a timely question. From the start I'd always intended to follow Johanna's route through Turkey. That meant travelling down the Gallipoli Peninsula, crossing the Dardanelles into Asia and then walking south to the port of Marmaris. At that point I hoped to board a ferry to Haifa on the Israeli coast. Then I'd met Rok and Irena in Slovenia:

'Oh, if you go to Turkey you must visit Istanbul. The Blue Mosque is *amazing*.'

As decisions go, it was definitely one of the bigger ones. If I went to Istanbul in the north, travelling south to Marmaris no longer made any sense. Instead, it pointed to a longer route—a walk straight down the Anatolian heart of Turkey followed by the Arab lands of Syria and Jordan. The prospect was tantalising, but did I have the courage to go for it?

After a while, I folded up the map and tucked it back into my rucksack. Istanbul, Ankara, Syria and Jordan: my mind was buzzing with the possibilities. Talk swung away from geography to distant girlfriends, to Turkish-EU politics and then back to the officious-looking proprietor. The old Turk must have a sense of humour to run this dump. I wondered if Mehmet agreed.

He glanced up from his bunk. 'I think so. The old man made a joke earlier.'

The whole hostel was a joke and not a very pleasant one.

'By the way,' he said, 'have you seen the showers yet?'

'Nope. Where the hell are they?'

'In the basement. Go back into the lobby, and you'll see a key on the wall.'

Mehmet lay back on his pillow and began to appraise another bunch of holiday snaps. I grabbed my towel, a sliver of soap and went looking for that key. Deep in the labyrinthine bowels of International Youth Hostel Thessaloniki, something stirred in anticipation of fresh meat. Was it myth or Minotaur?

As the dormitory door swung open, I caught Mehmet's grin. 'The showers are awful,' he said. 'I mean, really awful.'

Call me bull-headed, but I just had to see for myself.

And see the showers I did, although the push-button light on the staircase was less than helpful. It went off thirty seconds too early, plunging me into total darkness. In deference to Christ I restricted myself to minor curses. With outstretched hands I stumbled on toward the faint outline of a door. At the flick of a switch a yellow strip light spluttered into life, revealing a wall of concrete with creepy passages running off either side. What the . . . ? With mounting dread I turned left, then right, then left, then hard right again. Crikey, I thought. I'm going to need a ball of string to find my way back.

Finally, the full magnificence of the showers was revealed: two rusty showerheads nailed to the ceiling separated by a mildewed wall of cement. Old soap slivers and pubic hair lay tangled in the grates. And *la pièce de résistance?* There wasn't a door in sight.

Awesome.

I honestly can't remember the last time I whipped off my pants and shorts in a single fluid motion—pilgrimage is an unending list of dubious firsts. I ripped at buttons and tore off socks. Every few seconds I whirled in the gloom, expecting some nutcase to rush me with a knife, like the shower scene from *Psycho*.

At last, the dreaded moment came. Wrapping arms around my torso, I tiptoed across the clammy concrete toward the nearest red-painted lever. The showerhead rattled into painful life. *Ker-bonk! Ker-bonk! Ker-bonk!* A trickle of icy water came spluttering out. I gasped violently and bravely lathered up. I was still smiling stoically right up to that very first scream.

As the Greek hero Theseus might attest, a labyrinth can be a dangerous place. I'd just started to towel off when I noticed a flicker of movement on the upper ledge. Flipping hell! What's that? Do they have tarantulas in Greece?

Twelve eyes stared down from a silken lair. Two blue eyes stared defiantly back (I'm an easy-going bloke, but no one likes a Peeping Tom). Ignoring the incongruity of the moment, and the very real possibility that someone might catch me stark naked, I found the courage of Theseus and stood my ground. The mother of all staring contests was on.

One minute passed.

Two minutes passed.

Then, twelve eyes blinked.

'Haha! Gotcha!' I jabbed at my foe with infantile glee. That turned out to be a mistake. The spider was evidently a poor loser and had a brittle temper. In a flurry of rippling legs, the creature surged forward, driven by a frenzied bloodlust.

There are no visual records of what happened next. That suits me fine—my face would have made an interesting study in terror. Recoiling like a spring, I crashed back against the partition, the gargantuan spider tumbled to the floor in a heap of thrashing legs, then disappeared with a deeply satisfying gurgle among the swirling waters beneath the grate. Armed only with a sliver of soap I'd bagged my very own 'Minotaur'. Hurrah!

Fortunately, a ball of string was not needed to escape the horrors of the basement. Fiendish in their design, the location of the showers at last made perfect sense—all that cement was ideal for stifling screams. My vocal cords were totally scorched. I was still visibly shaking when I rejoined Mehmet in the dorm.

I tossed my towel onto the bunk. 'Crikey,' I croaked. 'You were right about those blinking showers.'

Mehmet grinned, but said nothing. *I told you*, said his smile.

On 29 July I left Thessaloniki behind and for the best part of a week travelled east across Greek Macedonia. I had mixed feelings about moving on. New friendships had been forged, and remembering the harsh sun of the northern plains, I felt far from enthusiastic. Such apathy nearly cost me my life. For ten frightening minutes I stomped up the motorway, eating tarpaulin from six-wheeled juggernauts before common sense intervened and I hastily backtracked down the hard shoulder. Even after such stupidity God stayed faithful. Outside a restaurant in Efkarpia I was instantly plied with beer by Stavros—an odd-job man wielding a garden hose. I didn't object; I was just glad to be alive.

With a growing sense of history, I continued east. I walked broadly in parallel with the old Via Egnatia—a 1,000 km Roman road that once stretched from modern-day Durrës on Albania's Adriatic coast to Istanbul on the Bosphorus. Caesar and his arch rival, Pompey, both marched this way during the final battles of the Roman Republic. Armies of the First Crusade did likewise, massing at Constantinople in a blaze of banners. St Paul had also trodden the Egnatia. He'd arrived by boat at Kavala (then called Neapolis) during his second missionary journey. That we were moving in opposite directions didn't dampen the excitement:

> Setting sail therefore from Troas, we made a straight course to Samothrace, and the day following to Neapolis.
>
> —Acts 16:11

From there Paul journeyed westward toward Thessaloniki in the company of Timothy and Silas:

> Now when they had passed through Amphipolis and Apollonia, they came to Thessalonica, where there was a Jewish synagogue.
>
> —Acts 17:1

Two thousand years stood between us, Paul travelling one way and myself the other. Could Christian fellowship span space and time? The hairs on my neck began to rise. For a few precious days in July, I was convinced it could.

These new feelings carried me first northeast to the town of Langadas. The main hotel is actually a spa and, in deference to the obvious marketing possibilities, could bear no other name than 'Alexander the Great'. Although five-star luxury was well beyond my budget, I quickly found another Good Samaritan. A German-speaking shopkeeper took pity and led me to a place more in keeping with dwindling resources. An ice cream cone was thrown in for free. Once again, I felt humility bite.

Oh God, do you see the goodness of these women? Will you make me worthy of their gifts?

As I wandered on through acres of withered straw it wasn't often I had something to cheer about. Above the roaring motorway serrated mountains loom and scratch, washing the sky in a sickly greenish haze. Olive groves neatly grid reddish-brown dirt. Little tortoises frequently blunder onto the road in search of interesting things to eat. I'd like animal charities the world over to know I must have saved dozens from instant death.

When civilisation reforms it arrives in small villages such as Kohilko, Analipsi and Mikri Volvi. Kerbs are high and edged with whitewash. Church domes the colour of sky-blue marbles bubble up beneath the sun. Because of the crippling heat nothing much happens, but when it does it's often memorable. At one petrol station I was invited to sit with the staff on the forecourt.

Some inquisitive customers joined us, and within minutes eight total strangers were jabbing fingers at dog-eared maps. As I rose to leave, a spontaneous collection occurred. 'For a hotel or nice meal in a restaurant,' said one. I gratefully took 30 euros from his hand. And the feeling bit even deeper.

Oh God, will you make me worthy of their gifts?

In great toil were those days lost. Chilly dawns brought goose-flesh to naked arms. Sunsets died in a ball of sparking rose fire. What lay in between was my shadow on the ground, dancing its way toward Jerusalem. Sleep came uneasily among the olive groves. I sought rest among the wild things of the Earth, among crickets and rasping grasshoppers, and sleepy tortoises looking up at my unshaven face with the eyes of newborns. These sweet innocents, I thought, no great deeds were being asked of them. They have no promises to keep.

Food-wise, I survived on tins of sweetcorn and pasta, and hospitality from smiling bow-tied waiters. Yet despite these gifts all was far from well. Fatigued by lack of sleep and rendered almost comatose by mind-boggling heat, I could feel the motivation ebbing from my soul. The thought struck like a dagger.

Without the will to go on, how can I succeed? How can I keep the promises I've made and complete my walk to Jerusalem?

Devoid of answers, I plodded on. Days melted together into a stupefying blur: tins of pasta eaten humbly by the reeds of Lake Volvi; six-wheeled tankers pumping poisonous exhaust among speckled green mountains; sapphire swells falling against orange beaches; milky-white pebbles rubbed smooth by the power of the ocean and the hypnotic rhythms of crashing surf. I like to think I picked up St Paul's route again by the four-metre-high Lion of Amphipolis—a stone statue sitting on its haunches with a lavish mane like a judge's wig. I collapsed onto a pile of nearby dirt. In feathered shade I prayed for the apostle's strength.

I stuck to my task, nailing myself to the road east and whatever it might bring. It brought eighteen-hour days of savage heat, enfeebling fatigue and, in the empty villages at least, a growing sense of isolation. Though I'd never contemplated walking with someone else, the advantages were obvious: greater security, shared decision-making, emotional support at critical moments. Companionship would have been priceless. Yet I carried no trace of regret. Travelling with another would have radically changed the dynamics of the journey. With my shadow alone falling on the ground, I grew to rely on God. And the God of Jerusalem grew closer as each day died, even as each was born anew.

It was shortly after Kavala that I finally took the plunge. The sea was maddeningly close; I could hear the waves crashing onto the pebbled shore just beyond the trees. When dusk fell I hacked my way through the thick vines strangling the beach, stripped off and sat naked among the shallows. The water was warm and soothing, the current strong; each wave nearly bowled me over.

I didn't care. I'd walked thousands of kilometres to bathe in the Aegean. I was a pilgrim walking to Jerusalem. And at the beginning of my days or the fragile, desperate end, keeping to that promise was *still* the only thing that mattered.

✳ ✳ ✳

Toward the end of the first week of August I gathered faltering strength and began my final push through the last big towns to the Turkish border at Kipoi. Having battled with giant tarantulas in subterranean showers, by the time I hit the outskirts of Xanthi I thought I'd seen the lot. I was wrong. On 4 August 2007, two amazing things happened:

1. Rain began to fall in Greece.
2. I developed an inexplicable interest in the music of Neil Diamond.

I don't know which caused the greater shock or, for that matter, the greater joy. Initially, it was probably the rain. A good downpour is extremely rare in these parts, and since water is great for cooling the air, it's well worth praying for. As for the strange

Neil Diamond craze, I attribute that to YouTube and the remarkable ability of music to lift the mood. Bizarre though it seems, watching Neil relentlessly growl out *Sweet Caroline* offered rare moments of happiness. The Turkish border and its huge uncertainties stood barely 140 km away. I figured I deserved some.

From the miracle of that first rain it took five days to tick off the remaining towns. I remember Komotini for its unnaturally large number of melon stalls and a pair of orange flip-flops I bought on a whim to appease sweltering feet. Wearing my new apparel I took to flaunting my blackened toenails and from then on always resented wearing boots. I found Alexandroupoli on the coast a fraction cooler. Hordes of blubbery Germans seemed to be the main guests, so in keeping with holiday legend getting hold of a sun-lounger after 6 a.m. proved impossible. The last outpost of Greek-dom was a small place called Feres. On arrival I found the entire town in the middle of a UNESCO world monument dig. (Either that or they were relaying the pavement. Like I said, it's almost impossible to tell in Greece.) Down to my last fifty cents, I stumbled past great heaps of earth towards a branch of the national bank. Aghast, I found it closed.

'Don't be so foolish,' she said. A studious-looking woman with horn-rimmed spectacles was watching from a particularly impressive mound.

What? Me?

Ms Studious waved a trowel at the glass. 'Just swipe your card across the door.'

After giving me a disapproving look, she turned away to carry on digging. She wasn't the only one. Children were digging with tiny spades. Skeletal tabby cats were digging. Slobbering Labradors were howling at the sky and frantically pawing the earth. Flailing trowels were everywhere. A fat bloke wearing a yellow sash caught my eye. He was trapped inside a taped-off crater digging his way to a massive heart attack. Crikey, I thought, is that the mayor? The whole town's gone mad.

I zipped open my travel pouch and with minor prayers began

to rifle. Assisted by a well-aimed Visa card, I'm pleased to report the door of the bank did spring open eventually.

Throughout these final days it was the plethora of gifts that kept me going. Orthodox priests were strangely elusive, but in their stead the common folk stepped forward, offering bananas, nectarines, free drinks and odd bits of cash. I accepted the lot, believing God would reward them in the hereafter. The most interesting gift materialised in Selero behind the trunk of a palm tree. A pair of darting eyes stepped out clutching a broom, muttered some unintelligible Greek and before I could flee, launched straight into blitzkrieg German. When I failed to respond they looked at me, puzzled.

'*Sind Sie Deutscher?*' A chubby finger pointed at my German-made Schöffel shorts. The guy was portly, snowy-haired and wearing a floral beach shirt so garish it would have been illegal even in Hawaii. Only the jasmine-blossom garland was missing.

I rubbed my sleeve across my sweaty forehead and grinned at him. '*Nein, Ich bin Engländer.*'

'Ahhh.' The old man leant on his broom and grinned back. '*Kaffee?*'

It was at least forty degrees in the shade. I didn't need much convincing.

Accepting hospitality is one of the more pleasurable aspects of pilgrimage. Stopping to eat this innocent out of house and home was indeed the right decision. I spent a pleasant half hour under a garage overhang, drinking coffee and eating an entire packet of mint humbugs. The sweets belonged to Efendi, a married man the wrong side of sixty with a house and wife in Düsseldorf. In between the usual questions, I found myself wondering about his name. It sounded Arabic, but his pale skin didn't suggest Arabic roots. I was still pondering the subject when he startled me by breaking into near-perfect English.

'You perhaps have a stick for walking?' He unfolded his arms and looked across at me earnestly.

I shook my head and stifled a chuckle. 'No, I don't.'

Efendi slapped hands on legs, excused himself and disappeared into the adjacent kitchen. I unwrapped another humbug, grateful for the opportunity to plunder. Minutes passed. What was the old fellow doing? I'm not sure whether my first response was joy or cleverly concealed horror. A fragile smile can hide many feelings . . .

'Here—' he said, stretching out an arm. 'This is for you!'

Mouth agape, I leant across the table and plucked the gift out of his palm. It was a length of mottled wood, light in the hand, about five feet long.

'Look at the top,' he told me.

I traced my finger along the shaft. On the thinner end the name 'Efendi' had been printed in neat blue letters. A smile started to play across my lips. I stood up manfully, gripping the staff, ready to part the Red Sea.

'Haha! I knew it!' said Efendi, and slapped me hard on the back. My legs almost buckled. 'I knew you were a real pilgrim, a real *deutsche Pilger!* Come here. Sit. Let us celebrate and talk of your journey to Jerusalem.'

Despite his enthusiasm, I wasn't entirely convinced. In England anyone with a walking stick is probably over eighty and has an oak casket on permanent standby. Nonetheless, I was too polite to refuse. As I trotted back to the road I must have cut a strange figure. With my bronzed skin, growing beard and a diet verging on the monastic, I was slowly turning into the kind of Old Testament prophet not seen since the days of Moses. If a cloud of locusts had flown by, I doubt I would have been surprised.

The last days ground on. I ate cold pizza on lonely hills. I met a Bulgarian woman with gold teeth. I saw illegal immigrants in twos and threes striding across straw fields with black shoulder bags. On the road more trucks appeared, transporting soldiers east to meet the threat of the great adversary. Turkey gradually approached: big, intimidating, alien—the mysterious yet alluring 'other'. With Efendi windmilling in my hands, I spent much of that final week thinking about it. Having never been there I pictured the usual stereotypes: belly dancers with swivelling hips, old men with drugged eyes sucking on silver hookah pipes. Everyone wore a crimson fez. (I was more convinced of that than anything else.) Yet as the border grew closer, darker thoughts began to encroach. Anxiety found voice in four simple words:

What would Turkey bring?

The very landscape begged the question. The Christianity of St Paul was waning and Islam gaining strength, Europe receding like a much-loved distant shore and Asia rushing forward, eager to embrace. Gone for good were the pretty plaster shrines that had festooned the plains of northern Greece. 'You're not alone!' they had cried, and I believed them. True enough, Christianity still reigned in the towns; but outside in villages of twenty cottages, near deep gullies swimming with turtles, within earshot of a herd of floppy-eared goats, it was the minaret that stabbed upward, and at night, alone among the grass, it was the muezzin that called the faithful to prayer.

I slept uneasily. Church bells stayed silent. And the question remained unanswered:

What would Turkey bring?

As I continued to pound the roads of Western Thrace, every day I saw more minarets stabbing the sky. So many blossomed among the hills I began to wonder if the Turks hadn't quietly annexed the country. Where are all the churches? I wondered. Where are the shrines? Suddenly, I saw myself plodding across Turkey with no church doors to knock on—a worrying prospect and not one I relished. Under the shade of an olive tree, I pulled out my diary and began to scribble:

1 Christian + 1,500 (km on foot) + frighteningly large country + 70 million Muslims + (history of Muslim vs Christian violence) – church support = disaster

The spiritual equation made for uneasy reading. I was heading towards a country so vast I could use the map as a duvet—and a double at that. Get a grip! I told myself. It can't be that bad! I staggered on, unconvinced. Each day church bells fell silent, the voice of Muhammad grew louder, and that of Christ, once a mighty roar, dwindled into a pitiful whisper. 'Don't forget me in the east,' he said. 'Don't forget what my Father and I have done for you.'

If I needed further fuel for growing fears, I found it at Sapes whilst waiting for another elusive Orthodox priest to show up. The silver-haired gentleman handed me a cup of coffee.

'So, you are going to Turkey?'

I took it from his trembling hand. 'Yep, if all goes well I'll be leaving Greece in a few days' time.'

'Where?'

'At Kipoi.'

The old gentleman frowned grumpily and pointed at my wrist. 'Then you should hide that cross.'

His waspish comment wasn't entirely unexpected. If you take minor geographical and historical liberties, the country I was about to enter had been fighting the country I was leaving since the Battle of Thermopylae. That was in 480 BC when three hundred Spartans died in a hail of Persian arrows. As for me, having come so far should I now skulk around Turkey like a thief in the night? The words of Matthew 10:32 held the answer:

Everyone therefore who confesses me before men, him I will also confess before my Father in heaven.

I thanked the old man for his advice, but hiding my cross was unthinkable.

At Kipoi I received a shock.

'No walking! No walking here!' The border guard rushed over, wagging his finger at me. I stood rooted to the spot.

Damn! I really wanted to walk. Before I could protest, a lorry pulled up, flapping yards of tarpaulin, and the angry guard frog-marched me straight into the cab. The driver—a whale of a man wearing a shark-tooth necklace and beer-stained vest—grinned at me through broken teeth. He yanked hard on the gear stick. A sudden hiss of exhaust erupted from the rear. Then we rocked and rumbled our way towards the bridge.

The River Evros is not a friendly place. Greeks with machine guns stare at everything that passes. Fifty metres on, groups of stony-faced Turks do the same. At the end of the gauntlet is a drop-down barrier manned by trigger-happy soldiers looking for trouble. They were in luck. On 10 August, they found it. In a moment of near insanity our driver surged to the front in a blatant effort to jump the queue. The eyes of the young soldiers narrowed. Two gun barrels rose in our direction. Only a quick-witted official waving his arms made them back off. The driver threw back his head and laughed throatily. I visibly blanched. I'd never been so frightened.

Finally, and after a severe scolding from at least six officials, we took our place meekly at the back of the queue. There was a terminal off to the left: anonymous, grey, oblong—a passport to the unknown. Was that the way in? I jumped down onto the crunchy gravel, re-shouldered my rucksack and nervously began to tighten straps. Beyond the stern soldiers with their trigger fingers, beyond the grey oblong terminal and its unseen trials, the Europe I grew up in no longer existed. I looked up at the heavens, feeling alone and anxious.

The hero—if he had ever existed—had fled.

Chapter Twelve

Turkey

The Land of Hospitality

I knew long before I jumped off the truck that Turkey was a big country.

It looks a lot bigger close up.

Five minutes after clearing immigration, I was striding down the hard shoulder towards a distant embankment painted gold by feathery corn. On either side of the dual carriageway bisected by T-shaped lights, beyond the fields of shimmering straw and the ubiquitous black-and-yellow Western Union money signs, were the humpback hills of Turkey, hazed blue and seemingly without end. I gripped Efendi tightly and, with hand on brow, squinted hard into the vastness.

Where would I find God here? How would I survive this huge country alone, on foot and without a single friend?

I needn't have worried. 'For everything there is a season,' says the Book of Ecclesiastes. The good book was right. On the long road to Jerusalem I'd found the greatest of them all.

I'd found the season of hospitality.

It was a glorious season, to be sure, and even after months of travel quite unexpected. What united a child's soggy ice cream, an impromptu picnic with smiling teachers, the cheery watermelon vendors between Keşan and Tekirdağ flogging *karpuz*, and about twenty-three glasses of tea, was the most wonderful hospitality anyone could imagine. I felt blessed. My good fortune was so great, even the Russian mafia plied me with food and drink. The oily-haired hitman was right; the 'real salted pork' from Moscow was delicious.

'Would you like to sleep over at my house?' asked the smiling assassin. He cocked his thumb and formed his hand into a mock pistol.

No. But thanks for the pork sandwich.

The heirs of the Ottoman Empire don't own much of Europe these days, but what they do offers a pleasing vista for anyone with nine days to spend on the road to Istanbul. It's a pleasant agricultural country. Watermelons (*karpuz*) are grown in vast numbers. Regiments of sunflowers carpet fields in saffron and burnt orange. There must have been thousands of these giants marching across the plains, like Wyndham's voracious triffids. Buffeted by vicious crosswinds, I huffed my way along miles of undulating tarmac pausing only to gulp water and photograph exquisite fluted minarets. Not even a knee-shattering 6 per cent climb on the approach to Tekirdağ could spoil the idyll. Instead, I reserved most of my curses for the Turkish Army—the nosy *Jandarma*. These young men carry guns and aren't the kind of people you want to mess with. Usually, I apologised meekly for walking on the hard shoulder, and then they would roar away in their jeeps wearing superior grins.

I remember it was around Tekirdağ the road first spun out to the coast. Sea breezes brought gliding gulls and the tang of seaweed. It should have been idyllic: languid swims in the warm waters of the Marmara, followed by camping on the beach. Alas, not. Several million Turks had arrived before me and bought up the entire coastline. The most I saw were razor strips of crystal blue. Maddening would be the polite way of putting it.

Frustrated by miles of gated black railings, I gasped my way around the coastal towns. Every few hundred metres I'd stop to drink another glass of *çay* (tea). Efendi was an absolute superstar.

Anyone who could wield a pen wanted to scribble their name. Soon I had a healthy collection of Turkish swear words (donated by young boys), football teams (mostly Beşiktaş and Fenerbahçe) and messages of support commending me to Allah. One enterprising individual even decided to add the name and telephone number of his hotel.

'You can't fool an old Turk, my friend!' A meaty hand gripping a pen began to wave in my direction. 'I know the good English!'

He did: just not the good English proverbs.

'It's a very bad wind that gathers no moss!'

Erm, quite.

With the gifts I gathered plenty of advice. One grinning café owner ran his hand across his throat. Apparently, some poor soul had fallen asleep in the fields and lost more than his money. On another occasion I was warned about the unhealthy practice of spiking drinks. Clearly discernment would be needed along with the kind of providence associated with massive lottery wins.

Perhaps it was the incredible hospitality, but I was eventually lulled into a false sense of security. Towns continued to come and go, and by 17 August I'd arrived at Büyükçekmece, only a day's walk from Istanbul. I was standing on the hard shoulder, eyes peeled for those annoying *Jandarma*, when a black sedan suddenly skidded across, shooting gravel in all directions. Two men looked speculatively in my direction. The grimacing driver: Neanderthal brow above a granite jaw; his skinny companion in a pink, short sleeve shirt, staring intently with weasel eyes. As I started to edge away Granite Jaw let rip.

'Police!' he yelled. 'Stay where you are!'

Brilliant. What the hell do these guys want? A plastic identity card appeared at the open window. A hand beckoned. I trudged over, glanced for a second at the card, unclipped my rucksack and let it fall into the grass. On the car no markings were visible. Neither man was in uniform. I felt my stomach tighten.

'Passport!' said Granite Jaw, whipping the card away and pushing it roughly into his shirt pocket.

Okay, okay ... My passport was trapped inside my rucksack. I knelt down and began to rummage. Was the driver's identity card genuine? There was no way of knowing. I regained my feet and reluctantly gave him the little maroon book.

'So ...' Granite Jaw began to casually turn the pages. 'Where exactly are you going?'

'I'm heading toward Istanbul.'

'And where have you come from?'

'Greece, just a few days ago.'

'I see,' he said, not bothering to hide his boredom.

I'd begun to think the interview was over when he suddenly pointed at my hand. 'What's in there? Let me see that bag.'

My passport had been inside my travel pouch. Granite Jaw dismissed me with his eyes and immediately unzipped the top. Nimble fingers began to rifle, drifting speculatively over credit cards and Turkish lira, flicking through US dollar bills. 'Where are the drugs?' he yelled. 'Where are the drugs?'

I stood gawping at the window. Drugs? What's this guy on about?

The frantic 'drug bust' continued. His weasel-eyed accomplice kept me occupied with a barrage of official-sounding questions. I never suspected foul play. At least the robbers had a sense of humour. Just before the car sped away, Weasel Eyes looked me squarely in the eye, grinned and cheekily asked, 'Is there anything we can do to help you?'

Yes, there is. Give me my flipping money back ...

An angry pilgrim relieved of 200 US dollars is entitled to let off a little steam. On the side of the D110 something dark and ungodly rose from English lips, then vanished behind a cloud of exhaust. From that moment on I kept my passport in my shorts and my money well out of sight. Lesson well and truly learnt.

✳ ✳ ✳

Although daylight robbery is never fun, after the shock and anger subsided I did discover some compensations. According to official statistics, a total of 23 million tourists visited Turkey that year. Thirteen-and-a-half million of those flew to Istanbul. Two Europeans walked in. Did either of these plodding stalwarts feel any pride? I can't speak for the other guy.

But I did.

You don't easily forget a day like that: oil slicks casting crazy rainbows on the hard shoulder; gleaming six-wheeled petrol tankers, all thunder and burning rubber; scores of canary-yellow taxis honking their horns seemingly for the sheer joy of it. The noise was deafening. Every kilometre another dolmus minibus swooped up to a crowded footbridge. New customers lurked beneath: moustachioed men with glum faces and hands in pockets, little boys scampering about in plastic sandals, flogging water for 0.5 lira a bottle. In huddled knots, Muslim girls stood gossiping in long blue-denim coats—the ankle-length *Jilbab* in deference to their faith.

And then, for one afternoon never to be repeated, there was a thin bloke in mud-stained shorts windmilling a very large stick.

I've got no idea how many pilgrims march across Turkey each year. I doubt the tally moves much beyond single figures. Even if I'm wrong, you can't plod about with a huge rucksack and not draw some funny looks; at each bus stop every eye swivelled in my direction. In the early days I may have felt some embarrassment. Not any more. I plunged straight into the milling crowds, flashing film-star smiles and striding boldly with my stick like an Old Testament prophet from the crinkled pages of Exodus.

'Long trip?' yelled a bobbing head from the throng.

How did he know I was English?

I spun around and without stopping shouted, 'Yes! Very long!'

And it was: 3,500 km long. Even here though, beside the noisy motorway, the marvellous Turkish hospitality never faltered.

'Mister! Mister! Water for you!' A small boy ran up to me gripping a bottle. I took it gladly as his father looked on.

'My friend, are you hungry?' said a portly street vendor twiddling a droopy moustache.

Was he kidding? He handed me a bowl of steaming rice and a pot of *ayran* (salty yoghurt), and I began to spoon it in. The only irritating moment came from the motorist who thought it was cool to overtake on the inside. To the driver who nearly took my legs off near the airport, believe me: it's not. An eventful day's walk finally ended around 7 p.m. Once inside the city suburbs, I hurried along the coast to the district known as Sultanahmet. It's a tourist's paradise full of hotels, hostels, smoky hookah pipe cafés, musicians banging away on bongo drums and, if you're keen on that kind of thing, swivelling belly dancers smiling at you with lustful eyes. Sightseeing is the obvious draw, and after a good night's rest I threw myself into the fray.

It was an exhilarating three days. There are four must-see attractions in Istanbul. I began with Topkapi Palace, the former imperial home of the Ottoman sultans, guarded by gun-toting soldiers and chock-full of fabulous treasure. Better writers than I have described the glittering gilt pavilions, but I stubbornly claim the record for leaving my breath on the largest number of display cases. 'Cor! Look at that one!' Rubies the size of Brazil nuts were winking beneath ostrich plumes. I'd never seen anything like it. For six surreal hours I gawped at emerald-encrusted daggers and priceless Ming vases. A suit of chain-mail armour dripping with gold appeared totally unbeatable. Then I spotted an 86-carat diamond and realised that each new case invariably displayed something more spectacular than the last.

The wow-factor continued in the adjacent Hagia Sophia. Up to 1453 this substantial Byzantine temple of Orthodox Christianity was the finest church in Constantinople. Then Islam came along, and it was converted into a mosque. Decommissioned as a religious institution in the 1930s, nowadays it's nothing more than a very effective money-making machine for the Turkish state. Even so, I heartily recommend the ten-lira entrance fee. In the cavernous upper galleries pensive paintings of Christ in flaky gold paint peer down onto the faithful, and bits of you begin to shiver that you never thought could. From here it's only a

fifteen-minute walk to the famous Grand Bazaar with its labyrinthine covered walkways. Again, it's another must-see, though
the high-pressure selling won't please everyone. All those shiny
trinkets are 200 per cent overpriced (at least). Every third guy
will try to flog you a carpet. Bargaining hard is essential.

I discovered the last of the big four attractions immediately
opposite Hagia Sophia. The Blue Mosque (Turkish: *Sultanahmet
Camii*) wasn't hard to spot. Most tourists were already heading
in the same direction with the same intent. I joined the throng
idling toward the main arch. The first images were almost Babylonian: great chunks of encircling stonework, hanging gardens
of crimson blooms. I glanced up at the sky, and 'jaw-dropping'
just doesn't describe it. The six minarets are of the 'Atlas Rocket'
variety. Triple balconies necklace the four largest, where a keen
eye can spot the speakers that announce the call to prayer. The
mosque's main dome rises in between—a charcoal-grey ribbed
colossus topped by a bulbous golden spire. A series of smaller
domes cascade beneath, opening up onto tiny stone balconies.
Slowly a question began to form. Had the Ottoman sultan ever
stood there in his beehive turban, reviewing his Janissaries or
waving to adoring crowds? It's quite possible. The giddy scent
of those crimson blooms coupled with an August sun is enough
to spark the dullest of imaginations, and I've got a vivid one.

I needed no imagination inside.

This pilgrim is firmly of the view that every Westerner should
visit *Sultanahmet Camii* at least once, if only to get an idea of how
the Divine might make an appearance among 20,000 handmade
tiles. The interior has all the familiar Islamic elements: spidery
Arabic script, golden and deeply mysterious; figures kneeling on
maroon carpets in their ubiquitous pill-shaped hats. Chandeliers
circle just above the head, though thanks to the stained glass
they are barely needed—scores of windows suffuse everyone in
a delicious kaleidoscopic haze. The giant marble pillars sprout
like trees. Fluted to beyond shoulder height, in the upper reaches
they link arms and explode into the mosque's trademark colours.

Among the interlacing arches lilies spring forth, and tulips and bowls of fruit in greens, reds and pretty Persian blue. Later, I discovered the tiling was completed in 1616. Its freshness today is still astonishing.

With camera in hand I spent hours among these marvellous antiquities. Outside the Blue Mosque it wasn't uncommon to see young Muslim men giving away copies of the Qur'an. I picked up an English version, flicked through and decided to keep it. I'd grown curious about Islam. The book, with its canary-yellow jacket, seemed like a good place to learn more.

I spent my final evening gathering information from a hostel computer on Akbiyik Caddesi. I knew the Middle East was fast approaching (about six weeks by rough calculations), and after that I would have to cross Syria on foot. The visa situation was already looking decidedly dodgy. As I stuttered forward on blind faith, the weakness of the plan was obvious:

What if the Syrians didn't play ball? What if they refused to let me enter the country?

For those unfamiliar with the region it wasn't such a stupid question. The politics of the Middle East are notoriously toxic, and it's standard practice for the Syrian authorities to refuse an entry visa to anyone travelling on into Israel. I remember the issue had become frighteningly real for Dutchman Thijs Postma. In 1998 Thijs had started walking to Jerusalem to raise awareness of global warming. Telling the Syrian Embassy in Ankara turned out to be a bad idea. The dream could have ended there, but Thijs was a gambler and determined to succeed. Discarding everything that might link him with Israel, he pressed on to the Turkish-Syrian border at Kassab, bluffed it out like a Mississippi poker player and, after an anxious wait, was finally awarded the legendary visa. I'm reliably informed by the great man himself that he never mentioned Jerusalem once. Good on him.

Less encouraging for me was the World Wide Web. 'A Syrian visa must be obtained before leaving the UK,' trumpeted the Foreign Office website. London was 2,000 km away as the crow flies; I had to laugh at the irony. Desperate for advice, I began trawling the travel websites. Some said I could get one at the border. Many said not. The most irritating posts said 'maybe' and it all depended on who was on duty at the time. Eventually, I realised there was a pecking order, with smaller nations breezing through and those considered hostile (i.e. the USA and the UK) getting special attention. 'Special attention' usually meant long delays or a polite invitation to buzz off. Americans had it worst of all and were sometimes rejected even with a visa. Entry to Syria seemed like a lottery.

I switched off the computer and went upstairs to the dorm. I knew what awaited on the streets: the churning crowds seeking spectacle, peppermint tea taken on tasselled couches, clouds of apple-flavoured smoke, and hot coals burning in silver hookah pipes. If I stepped outside, the great mosque would be bathed in colour—blue, green and purple spotlights splashing across the six rocket-like minarets. Slack-jawed tourists would be watching the show. Parents would be lifting children onto their shoulders for a better look. A dozen nationalities would be chattering in a dozen tongues. This was Istanbul at its best. This was a city made for fun.

And yet, had I travelled so far just to be entertained?

I sat down on my bunk and thought of the promises I'd made in twelve countries. I thought of the hospitality I'd taken from countless strangers and tiny hands with hearts like lions. Even if getting a Syrian visa was impossible, I still had to try. I still had to do them justice.

No. On my last evening in Istanbul I did not go outside. This pilgrim stayed in. And somehow, *some way*, I knew I had to get through.

✳ ✳ ✳

From a windy quayside at Beşiktaş it was a short hop across the Bosphorus to Asia. I entered Istanbul on foot. On 22 August, I left it by ferry. One hundred and seventy-one days of European sweat and toil ended in ten minutes and twenty-three seconds. Yes: I timed it. The swiftness of the end seemed less than fitting.

While the journey lasted I sat beside the railings, clutching a 1.3-lira ticket and hugging my rucksack close. Above the choppy waters squawking gulls were dive-bombing the deck in search of scraps. The opposing bank slowly advanced in a thick bluish haze: more Ottoman domes, yellow cranes laddering the sky, red parasols dotting the quayside—Asia appeared terrifying in its ordinariness. I gazed back thoughtfully towards Europe, hearing the steady drone of the engine, feeling my feet shudder on the planks, watching everything that had defined me—school, work, family, and friends—disappear behind V-shaped, frothing surf. Up to that moment I'd always felt more English than European. Now I wasn't so sure.

When jettisoned onto a new continent there's no knowing how you're going to react. For much of that first day I seemed to be afflicted by a strange kind of debilitating uncertainty. Grim-faced and wide-eyed, I wandered through the streets of Üskü-dar and Kadiköy with Efendi thudding gently on the pavement. Confidence fled in the face of hard Asian stares. I also stopped asking for directions, which isn't a great decision when you're carrying a map that only shows the main streets. Surrounded by a million strangers who knew exactly where they were going, I slumped on a wall to chew a circle of simit bread. I guess land-ing in Asia isn't such a big deal if you end up hopelessly lost.

Thankfully, I'd bounced back by the morning. By the grace of God and a string of bus-stop maps I eventually reached Maltepe, checked into a painfully expensive hotel (the suburbs were solid concrete, and there was nowhere to camp), and after about ten cups of coffee finally started to make some serious headway out of Istanbul. I was threading my way past bustling bodies when I spotted a tall man holding a basket standing patiently beside a mossy wall. Conservative pale-charcoal suit, chaste white shirt, unassuming blue tie, and an unnatural cheeriness that seemed to defy all reason: I totally missed the first clue.

'We like the English people,' he said pleasantly. 'Do you want some water?'

The day was a scorcher, and it would have been stupid to say no. I took the proffered bottle with a smile and in between gulps glanced down into the basket. The second clue was the clincher: pictures of godly men and women gazing pensively at unfurling scrolls. Wow, could it really be?

Yes it could: the infamous *Watchtower*.

I've got no idea how many Jehovah's Witnesses live in Turkey. It can't be many. Maybe there's just one lurking by the railway in Kartal and by some quirk of fate I'd been destined to meet him. It's not a question I often ponder. What I do know is that Witnesses in the United Kingdom like to wander door to door to win fresh converts for their particular brand of Christianity. Then the *Watchtower* is invariably to hand, a dreary pamphlet full of sober thoughts and airbrushed faces looking impossibly pious. This guy had stacks of them. Sensing that I was ripe for salvation, he immediately sprang into 'convert mode'.

'Have you heard the good news?' he asked, just as the water ran out.

'What news is that, mate?'

'The news about Jesus Christ of course.'

'I certainly have,' I told him; then tried to imagine myself as a Jehovah-approved servant condemning the moral outrage of golden-bowed Easter eggs. (It was a bit of a struggle.) Eager to move on, I proudly held up Johanna's little string cross, proof certain of my impeccable Christian credentials. Alas, the glittering prize of salvation couldn't be so easily brushed off.

'Yes,' he continued, with a self-righteous smile, 'but are you ready to accept Christ as your Lord?'

Erm . . . I thought I just said that. I only managed to get away when I agreed to 'avoid all base desires' and accept my copy of the *Watchtower* with 'a pure and joyous heart'. One of those commandments proved much harder than the other, but I'm not telling you which.

I walked harder and faster during the next two weeks. The capital—Ankara—grew steadily closer, and in quieter moments I was still obsessing over the Syrian visa, which had started to assume a quality somewhere between myth and legend. I might have thought of nothing else if it hadn't been for the amazing hospitality of those northern towns. Gebze: four glasses of tea, biscuits and a can of fizzy orange. The Pendik Marina: tea plus a chicken dinner with a group of workmen. Körfez: a free hair wash in a barber's shop and a two-kilogramme ashtray shaped like a human skull (tactfully discarded when out of sight of the donor). A cement factory was a particularly unexpected source of nourishment. At dawn a guard came to my tent and politely handed me a breakfast tray. (Three baying dogs had kept me up all night, but you can't have everything.) Of course, not all gifts were edible. Without even trying I picked up two roadmaps, a stack of cloths, baseball hats galore donated by petrol stations with a nose for free advertising, and a neck whistle—great for scaring off bounding dogs just before they attack. One day, I told myself, I would sit down and add it all up. Turkish hospitality would surely total many hundreds of pounds.

As the days fled by I began to deepen my knowledge of this vast country. Its people provided the greatest fascination. Everywhere young women wore long denim coats and headscarves, even at the height of summer. It must have been forty degrees in the shade. I wiped the sweat from my brow with amazement.

The sleepy, dust-blown towns were full of similar novelties. Little boys scurried about carrying glasses of tea on silver trays. The usual recipients were old men running obsidian beads between their fingers. There are a lot of old men in Turkey. They fill the roadside cafés, guzzle tea from dawn to dusk, and point at that picture of President Atatürk hanging, shrine-like, on the wall. I followed a bony finger and gave another appreciative grunt. Small-winged collar, tightly knotted cravat, old-fashioned morning coat: in the mind of Turkish artists, at least, Atatürk is forever doomed to live in the 1920s.

My learning curve continued at a frightening pace. I absorbed every detail and made copious notes:

(ULTRA VITAL NOTE: Turks don't like Greeks, or Kurds, or Armenians!!!) ... Simit bread is carted around on barrows and seeds get stuck in your teeth ... Absolutely no one wears a Fez (except tourists in Istanbul).

merhaba means hello
karpuz is a watermelon
baklava is a nut-filled pastry soaked in syrup
Yunanistan is Greece (but better not to mention—see above)

The road continued to throw up surprises. It was on this leg I met the largest grower of azaleas in Turkey. Inside a steamy hothouse full of purple blooms, I learnt that 20 per cent of Turks are doing well, 80 per cent are not, and that Sakarya was seething with Islamic fundamentalism and had been rocked by a 7.6 earthquake in 1999—thanks Dunder, you're a fine bloke and I'll always be grateful for your help. On another occasion spiritual matters came to the fore. While tucking into rice in a roadside diner, an Arab sheikh turned up and demanded we discuss the Qur'an. Heck. What could I do? The pious sheikh read a passage in guttural Arabic. I took out my English-language version and babbled like a good *Sarfender*. Our waiter translated my stuttering German into Turkish. It was totally crazy, but somehow it all worked. Although I found the local language unfathomable, I was surfing a cultural wave and scribbled everything down:

benim adım Tony = my name is Tony
kavun = melon
hoş geldin = welcome
çok güzel = very beautiful
teşekkür = thank you

From such richness of vocabulary I formed the immortal line:

'Hello. My name is Tony. Your melons are welcome and very beautiful. Thank you.' Scattered well-wishers from Maltepe to Kazan found it surprisingly amusing.

At Düzce I stopped over for a few days to rest and refit. I didn't have any choice. A pair of walking boots will only get you so far before the services of a cobbler become vital. Somehow I managed to find one who in the best traditions of the word 'cobbled' together a new heel. A mountain of glue got me as far as the massive army base in Ankara's suburbs, which is the best one can say about it. While in Düzce I also acquired my first haircut since Munich and, due to the ravages of sun and sweat, a T-shirt from the ten-lira rack. Despite my new top being a tasty little number stamped with '214' and crude orange slogans, it was still Efendi that caught the eye. Dozens thought it would make a very effective bludgeon. They were normally male, barely four feet tall and under ten years old. In the mind of young boys a stick has only one purpose, and it's got nothing to do with walking.

'Here!' yelled the grinning tyke. 'Take that!' and swung Efendi inches from my head. I nimbly dodged the blow and accepted a partially crushed pear as recompense.

Still other fingers resorted to the pen, scribbling names and rude Turkish words that have no place on such a sober journey. Later, it's quite a shock to discover 'Volcano thinks you stink!' The only irritations as I drifted relentlessly towards the capital were the head-to-toe stares of some folk who appeared to be mentally calculating my net worth (mainly to themselves) and the practice of hotel owners to double the price at the sight of a European face. If you've ever been to Turkey, you'll know what I mean ... Other than growing fatigue and the now perennial visa worries, I had little to fret about. Life was kind, and what hospitality came my way, it flowed freely.

I don't want to look like a wet blanket, but the triumph of crossing into Asia never really came, not even in the Turkish capital.

Ignoring my cardinal rule of not entering major cities after sundown, on 5 September I marched straight in, accompanied by screaming traffic and the stationary planes and helicopters of Ankara's big army base. A few of the sentries shouldering rifles shouted a friendly *'Merhaba!'*, which at least made the dark a tad less intimidating.

Dawn brought the immediate challenge of finding new boots. To the guy from the hotel in Kizilay who chaperoned me to a sturdy pair of brown Caterpillars: huge thanks and I'll always be in your debt. This chap was an absolute gem. He even waited in the shop while I tried on every conceivable make and colour. Try getting that kind of service in Europe.

Then, on the third day, the inevitable took place. I offered up an enormous prayer and went hunting for a visa at the Syrian Embassy. The voice behind the metal grille was female and the irritation obvious.

'You must complete this form,' she said fussily, 'and get a letter of recommendation from your embassy.'

I stared at the peeling white paint. Arab eyes stared back, and a sheet of paper was shoved under the grille. From previous research I knew the letter cost £50, a high price for something the British Government could print off for ten pence. I was far from pleased. Then came the nasty coup de grâce.

'If your application is approved, it takes ten days for the visa to come through.'

Err . . . *if* your application is approved? I took the form with a mumbled, 'Thanks.' Later, I decided it sounded more like a strangled gurgle. To be frank, I doubt she cared.

I spent that evening debating the options. The obvious choice was to grab a hotel room for ten days and pray the visa turned up—obvious yes, but also costly and extremely boring. Ankara, for all its importance to the Turks, is not really a tourist's city. I'd already traipsed around Atatürk's Mausoleum, and apart from the Museum of Anatolian Civilisations, there wasn't much else to see. Yet was there any alternative to waiting? If the embassy was to be believed, I would probably get what I wanted. *Probably.* The easy choice was to sit tight. Hard logic really demanded it, and I would have done—except for one small detail.

The heart spoke otherwise.

In the end, I'd always known how this would go. For over 180 days God had stood by me. Together we'd battled our way across Europe and Asia, and faith so brittle at the start had been forged strong as Sheffield steel. Surely, I reasoned, when I needed him most he would stand by me still?

The decision was made. Forsaking the easier path, I would place all my faith in God. I would discard all maps and documentation linking me to Israel and walk to a tiny outpost on Syria's northern border. Like Thijs Postma before me, the brave eco-pilgrim who wanted nothing more than to preserve this beautiful world we all live in, I too would gamble everything and try for that precious visa at Kassab.

For two weeks beneath a waning sun I carried those hopes and dreams toward Tarsus—the birthplace of St Paul—bisecting, as I did, the 180,000 square kilometres of central Anatolia and the vast swathe of nothingness that makes up the agricultural plains. On two of those days I had the good fortune to camp on Tuz Gölü, a large salt lake shimmering like a pool of molten silver. I can still remember that first dusk. I pitched eagerly on the flats, pushing tent pegs into a brown, crunchy surface rather like a freshly baked meringue. There wasn't a rock or stone in sight—a welcome change after so many sleepless nights. Before retiring I stepped outside for a final look at that glittering velvet heaven. How wonderful, then, to be a speck before such beauty. The sky was crisp and clear like a winter's morning, and every star a giant. For what seemed like hours I stood barefoot on the warm salt, feeling it squish between reddened toes, watching yellow light fleck the highway as crosswinds swept from west to east to ruffle hair and test guide ropes so carefully placed. The winds eased off at the rise of the midnight sun, and I slept better than I had in weeks.

Slowly, in small determined steps, the seasons began to turn, bringing me full circle. The middle of September came and went, and quite suddenly my favourite time—autumn—was at hand. Cold mornings followed colder nights, and I found comfort in my fleece, zipping it right up to the neck. The sudden chill came as a surprise, but Turkish farmers knew better. Anatolia's vast wheat fields had already been gathered in, and the yellow stubble lay like sand on every slope and every horizon. Hand against brow, I stood alone, blinking at the vastness.

With Efendi thudding on the hard-shoulder gravel, I hurried south. Small towns fled by, delightful tongue twisters such as Akörençarşak and Şereflikoçhisar. I took what little I needed and moved on. I came to know loneliness well in those days: every ten kilometres a brief word in a petrol station, every twenty another, and a bowl of rice in a diner where I was the only guest. Donkey riders crisscrossed the hazy plains, but they rarely came near the road. Old truck tyres lay shredded by the roadside, cast off and forgotten. Death fed the breeze: rotting donkeys with distended stomachs, shrivelled sheep carcasses, dogs lying sideways, stiff-legged and glassy-eyed. The stench was dreadful. I'm certain my spirits would have crashed if it hadn't been for the steady line of heavy goods vehicles that thundered past. I can't remember a single driver not honking their horn. As they did, I raised Efendi in salute, then the fleeting moment was gone. The comradeship of the road? Yes, it really does exist.

At Pozanti my burden unexpectedly lessened. 'Hallelujah!' I cried to advancing trees. With lips cracked beyond the healing power of any lip balm, I staggered out of my Anatolian 'desert' like a Legionnaire who'd become lost in the dunes. Hunger had depleted my strength; I made straight for the big Shell diner, finding new life in heaps of salad and steaming rice. Once there I found it hard to leave.

Swinging right, the D750 highway dipped and rose, threading

one walker and a dozen cars between broken mountains dark-green with conifer plumes, pines and firs. Skittish grey horses crisscrossed the tarmac, snorting then galloping indignant into the trees. Tamer animals worked the hilly villages: droopy-eared donkeys shouldering huge urns of milk. I patted them gently as smiling owners looked on. For the only time in my life I pitched camp among those splendid heights. Thousands of fir cones littered the soil like unexploded grenades. Pine needles crackled underfoot, spawning rivers of scent. At twilight I inhaled deeply and instantly felt a million times better. Lower down I camped by babbling brooks, basking in the late afternoon sun as dandelion seeds floated by on tepid breezes and rushing water soothed aching feet. I towelled them dry just as the sun disappeared in shards of crimson. Once again, I knew it was good to be alive.

The conifer forests ended abruptly after Çamalan. Those feathered giants of the north, so cool in the morning and fragrant at dusk, retreated into the uncertainty of pilgrim memory. I quickly came to mourn their loss. There's real peace to be found in the wilder places of the Earth. Time to think and reflect. Time to be thankful. Time to plan new adventures, confess to scribbled diaries burgeoning with great fears and greater hopes, and at the howling of the wolf ponder how many shades of red are born at the death of each hard-won day. There's plenty for those that look.

The moon was a giant that night. I sat on a log, coffee in hand, as it hung above me like a tarnished silver dollar. Stars were burning the heavens: smudges of yellow, pulsating orange, soft twinkling white. Sparking comets created at the dawn of time struck the blackness, leaving trails of ghostly blue. On my last night in the forest it occurred to me that I should write these things down. So I did, adding as a footnote: 'Perhaps one day some of this could be turned into a book . . .' The biro dried up, and the thought, like false hope, seemed to die with it.

On the road to Tarsus a new Turkey ran forth, and the great plains of that hazy south beckoned hot and dry as a crunchy hayfield in the week of harvest. I met the challenge with vigour and determination, as I always did. Savaged by the sun, I plodded on between hills sharp with flashing flint and the prickled splendour of purple thistles. All along the hilly ridges clouds fluffed white as goose down drifted in an ocean of powder blue. More than once I looked up in wonder and saw faces of friends appear like magic, then disappear just as quickly. I saw none on the road that day except for one occasion. Two hours out from Tarsus I spotted a black speck bobbing around in the distance. I squinted, hand against brow. Every so often the speck would suddenly halt, drop to its knees and poke at some unseen object lying in the grass. I figured it was a man, probably a poor one, scavenging for goods. With nothing else to do, I lengthened my stride and hurried to catch up.

I was right on both counts. At close quarters the speck became an elderly gentleman, weary eyes dimmed by the struggle for existence, scuffed trainers open at the toe and a black suit once good but now frayed and torn. I was briefly reminded of Charlie Chaplin, but there was no mirth here. He caught my eye and I saw myself and a million others looking back—a fellow traveller with needs, wants, hopes and dreams, and not all of them yet fulfilled. Afternoon shadows were already clipping the hills and Tarsus still 10 km distant. I was on the verge of pressing on when compassion struck. I couldn't leave it there. Not now. Not after receiving so many gifts myself. I reached into my bag and gave him my last bottle of water. In the heavens a thousand angels cheered. The old man downed it in five tremendous gulps. And me? Never before or since have I felt more joy from watching someone drink.

I might have forgotten that moment if not for another brief encounter. A few days later I strolled past another village, and a man of similar age and bearing approached me in the sun. He smiled, muttered a few words in Turkish, then pushed a one-lira coin into my hand. I have no idea what he said, but I took it gratefully. Later that evening I pulled out my New Testament.

As I flipped lazily through the crinkled pages, they fell open on Luke 6:38:

Give, and it will be given to you. For with the same measure you use it will be measured back to you.

Insight struck like lightning. One fine day in September I gave away a bottle of water worth one lira. Not long after I received a gift of equal value. In Heaven, I realised, no act of kindness is ever forgotten. For in this life or the next, you get back what you give out.

✳ ✳ ✳

Abandoning the soft beds of Tarsus for the spiritual rectitude of rock-hard ground, in the last week of September I re-shouldered my rucksack and turned my head towards the capital of Hatay Province—the biblically historic and Christian-friendly Antakya. Once again, I wasn't surprised to find myself following in the footsteps of St Paul. During another of his famed missionary journeys the apostle had visited the city (formerly Syrian Antioch), taking much the same route. His purpose then had been a noble one: to strengthen the faithful and win fresh converts for Christ. Astonishingly, one wash in fifteen days and a rucksack of grubby underwear had recently tempered my enthusiasm for the evangelical life. I'd only one message for the good churches of Antakya: 'I'm a pilgrim. Can you please give me a shower?'

Seven days of hard walking were needed to answer this vital question. With my usual doggedness I ignored another growing blister and powered on in an east–south arc around the exotic-sounding Gulf of Iskenderun. Mehmet was right about Adana: it really was hot. I gratefully left the city with a healthy stash of US dollars to pay for the legendary Syrian visa. All the camping was dreadful: barking dogs, bumpy cornfields, gunshots splitting the night; walking 35 km a day on four hours sleep is not much fun. I had better luck in Dörtyol where I took a two-room suite in a residence for teachers. As I left the town the sound of schoolchildren at play caught my attention. I soon caught theirs.

'*Turist!*' screamed the boy, frantically jabbing the air.

A forest of seven-year-old heads turned to face me. Skipping ropes and footballs were cast off. The playground erupted in a tremendous cheer. Twenty grinning faces stampeded toward the fence, eager to shove their fingers through the gaps. I'm not sure who experienced the greater joy: the yawning pilgrim startled by unexpected superstardom or the massed ranks of saucer eyes. Whatever the answer, the playful energy of the children did a lot to keep me going.

My popularity remained surprisingly high that day. Sometimes there would be long stretches with no one to talk to. At others the whole world was queuing up. An hour from Iskenderun, while slumped beneath a crumbling bus shelter, I spotted a bicycle climbing the hill flying a crimson pennant from the rear. This guy is no Turk, I thought, rising to shake another hand.

Seeing me wave, the bike veered over and a young man in his twenties jumped off: curly blond hair, bookish spectacles, orange T-shirt, grey cargo pants. 'Yesterday I asked the Lord for some-one to pray with,' declared the solemn-faced youth overflowing with the Spirit.

Funny. I bet he never expected a balding forty-three-year-old from the sewerage-ridden coast of *Sarfend-on-Sea*. Truly the Lord works in mysterious ways. Luckily, my tendency to pronounce 'outh' like 'arf' didn't spoil our friendship.

'Andreas, what's wrong with your marf?'

'Marf? What marf?'

I pointed to his swollen lip. 'Your marf, mate, your marf.'

'Ah,' he said, nodding, 'you mean my *mouth*.'

'That's what I just said!' Accents can be so much fun.

It felt good to meet a like-minded individual. Andreas was a charity volunteer from Switzerland pedalling toward Jerusalem. He'd been chased by a bear in some woody part of Romania and sported a swollen lip the size of a truck tyre. Other than that, the young man from Zurich seemed in pretty good shape. As we sat guzzling water I gazed with envy at his massive panniers crammed with kit. His bike was one of those expensive recumbent types where the rider gracefully reclines before crashing into a tree. Andreas shook his head firmly and laughed. 'That's never happened to me!'

Together we trudged slowly toward Iskenderun, dragging his bike up the steep pavements, grateful for the coastal palms and dappled shade. Talk was of home, work, anxious parents and to my surprise—other pilgrims travelling on foot.

'I met Cyril near Izmit,' said Andreas. 'I saw him on the road, a black guy with a big rucksack, and we stopped to talk and he was telling me stuff, about all the stuff he'd done.'

'Did he have a walking stick?'

'Ya, a big stick like yours.'

'Really?' I was gobsmacked.

'Sure. I'm telling you, I saw the guy near Izmit, and I'm one hundred per cent certain he is walking to Jerusalem.'

I paused to think. 'Okay, so you must have seen him in the north. In which case he must be about thirty days behind me. I wonder how far he walks each—'

'He walks quickly like you. He told me he started from Santiago de Compostela.'

Santiago was the famous pilgrimage cathedral in northwestern Spain. 'Blimey,' I muttered, 'this guy must be walking, what? At least eight thousand kilometres?'

'I know,' said Andreas, and rolled his eyes. 'You walkers are a mad lot!'

I laughed. Sometimes I had to agree.

We parted company the following morning. Andreas had a strong preference for the coast ('the nice flat route with lots of beaches,' as he quaintly put it), and I tackled the steep and windy Belen Pass, arriving in Antakya two days later. Spirits were high as I roamed the streets around the River Orontes. The city was full of familiar sights and sounds: minarets spearing the sky, portraits of Atatürk grimacing in his 1920's frock coat, rainbow spice markets assaulting the senses, the melodious call to prayer. The women were the real surprise. With Islamic Syria just over 100 km away, I'd expected an extremely conservative city with a high preponderance of head-to-toe burkas. Boy, I got that wrong. Although many women wore headscarves, a large minority didn't, and quite a few wore skimpy tops and jeans that would have caused a riot in northern towns. Packed to the rafters with Sunni Arabs, Alawite Arabs, Orthodox Christians, Catholics, Protestants (the minister hailed from North Korea, no less), and the odd Armenian shopping for a new broom, the modern Antioch was far more cosmopolitan than I thought.

I had the friendly Korean minister to thank for sending me to 'Peace House'. Promoting world peace is a worthy cause, and in Antakya that noble charge is led by Barbara, a German Catholic nun who likes to sing and play guitar. We first met at her home on Gazipaşa Caddesi. After shoving open a studded-iron door that would have graced a Crusader fortress, I stepped cautiously into a walled garden festooned with Persian rugs and terracotta urns. The minister had promised me a nun in traditional black habit. Instead, I discovered a woman as tall as I was in a practical charcoal tracksuit with auburn hair flowing to the shoulder. I summarised events so far, hoping for a bed plus shower.

Barbara unfolded her arms and, with rocking hips, eased herself off the edge of the table.

'I think I understand . . . and when do you arrive in Jerusalem?'

'That's hard for me to say, but I'm hoping it will be sometime in November.'

With all the disappointments of the past I was half expecting another brush-off, but she merely said, 'Well, we have a spare house that is empty. We have some exchange students from Germany here at the moment, but as a pilgrim you are welcome to stay.'

I mentally sighed with relief. As a pilgrim I was more than happy to.

In retrospect, turning up at Peace House was one of my better decisions. For six lazy October days I embraced the charming old quarter, a confusing maze of gullied alleyways roamed by hungry toddlers in nappies and packs of anorexic cats. Gauntlet-shaped doorknobs were de rigueur, perhaps a nod to the city's Crusader past. All the houses were sheer enchantment. I remember well the thrill of turning the key and shoving open my very own studded-iron door. A horseshoe courtyard beckoned. Swirling leaves, scarlet and gold, teased an idle broom. All around the upper gantry secretive panes of glass peeked shyly beneath bark-brown terracotta tiles and lime-green vines. 'Dorms are on the upper level,' Barbara said to me. I raced upstairs, finding a pair of steel bunks, some diamond-patterned rugs and lattice windows on three sides adorned with lacy drapes. Every floorboard was a different size, and there wasn't a straight line in sight. Its quirkiness appealed. I instantly fell in love.

I wasn't surprised when the feeling grew. At dawn, first rays, warm and welcoming, suffused the room in golden light. The sound of shifting drapes was like the flutter of doves, and in the alleyway below tiny children laughed with the innocence of angels, as a distant piano tinkled chaotically and Schubert's notes fed the breeze. The name of the organisation was fitting. I'd never felt greater peace.

For breakfast I munched on toast and marmalade in the courtyard. Lunch was taken at Barbara's house. At the garden's rear there was a cave-like chapel laid out with wooden stools, peace slogans and a music stand. Every evening at six we gathered for a service, and Barbara would sing while strumming her guitar. Normally, I'd read something absurdly deep by Rumi, a popular Persian mystic who wrote clever parables about cows kicking over their own milk. I must admit, I never did understand them. Word of my triumphant arrival swiftly filtered down the Christian grapevine. Suddenly, every pilgrim within a hundred miles wanted to know me.

'*Mon Dieu!*' he cried. Up tottered a snowy-haired Frenchman with gaping arms. 'Is it true?' he gasped, and before I could get a word out began to kiss my cheeks with frightening passion.

Barbara nodded thoughtfully in my direction, and the ancient Frenchman kept on kissing. Yep, I really was walking all the way to Jerusalem. I found the local press more restrained: no kisses, not even a friendly hug. The *Hatay Kent* got the scoop. We met in Barbara's courtyard around a wooden table sprawling with white china mugs and dog-eared maps. I shook hands politely with a chubby guy in a turquoise V-neck sweater.

He smiled at me and said, 'I'm Tamer, the journalist.' Then he flicked on a tape recorder, and the friendly interrogation began.

'Why are you walking to Jerusalem?'

'How far do you walk each day?'

'When do you expect to arrive?'

I stuttered on, wondering if the answers made any sense. His final question caught me by surprise.

'Okay, that's great,' he continued, jotting copious notes despite the recorder, 'and now, do you have a message for our readers?'

I wasn't sure I did. Instead, I mumbled a few weighty words about the need for peace in Jerusalem, and then the recorder was promptly switched off. As they say in the business: it was a wrap. Afterwards, came the photos. While I remained seated, Tamer handed me an old copy of the *Hatay Kent*. Apparently, thanks to the blessing of divine forces I could now read Turkish . . .

A mischievous grin started to play across his face. 'Oh, don't worry about that,' he said. 'It's just for show, and our readers will never know.'

Clever journalists. They seldom let truth stand in the way of a good story. Other pictures followed: me gazing pensively at a smudgy map of Syria, group shots with Tamer and Barbara. The iconic shot was taken in the street outside. We must have spent at least twenty minutes trying to capture me in full flow with my stick and rucksack while waiting for a freak gust of wind to open a Turkish flag dangling from a pole. When the photos were finally in the bag we returned to the table. In a few days' time I would be attempting to bluff my way into Syria. Could the paper delay publication?

'No problem!' said Tamer, shooting me another of those mischievous grins.

I had no idea if the Syrian guards read the *Hatay Kent*, but it seemed wise to play it safe. If they knew I was heading to Jerusalem, they would never let me in.

For the rest of that week I remained a guest at Peace House. I idled away the time chatting to the German foreign exchange students, roaming the vibrant bazaar and generally enjoying life behind a studded-iron door replete with gauntlet-shaped doorknob. Then, on the morning of 8 October, I finally bit the bullet and struck south toward Yayladağı, the southernmost town in Turkey. Naturally, there were a few minor irritations to get the blood up. After Harbiye I discovered the main road was closed for repairs, and I spent an interesting fifteen minutes up to my ankles in shifting gravel chased by a madman on a donkey. I do love animals, but I was quite chuffed when the beast collapsed from exhaustion.

Once back on unyielding tarmac I quickly encountered my old nemesis: lack of water. Inspired by some dubious Montenegrin survival skills, I plucked a discarded water bottle from the roadside and drank. Then I wished I hadn't. I powered on with all the intelligence of a clockwork robot. Yayladağı stood in the valley below, a green and dirty-white checkerboard sprawling beneath hazy hills. I meant to get there, and no one was going to stop me. Well, no one except the nosy Turkish Army.

First, I pleaded: 'Yayladağı?'

Then, I begged: 'Yayladağı . . .'

Finally, I shouted: 'Yayladağı!'

A quartet of puzzled faces sat inside the jeep. Don't these guys know their own country? I asked myself. Suddenly, I had a light-bulb moment. 'Suriye!' I cried, and started jabbing frantically at the south. Inside the heads of four unwilling conscripts from small-town Turkey, the light finally came on . . . 'Ah, Suriye!'

At last free of the meddlesome army, I descended the final hill accompanied by a cost-conscious motorcyclist freewheeling in tepid sun. Once in town, finding lodgings was the top priority. By now I'd been interrogating innocent bystanders for months. This crumbling dustbowl in the middle of nowhere would be no problem at all.

'Oh, Oh,' stammered the driver, with rabbit-in-the-headlights eyes, 'try over there.'

Cheers, mate. I will. 'Over there' was a pretty pink building that turned out to be another residence for teachers. Twenty-five lira bought me a tiny room bounded by motorway corridors and a referential portrait of Atatürk the size of a garage door. Great. Job done.

After a brief nap I ventured outside to gather supplies and get a final look at everything I was leaving behind. Anyone coming to Yayladağı should try the apples. They're firm, vivid green and ridiculously sweet; the best I've ever tried. As it was still early afternoon the locals were out in force. On dust-blown pavements schoolgirls clutching books were returning home in their navy-blue dresses and white knee-length socks. Hordes of old men in coal-black blazers and pill-shaped hats meandered about, gazing up and blinking in the sun like lost Grecian tortoises. At some point the call to prayer shattered the skies, reminding me that St Paul's efforts in this part of the world had ultimately been in vain. This was their town, their country, *their faith*. Yet again, I was just a stranger passing through.

On 10 October 2007, I trudged the last few kilometres to the Syrian border. It was my birthday. I was forty-four years old.

The climax of a 1,500 km march across Turkey lay in the balance and more than that, the fate of my pilgrimage. The previous evening I'd sunk to my knees promising the Almighty endless devotion. As the words poured out I'd meant every word—the desperate always do. Would God, I reasoned, bring a man so far only to let him fail at the last hurdle? It was the question of the hour. It was the only question that mattered.

In the great forests that clothe the border an answer was now imminent. Life, the impassive witness to the demise of empires and kings, continued oblivious to the impending drama. Birds twittered. Grasshoppers sang. Surging winds whooshed through the upper pines, sending them into a Mexican wave. As Syrian immigration approached I felt apprehension bite. 'If I saw you with that enormous walking stick,' Andreas had laughingly told me, 'I'd immediately think this guy is a pilgrim walking to Jerusalem.' The recollection sent a shiver up the spine.

For all its mythical connotations, Kassab's small immigration compound was entirely ordinary. Black padded benches occupied both left and rear. Directly ahead, two soldiers in khaki bobbed about behind a waist-high counter, tapping ponderously on keyboards. Just right of the entrance stood an office of grey-paned glass where a muffled phone was trilling. With a mouth like sandpaper, I strode forward unconvincingly. The voice of doubt was a mocking sneer, 'Perhaps you should have waited in Ankara for your visa?' Perhaps you should shut up!

I dropped my rucksack to the floor and leant my stick gently against the counter. Slowly a mop of black hair began to rise. This was the moment. The coin was in the air, the die had been cast, the roulette wheel was spinning and could no longer be stopped.

'Yes?' the guy said.

Chapter Thirteen

Syria

The Land of the Unfinished House

When I began descending stoically over rainy holes in Western Europe I never dreamt I'd have to blag my way into the Syrian Arab Republic. It's not the kind of thing you anticipate when you're at home stuffing a rucksack with random junk. But there I was, freshly shaved, wearing my cleanest clothes, gripping my EU passport white-knuckle tight and hoping my birthday would somehow win me favour with the authorities. My do-or-die bid to get my grubby hands on a 100 per cent genuine Syrian visa began around 8:30 a.m., local time. It began badly.

'Big problem, Mister,' he muttered glumly. *Tap-tap-tap, tappity-tap-tap.* 'Big, big, visa problem. We have here very big problem for you.'

The guard on the left had the shoulders of a Rwandan gorilla. He'd dismissed me with his eyes a few seconds ago and was tapping laboriously on a keyboard. I fell back into defiant silence. I'd lugged a 30 lb rucksack across twelve countries to reach this counter. No way was I going back to Ankara. Not today.

The second chap was shorter, with yellow braid on his epaulettes. So far he'd ignored me. I coughed politely, 'Excuse me.'

Arab eyes slowly rose and threw me a head-to-chest appraising look.

'As I just said to your colleague, I'm sorry I don't have a visa. I'm an Englishman travelling to Jordan. Today is my birthday, wouldn't it be a wonderful gift from your country to mine if you could—'

The guard looked at me oddly. 'Mister, do you actually have a passport?'

'Sure. I mean, of course. I've got my passport here—' I slid it quickly onto the counter before he could change his mind. 'And I've brought these American dollars to pay for my visa, here at Kassab. I hope it will be enough.'

Yeah, like it could be otherwise. Three hundred dollars in tens, twenties and fifties sat in a springy stack. I hate to give Dave any credit, but that travel superman from the bizarre youth hostel in Skopje was right.

The guard's eyes never left the money.

I'm not the first desperate tourist to oil the wheels of Syrian immigration, and this side of the second coming I won't be the last. Stuffing my passport with wads of cash would have been far too brazen, so I simply let it sit on the counter and waited for a response. I was starting to think I might have made a mistake when he said, 'Okay, Mister. You want a visa?' I nodded eagerly, eyes all glassy and intense. 'Then you must wait while we send a fax to Damascus.'

That's more like it. I'd learnt from various travel blogs that when they start blabbing about faxing Damascus a visa normally follows.

'It could take many hours,' he added, pointing at the padded benches. 'Take a seat and we'll call you.'

Fine. I would have camped outside for an entire week if necessary. I scooped up the money, pulled my English Qur'an from the depths of my rucksack and slumped with renewed hope on a bench. I'd barely hit page three before I found myself in the Mother of all Visa Battles with the centre manager—Saddam Hussein's toad-like twin. Marvellous. So much for that wretched fax.

For twenty minutes the battle raged. Thick moustache, oily skin, flapping jowls: Saddam didn't seem very pleased to see me. Nor for that matter did his interpreter, a sly, silver-haired fox with a smile like a cut-throat razor; a joke here would have been rarer than an Iraqi weapon of mass destruction. While Saddam puffed heavily on a long cigar, the interpreter reclined on a sofa and I stood rigid before both, nervously clutching my Qur'an. I watched Saddam's eyes travel across its yellow cover. Yes, I thought, let him wonder. Why did this Englishman have a copy of the Qur'an? Was he a Muslim? It never hurts to sow confusion in the mind of the enemy. The interpreter quickly cleared his throat.

'What is the purpose of your visit to Syria?' he asked.

'I'm travelling to Jordan, and after that I intend to visit Petra, the ancient city in the desert.' (A good cover story, I thought.)

'I see, and how long do you intend to stay in Syria?'

'I'd like to stay as long as my visa allows.'

'Okay, and what please is your profession?'

I had some trouble with this one. Somehow the interpreter misunderstood, and from being a charity worker raising money for young people with mental health issues, I became a junior doctor complete with stethoscope. I didn't have the patience to put them straight. The killer question was thrown in at the end. Since conventional methods had failed to unnerve me, Saddam finally reached for the nuclear option. I guess it just runs in the family . . .

'Now, tell us please.' The interpreter narrowed his silver eye-brows. 'Are you travelling to Israel?'

The sly old fox edged forward in his seat. I turned back to face Saddam who was puffing excitedly on his monstrous cigar. There was only one right answer, and every Joe from here to Timbuktu knew it. My response was a poker-faced, emphatic 'no'.

The tension eased considerably after that. Saddam slumped back in his big-boss black-leather armchair. Turning to his inter-preter, he muttered something guttural, took another lengthy drag on that huge Cuban and, with a final calculating stare with those toady eyes, dismissed me in a bluish haze. At the door the interpreter caught up. 'I think it will be okay,' he told me, suddenly finding a smile. He was right: it was. Ten minutes later I was striding briskly toward Latakia. At $52 I'd probably overpaid, but I didn't give a damn. The whole process had taken less than thirty minutes, surely a record for any Briton.

In the quiet corridor of trees that led away from the compound relief turned to joy and then to the prophetic words of 1 Samuel 2:30:

Those who honour me I will honour.

They seemed written for this very moment. Strict immigration rules demanded I apply for my Syrian visa in the UK. I didn't. Later, I should have spent ten days burning up cash in Ankara's hotels. I didn't do that, either. When the moment came I put all my faith in God, believing he would honour the 5,000 km beaten out with size nine boots. Are those that honour God remembered? Had that incredible gamble been worth the risk?

At Kassab I had the courage to throw a coin in the air, watch God catch it in mid-air, and then slam it down heads up.

I'll let you decide.

✳ ✳ ✳

Despite the jubilation that accompanies such a mighty victory, wringing a visa out of the authorities was not the end of my Syrian adventure—merely the next step to greater wisdom. Of all the lessons I learnt that first day the most important was to ignore my own xenophobic press. Only six years earlier Muslim jihadists had crashed planes into New York's Twin Towers, killing thousands. Hadn't one of the hijackers come from Syria? An hour after talking my way into the country the euphoria had all but evaporated. Flag-burning extremists lurked behind every tree. I mean, these Arabs were all terrorists, weren't they?

'You are welcome in Syria!' cried a crinkled old grocer, as he backslapped me into a chair.

Well, not exactly; and with that slanderous accusation quickly went a bunch of other long-cherished myths. There was no desert to gawp at. No crescent sand dunes. No French Legionnaires in the famous *Képi Blanc* firing at the revolting Berber from white-washed forts. Worst of all, there wasn't a cud-chewing camel in sight. I knew what I was expecting, and this wasn't it.

'You are welcome in Syria!' declared my host's giggling daughters, as well as two bemused women sorting oranges and Mrs Bashir who'd seen a frightful commotion in the grocer's shop and rushed over to see what was going on. They were right. The forest was thick with friendly Armenians, Christians like myself, flogging fruit and vegetables in the wooded valley that feathers the northwestern coast. A few spoke English, others French—a legacy from the country's colonial past. Linguistically, *le français* wasn't my strongest suit, but I gamely persevered, dragging out from the depths of my childhood *qui, non, merci,* and what must be every schoolboy's favourite: *'Ouvrez la fenêtre!'* (For anyone under sixteen the French command to fling open a window has almost legendary status. Once learnt it's never quite forgotten.) As well as being grossly overfed by elderly grocers, I was digging deep into the ethnicity of my sand-less, camel-less Syria.

Another crinkled face began to ease my shoulders into a chair. 'There are many Alawite Arabs here,' he said, smiling pleasantly and handing me a bunch of purple grapes.

'Eh? Are you sure?' I quickly scanned the reddening pomegranate trees, hoping to catch a glimpse of such an elusive creature. I had no idea what an Alawite Arab looked like, or how he/she/it differed from any other, but to an ignorant Englishman it all sounded incredibly cool.

For the rest of that day I continued down the swerving road toward the port city of Latakia. The fertile valley delivered much that would never be seen in England. Beneath succulent green leaves clumps of oranges waited to be plucked. The ripening fruit of the pomegranate tree did likewise, dotting wrought-iron bal-conies in pinkish red. Although I don't care for them myself, in Arab lands pomegranates are highly prized for their taste, and in autumn the stepped hills are teeming with them. As for the local housing, I found some of it distinctly odd. Without doors, windows or roofs, these ugly constructions reminded me of a Spanish off-plan build that's run out of money. Quite a few that seemed otherwise complete still had the steel supporting rods poking up through the concrete columns. The sight of these un-finished eyesores irritated my Anglo-Saxon desire for order. An unsuspecting German might have been outraged.

I'm not sure when the hospitality began to dry up, but it must have coincided with the gathering gloom. An hour before dusk I thought I'd finally run out of company when on a grassy bend I spotted a skinny purple-shirted youth hammering nails into a wooden shack topped off by a corrugated iron roof. After jok-ingly telling him, 'I've come a long way, and I don't just mean the border', courtesy demanded I fill in the blanks.

'You walked from Europe?' The builder draped his hammer over his shoulder, dropped to the ground and rose holding a jam jar filled with nails. 'Is that possible?'

'It's possible,' I grunted, 'though next time I'm going to take the plane.'

The young builder whistled and broke into a grin. '*Masha'Allah!* Then you truly are a long way from home!'

As he continued to stare at me I gave him a tired smile, feel-ing some of the fatigue lift. When it came to hospitality I could out-sniff a bloodhound. I sensed a new grocer in the making.

'I've got some cans inside,' he said. 'Would you like one?'

Bingo! Unclipping a few chest straps, I cast off fear and bear-hugged my monstrous rucksack straight into a twelve-by-eight swaying shack.

Sitting on tiny stools sipping someone else's cola is not an un-pleasant way to spend an hour. The hospitality was everything I'd come to expect, and then some. By the end of the first can

I'd discovered Mustafa was happily single, eighteen years old, living nearby among the pomegranate trees of Zgreen, and a bull-headed Taurean—the latter implying great skill in all things practical. I looked up at two crooked shelves and in a moment of astonishing clarity realised astrology was total bunkum. By the second can he was in full flow. Intending from an early age to study medicine in Damascus, the stethoscope had been kicked into the long grass when his grocer father had suffered a fatal heart attack. To shore up the family finances he was aiming to make 'big money' selling groceries in very small potting sheds. I couldn't envisage a large clientele.

It was on the third can that the conversation took a surreal turn. I'd been waffling on about camping in Montenegro and the menace of snakes when he said, 'Mister, would you like to see one?' His eyes were dancing with childish glee.

I sat bolt upright. 'What? Do you mean right now?' I was about to change that to an implacable 'no' when he dipped below the table, rummaged in a cardboard box and rose cradling a sizeable plastic bottle. It had been inches from my feet all the time.

Marvellous.

He snickered and shoved the beast even closer.

'Is it dangerous?' I croaked, face white as chalk.

'Mister,' he said, tapping the bottle with pride, 'this snake bites many cats and dogs in our village. They all die in terrible agony.'

I took that as a resounding 'yes'.

Other than the sun-loving viper, there are very few danger-ous beasts roaming England's green and mostly pleasant land. I inched closer, mesmerised by nine inches of silver scaling and a flickering forked tongue. If camping in the forest was perilous, then walking the road was damn near suicidal.

Mustafa grinned evilly. 'Mister, I do not think that is so good for you. This road is very bad at night, very, very bad.'

Ha-ha. Of course, it had to be.

'Bad men in cars drive up and down looking for people to rob.' He ran his hand across his throat to make sure I got the point.

'Yeah,' I countered, 'but what about the police? I mean, they must have patrols and all kinds of—'

'The police?' He rocked back on his stool, slapped his knee and laughed. 'Listen, Mister, the police do not care about foreigners. Sure, if a Syrian dies, if one of our people dies, they will invest-igate. But if a tourist dies they will do nothing.' He shrugged his shoulders. 'That is the way things are in Syria.'

Marvellous. So if the snakes didn't pump me full of poison, the robbers would slash my throat. And the police? They would mark it up as suicide . . .

After draining the third can I decided to leave. It was excellent timing. Talk had swung round to the Israeli-Palestinian conflict, to dubious Western military interventions ('You invade Iraq, many Muslims die, was it for the oil?'), the inhumanity of the Gaza blockade, and suicide bombers in dynamite vests.

'Look here,' he said, lifting his shirt.

I glanced at his skinny ribcage.

'See? No dynamite.'

I shifted uncomfortably, and his voice began to squeak with exasperation.

'Why do you accuse us of terrorism? Why? We become angry in Syria when you make these unjust accusations.'

I nodded vaguely, trapped by my own prejudice. The goodness of the people just didn't compute, nor could it. Like millions of others I'd bayed for Arab blood as the Twin Towers fell and the last phone calls of the victims were replayed on television. The unscripted panic of clattering chairs and trembling voices still haunts. Now I was starting to see the world as it really is. The voice of truth so lost on the coast of Holland, beneath corru-gated iron roared louder than any lion.

It would roar louder still.

I walked on for another hour, eventually finding sanctuary in the house of Momdoh Hrez, a local butcher as broad as he was tall. As twilight fell we gathered on the verandah overlooking the pomegranate trees: mum, dad, one hungry pilgrim with a generous plateful of chips, and three knee-high kids drinking lemonade.

'You are welcome in Syria!' cried five-year-old Della, raising her tiny glass in salute.

Deep shame accompanied every bite. It hit me, then, and that veil of ignorance I'd worn for so long was shredded before my eyes.

I was welcome in Syria.

Not all Syrians were terrorists.

And the hands that beckon in your darkest hour are those you'll always remember.

✳ ✳ ✳

For the remainder of that first week, and up to the following Sunday, I walked south along the coast towards the city of Tartus. It was a smashing time to be on the road. Never once did Syrian hospitality falter. Beaming shopkeepers let me walk out laden with packets of figs, and more than one stranger handed me money. In a typical encounter a man on a corner demanded I accept 200 Syrian pounds (about £4), before letting me walk on. Informed by late-night readings of my Qur'an, I realised the desire of the Muslim was to obey the words of the Prophet, and the teaching was clear:

> They ask you what they should spend, say: 'What you spend out of goodness should go to your family and the relatives and the orphans, and the needy, and the wayfarer. And any good you do, God is fully aware of it.'
>
> —Surah 2: Al Baqarah

Such was the people's generosity there's no denying God had plenty to be aware of. Without being an orphan or relative of the donors I doubt the words could have been more appropriate.

The end of Ramadan further favoured my endeavours. Fasting ended on 12 October that year, and immediately afterward came the feast of Eid when Muslims traditionally celebrate. More gifts followed in frightening abundance. Efendi, always popular with the young, became smothered in Arabic as whole families lined up to sign their name. Babies smiled and laughing toddlers punched the air; genteel housewives in silver headscarves served coffee. I told them the Arabic script was beautiful, and it was. But in truth it was these simple moments of sharing that held the real beauty.

One by one I graced the coastal cities with my hungry, unshaven presence. First up was Latakia, a windy port of waving palm trees and grinning crooks masquerading as tourist-friendly hotel managers. Red and blue containers stamped *China Shipping* and *Maersk* littered the quay like giant Lego bricks. There was no obvious reason to hang about. I blew $30 on a room overlooking a big container ship called *Mighty Michalis*, then promptly marched on to Baniyas. The quintessential Arabian third-world disaster, I remember the city unfondly for its water-stained concrete, looping telephone wires, dead looks of semi-despair and its lone camel, which looked even more dishevelled than I did. I've never seen a more depressing place.

It was just after a tour of Jableh by a three-star general (I moved in exalted circles in those days) that I managed to swap car exhaust for refreshing sea air. On lonely back roads I meandered around stony beaches, dodging squawking seagulls and some surprisingly large cacti. The latter reminded me of those Arizona giants always shown in Hollywood Westerns. A fall here would have been a painful experience and well beyond the remedy of any first-aid kit. Gradually, the great forest gave way to sand. I saw the apple-red pomegranates no longer, but greenhouses by the score for almost to the breakers farmers had made the tomato plant their god. Humid cathedrals of polythene and cane covered every inch of ground. I counted fifty before giving up.

Then I hit the old Crusader city of Tartus, notable in medieval times for being one of the last Templar strongholds. Among zebra-striped pavements I found myself embracing gloriously wide avenues and the novelty of pencil-grey guns silhouetting the Mediterranean. I didn't dare take a photograph (for obvious reasons) but was quite excited to see my first Russian naval base.

I had less luck with the churches. All were bolted shut or surrounded by towers of scaffolding. The happy exception was a walnut-doored cathedral presided over by the bishop himself. A small, rotund fellow in silky white robes and matching skullcap, I watched his mouth twitch into a nervous smile.

'We shall see if we can find a place for you,' he told me.

The olive-skinned ambassadors of Italy and Spain stood beside us and were studying him intently. The old fellow could hardly have said otherwise.

Through the dwindle of those October days, my heart warmed further. In the hospitality of the Syrian people I often saw Turkey looking back. Cups of coffee deputised for Turkish tea, and the greeting *merhaba* was replaced by *marhaba* and a guttural sound hitting the roof of the mouth. I'd like to think I didn't embarrass myself too much in the pronunciation.

I saw much that typified the Middle East. The coins of Syria have no decimal numbers, which poses a particular challenge for those who can't read Arabic. When paying for goods I simply held out my hand, hoping the shopkeepers wouldn't rip me off. I'm pretty sure no one did. Of course, all the women and older girls had their heads covered. But so did many men, favouring the chequered headscarf (or *keffiyeh*) popularised by the late Yasser Arafat. Later on, I found out these simple garments are colour-coded. Red-and-white are worn by Jordanians, black-and-white by Palestinians. In the Levant, where politics is about as explosive as it gets, what you wear on your head speaks volumes.

After Tartus I swung away from the Lebanon. I felt happy with the decision. The British media had drilled into my psyche that Beirut was a fearsome place governed by bearded fanatics where rocket-propelled grenade launchers were de rigueur. Although I'd learnt enough to know that was probably nonsense, I had no great urge to prove the media wrong. In any case, I had Krak des

Chevaliers in sight. As a history buff I couldn't pass up a visit to the famous Crusader castle. With a dozen new signatures on my stick, I swept down into the hilly Wadi al-Nasara—the so-called Valley of the Christians.

And despite one notable exception, I'm glad I made the effort. I found the valley to be an agreeable place. Fertile, not unduly hot, blessed with pomegranate trees, blessed with the cross of Christ—in a land where 90 per cent of the population is Muslim it's rare to find an area where Christians actually make up the majority. Wiping sweat from brow, I meandered across steamy dirt terraces, dodging propeller-shaped cacti lurking on dipping roads and squinting hopefully at sun-bleached Melkite stone. In between the now ritual stick-signings, I discovered the best of Syrian Christendom hidden in the convent at Mashta Azar.

'*Avez-vous faim?*' she asked quietly with upturned eyes. A wrinkled face was peering up at me beneath a nun's black habit.

After two hundred days eating mainly cold food it's a foolish pilgrim that rejects a cooked dinner. A sweet old lady with grey eyes like October skies, Sister Marie-Anne was one of only two nuns in attendance. In another life she would have made a fine granny, the doting kind that knits oversized sweaters at Christmas. In this incarnation she'd devoted herself to the church, and that meant giving me a slap-up meal.

'*Bon, très bon!*' I pushed back the empty bowl and patted my stomach to show appreciation. It was a pleasure to see her smile. Turkish coffee followed in a blue china cup rimmed with gold. I took the cup from her hand, sipping eagerly, feeling the steam tickle my nose, avoiding the gritty sludge that always forms at the bottom. I left bloated with lamb stew and a blessing in lilting French. Yet again, I'd found a Good Samaritan to lean on.

Unfortunately, not all souls in the valley were disposed to helping travellers in need. A few hours later, I found the worst of Christendom beneath the vaulted arches of the Monastery of St George. A tall guy with a lavish beard, ruddy cheeks and coal-black hair that really needed a good brush, he seemed to float towards me in a black overcoat that ran to the ground. With an abundance of rooms and only three monks in residence, surely there would be a place for a pilgrim here?

'Oh, excuse me,' blustered the priest, clutching his chest as if mortally wounded. 'Excuse me, but we do not receive anyone here.'

'Really?' I eyed him squarely. *You do not receive anyone here?*

Cue a stupefied pause while I mentally checked I'd just crossed Europe and Asia Minor on foot only to be brushed off like a cold-caller selling double-glazing. Yes: I had. Wait a moment, I thought, let's get this straight.

You are in the pay of the church . . . and you do not receive anyone here . . . in this enormous monastery . . . with at least twenty rooms?

The guy even refused to offer me a cupful of water. What's wrong with him? I asked myself. If Jesus had asked for shelter, would he have received the same treatment? And if not, why was it acceptable to turn away others? The monk's lack of charity seemed callous and ridiculous in equal measure.

I spent that night in the fields and the next day more happily doing what any tourist in these parts is virtually obliged to do. On the heights above al-Husn sit the hulking ramparts of Krak des Chevaliers. The early Christian Crusaders were quick to see the original castle's potential. When the Knights Hospitaller took control in 1142 they immediately began reworking the site. For 130 years the heavily strengthened fortress provided unprecedented views of the Gap of Homs—the low agricultural plains linking the Mediterranean to Syria's interior. The fort's concentric design, mammoth towers and five-metre-thick outer walls made it almost impregnable. Quartering 2,000 foot-soldiers and providing stables for 1,000 horses, not even the mighty Saladin could breach the defences. With that kind of pedigree a pilgrim might spend hours there. Six to be precise.

'Batteries, Mister?'

I spun around to face a cloud of toxic breath. It was another souvenir vendor, sagging at the knees with throw-out packs of postcards. This guy was at least fifty, wheezing badly and in need of serious dental work.

'Err ... No thanks, mate. I'm fine. Try over there.' A huge blond woman with arms like an ox caught his eye, and he stumbled off in search of a sale.

With hindsight six hours weren't nearly enough. If you can avoid being stalked by wheezing souvenir vendors (which is most of the adult male population of al-Husn), the Krak is everything the guidebooks brag about. Outer ramparts provide the thrill of the dark—a honeycomb of rock-strewn tunnels, arched corridors with cross-slitted windows, and secretive staircases spiralling down into gloomy nothingness. Roosting bats can be seen by anyone with the courage to plunge into total darkness with a flickering head torch. I did, and saw plenty.

The inner fortifications are different again. Dusty courtyards lead to vaulted archways and there are plenty of windy turrets to climb providing skyscraper views. It's strange how height always conveys a sense of power. For one day in October I was Lord of the East, a diminutive checkerboard of russet red and bottle green, and in the distance rolling coffee-hued hills washed with bluish haze, extending beyond even the falcon's eye. The view alone was well worth the entrance fee. I finished a marvellous afternoon in the Princess Tower restaurant dining with a crowd of Japanese. English fish and chips, in Syria, in a nine-hundred-year-old castle once besieged by Saladin himself? I was becoming blasé; the incongruity of the moment completely passed me by.

Whilst the image of crinkled Armenian grocers backslapping astonished tourists into chairs is a charming picture to present in travel brochures, there was a darker side to my Syrian adventure. During those first nine days of travel everyone wanted to know me. Over the next sixteen they still did—but for all the wrong reasons. At the head of this growing queue were the nation's bad men. How do I know?

Because they were right behind me.

The first sign of trouble occurred on the main road at the base of the castle. I was returning to my hotel, mind buzzing with mossy parapets, when I happened to turn and notice the silver bonnet of a car following discreetly behind. At first I thought it was my imagination, but no; every time I stopped, so did the car. Strange. Why would anyone want to follow me? I'd paid for a room that night as I needed to wash some clothes. On TV a female newscaster wearing too much make-up was wittering on about 'Occupied Golan'. After hanging up the third pair of dripping socks, I switched it off and forgot the incident.

I wasn't feeling so calm in the morning. On the highway to Homs I quickly picked up two drivers in a white van creeping stealthily up the hard shoulder. I stopped for a rest; they stopped. I started; they started again. It was no coincidence and all very James Bondish. All I can say is thank God for the roadside trees. Towards the end of the afternoon I grew tired of pursuit and ducked down into their protective embrace. Within seconds I saw two faces above, frantically scanning the forest. I still don't know how I gave them the slip.

The evening brought fresh angst. Usually, I would have been happy to pitch camp. On this occasion a clear line of sight was essential. I slept under the stars, fully dressed, boots on, with the zip of my sleeping bag down in case I had to scramble into battle at a moment's notice. A full moon can light up an object on the ground like a torch. That night there wasn't a trace. I counted myself doubly lucky.

Then, at the entrance to Homs, new faces awaited.

Blimey, I thought. I've done nothing wrong that I know of. Who are these people? What do they want?

The first of the new batch of stalkers was a bearded motor-cyclist wearing a military flak jacket and black goggles. Whatever his orders, they didn't include subterfuge. He brazenly tracked me down the road always staying about twenty metres behind. Seeking some means of escape, I hurried to the other side where trees crowded the pavement. For ten minutes I sat on a broken wall, gulping water and wondering what to do next. Before I could settle on a plan a sleek black sports car pulled up.

Blast! Now what? I glanced across at the red-and-white chequered headscarf, the questioning eyebrows and the thin black moustache shaped like a bow. The driver's razor smile carried all the charm of a cobra. As he looked me dead in the eye I felt my stomach tighten. He raised his hand and gave it a twist in a 'What are you doing?' kind of way. I decided to play dumb.

'Thank you,' I called out, just loud enough for him to hear. 'Thank you.'

I bowed politely, clutching my chest with false deference. Yes, I thought, thank you friend . . . and buzz off. After a while he obviously realised I wasn't going to approach the window. The black sports car rolled forward. *One inch at a time.*

I walked on into the centre of Homs with the motorcyclist in dogged pursuit. Given the sinister nature of these developments I immediately went looking for somewhere safe, which unsurprisingly happened to be the nearest church. Tall and regal with furry eyebrows that seemed to meet just above the nose, Father Harron wore traditional black robes, as all good Jesuits should. On arrival I was given a box-room overlooking a Y-boughed mango tree; at lunch, a steaming bowl of chicken soup. As we dined in the monastery I recounted all the strange events that had occurred since leaving the castle.

'Be aware,' he said evenly, 'that we have many secret police in Syria. They call on us from time to time to see if we have any problems. It is quite normal here. Perhaps,' and he waved his spoon airily about, 'these people are the police working for your protection?' I looked at him stonily, totally unconvinced. 'After all,' he continued, 'it would be bad for the Syrian Government if something happened to you.'

'Yeah,' I conceded, 'I guess that's true. On the other hand, I didn't want to mention this but—'

'Yes?' He looked up from his bowl, and I just spat it out.

'Isn't there a danger of terrorism in Syria?'

He shifted uneasily in his chair. 'Yes, unfortunately it's possible. As a British citizen your value to these people, to terrorists, is very high.'

It was a chilling confession. During 2004 a nasty crowd in neighbouring Iraq known as Tawhid and Jihad had been taking hostages and cutting off heads. Other Islamic groups had been quick to follow their murderous example. Chances of release depended on a peculiar mix of faith (Muslims fared better than Christians), money (millions of dollars in ransom helped) and above all, involvement in the Iraq War (citizens of the invading countries got off worse). According to the only statistics I could find, a kidnapped Briton had a 50 per cent chance of ending up dead. For the only time in my life I wished I'd been born a Muslim to millionaire parents in neutral Switzerland.

In the evening, concerns continued to grow. Seeking reassurance from my own kind, I borrowed a phone from one of the priests. The response of the British Embassy was just plain daft.

'But has anyone tried to attack you?' she asked.

The voice was female, unsympathetic and bored. I envisaged a blonde in pink lipstick, filing her nails.

Has anyone tried to attack me? Of course not! If they had, I would already be dead, or trussed up like a pig and on my way to Iraq! I shook my head with disbelief. As far as the British Government was concerned, I was on my own.

I spent the last night in Homs weighing up the options. Father Harron's advice was well-meant, but it wasn't overly reassuring. The capital—Damascus—lay 165 km to the south. I'd crunched the numbers, and it looked like a six-day march; maybe five if I really pushed it. The risks were obvious: day after day on the open road, alone, with possibly nowhere to hide and no phone to summon help. All I could think about was Ken Bigley. Only three years earlier the civil engineer from Liverpool had been abducted and beheaded in Iraq. That blighted country stood 200 km to the east—less than four hours' drive. It focused the mind.

On 21 October I bade farewell to the safety of the monastery and struck south toward Damascus. The highway running from Homs is a wide, handsome road with a decently sized central reservation overgrown in parts by conifers. On either side strips of forest provide cover for 40 km before eventually thinning in the west to reveal the smudgy coffee and charcoal hues of the Anti-Lebanon Mountains. As helicopters buzz the peaks like angry wasps, so sandy plains with clumps of brittle grass rapidly become the norm. There's not a lot else to see. Here and there, Syria's glorious leader, Bashar al-Assad, waves heroically from blistered billboards. Palestinian Vipers slither about in the dark. (Sleeping under the stars, as I did, it's a miracle I wasn't bitten.) On the road you tend to smell the dead animals long before you see them. While tying a shoelace I spotted a donkey, lying sideways, belly distended with gas. There was a hunting knife embedded in the poor creature's skull. I remembered the look of horror on its face all day.

More drama swiftly followed. The horror might have ended there, but this was the road to Damascus, not Notting Hill. Until I saw the blue road sign to Iraq I was adamant that the shock value of rotting donkey plus embedded knife couldn't be beaten. I was wrong. In a moment of pure surrealism I stood quietly sipping water watching the odd car make the big left-hand turn toward Baghdad. As a Westerner it seemed incredible that anyone would want to. Then I realised the drivers were probably Arabs with relatives or friends to visit. It wasn't so strange. No matter what the death toll, no matter what atrocities take place under this banner or that, life always goes on.

For five days I marched straight down that arid, evil-smelling hinterland. Death was never far away. It lingered in the dust and sweltering air. It waved to me from roadside billboards. It was in the minds of men obeying dubious orders. A little after midday on the second afternoon, the inevitable happened—another motorcyclist appeared and began to trail me down the motorway. On a couple of occasions he sped past, and then the hunted came within inches of the hunter: the same green flak jacket, black goggles, and red-and-yellow tasselled rug slung over the seat. He zipped by as if I didn't exist. I grew to hate the *put-put* sound of four-stroke engines.

Slowly the problems began to build up. Even when I wasn't being followed about (which was most of the time) I avoided the maze-like towns, fearful of what lay within. Consequently, I ate poorly. For nearly a week I survived on two meals from road-side diners supplemented by a glass of tea and an apple from a friendly gardener near al-Qutayfah. Stomach cramps gave me a new appreciation of food. I also had to forego visits to many monasteries, including Mar Sarkis at Maaloula where Melkite Christians continue to speak a dialect of Aramaic—the language of Christ. Mar Musa was another unfortunate casualty. During mid-afternoon I arrived at the outskirts of An-Nabek, a town about 65 km north of Damascus. A second motorcyclist pulled up immediately.

He lifted up his goggles. 'Speak English?' he grunted.

My new inquisitor wore a black leather jacket wearing thin on the arms. I looked at him sourly, hoping he would shove off.

He leant forward onto the handlebars. 'What's your nationality, Mister? Are you alone?'

No comment.

With darting eyes, I pushed on through the town. Beside the central mosque men in headscarves huddled around stone steps. Some were standing, others were sitting; I could feel their eyes drilling my back. In a nearby grocer's shop I stopped for some supplies. Apparently, Mar Musa lay on the heights 15 km up a narrow road. I would have loved to go there, but it seemed like suicide. Instead, I thanked the shopkeeper for a partially melted Twix and trotted back to the relative safety of the main road. A few hours later, I'd just passed the gigantic chalky statue of Hafez al-Assad (the former president of Syria) when I noticed a white van about twenty metres distant and a guy shouldering a huge camcorder filming traffic, filming *me* . . . What the heck?

I came to a halt about six inches from his face. 'Look,' I said sharply. 'What do you want?'

The cameraman was an Arab about my age, a few inches taller, with a ragged grey beard forming a point below the chin. I was trying to decipher the plastic clip badge on his shirt when he dropped the camera to his waist and said, 'Please, my friend, let me explain our intention.'

'Yes,' I growled, arms tightly folded, 'please do.'

The cameraman blinked. 'We are a well-known Slovenian TV company collecting news for Syrian television. We saw you walking along the road and thought—'

'Thought what?'

Before I could react, he leant inside the side door, ditched the camera and began to unravel a microphone. It was one of those black fluffy types used by reporters.

He spun round, 'Please, my friend, calm down. Would you like to make a statement?' The mike was shoved aggressively under my nose, and I instinctively took a step back.

'Do not worry,' he said soothingly, as a female Arab from the open side door began frantically shooting me with a digital camera, 'our news reports are only recorded for a Syrian audience.'

Wow! Great idea! Let's tell everyone I'm walking to Jerusalem (probably an offence requiring immediate arrest, but hey . . .) and in the process invite every terrorist in southern Syria to join me. Then, on the way to Iraq, someone can measure me up for one of those nifty orange jumpsuits. I'd heard enough.

'You must be joking,' I said bluntly. 'I'm not giving you any information. Just go away. I don't have anything to say.' I threw up my hands and, without looking back, stormed off. My life was on the line. I didn't give a damn if he got upset.

In the long days since, I've sometimes wondered whether I misread the situation. After all, a solo pilgrimage is an intense experience, and the stress of constant surveillance can get to anyone. At these times I simply ask myself this question:

How many Slovenian television companies with Arab film

crews are likely to be randomly cruising the Homs-to-Damascus highway looking for news items solely for a Syrian audience?

If you happen to work for Syrian Arab Intelligence and think you might know the answer, please don't write in.

✳ ✳ ✳

Despite the attention of dubious Slovenian TV crews, the secret police, terrorists by the dozen, the odd al-Qaeda operative, and anyone else who had nothing better to do than follow me down the motorway, I did indeed make it to Damascus. Alternatively known as Dimashq and ash-Sham, the city where St Paul had narrowly escaped death by descending in a basket from the Kisan Gate offered a welcome respite from the rigours of the road. At the beginning of another warm evening I marched with deep gratitude into the swanky four-star Damascus International. The manager was a wrinkled fellow in a shiny black waistcoat.

'One person for one night?' He peered at me over his glasses. 'Can you afford seventy-one dollars?'

I hadn't shaved in days, and my Moses-style walking stick was nearly as tall as he was. I could understand why he might have a few doubts.

I ended up staying five days in the Syrian capital. Four-star luxury was well beyond my budget, so for the next few nights I found cheaper lodgings at the Future Tower Hotel. The inhabitants of Damascus were a diverse crew. Every crooked taxi driver is called Suleiman, and they're all on the run from ICC arrest warrants. Outside the posh hotels soldiers gripping AK-47s sit on chairs. I assumed their main function was to deter crime, but if they gunned down a few bearded motorcyclists wearing flak jackets, that was fine by me. It was here I often saw the poorer folk sitting nearby. From wooden crates middle-aged 'shoeshine boys' look up at Europeans in Armani suits and mega-rich Arabs streaming past in their white ankle-length *dishdashas*. Twenty-five Syrian pounds (fifty pence) is all it takes to clean a pair of dirty pilgrim boots. It's amazing what some people live on.

reside here? Many Arab women clearly thought so. I watched several sobbing quietly, heads pressed against the dusty glass. In that peculiar emerald twilight I found only disappointment: no tears and no severed head. Oh, well.

I stayed holed up in the city until the morning of 30 October, then, terrorists or no, bade farewell to the safety of the capital and walked steadily south toward the Jordanian border and the big Syrian transit centre at Nasib. In spite of all the unwelcome attention I'd received since leaving the castle, for the first few days nothing much happened. I dug Efendi into the gravel of the hard shoulder. Dawns grew markedly colder. Dusk descended earlier. The big wheels of life continued to turn—and not only for the seasons. Like the innocent I'd once been, walking slowly beside the windmills and canals of Holland, I lanced blisters and accepted gifts from strangers. Unlike that innocent, never again would I take to the pilgrim road and with gratitude shake their hands. The walls of Old Jerusalem stood little more than a week away—one week to reach the gates I was risking my life to see. Would God himself not greet me on the other side?

I trudged on, hoping for divine inspiration, or at least some of the earthly kind to justify the enormous expense and obliteration of four pairs of walking boots. I didn't get either from the boring view. About 40 km out of Damascus it was all barren farmland—freshly ploughed fields littered with clods of earth shaped like horses' hooves. The landscape seemed more Europe than Middle East. If I ignored the odd Arab boy skipping down the central reservation collecting aluminium cans, I could well have been plodding through any English shire county. I glanced about with the wide eyes of an anxious foreigner. Sometimes I spotted a Bashar al-Assad poster pasted to a column; at others, a bit of familiar greenery. In places the red fruit of the tomato plant were very common. Every few minutes another flatbed truck rattled north laden with wobbling polystyrene crates. I didn't think twice about picking up the strays. For eight months I'd lived the life of a true pilgrim. Survival was in my blood.

Such were the events of the next twenty-four hours I soon had ample opportunity to call upon such resilience. Since leaving Krak des Chevaliers I'd found myself under increasing scrutiny. I'd been stopped twice by Syrian Arab Intelligence, questioned by unidentified individuals on numerous occasions and stalked for days by unknown parties in every conceivable vehicle. The nightmare scenario became dangerously real a few kilometres on from al-Kiswah. It began to grow dark, and I had another motorcyclist tracking me down the highway. I knew I wouldn't be able to shake him off.

What should I do? I asked myself. What *can* I do? I pulled off the hard shoulder and turned left onto open farmland. I had to find a plan—and quickly. A desperate idea began to form. I could pitch my tent in view of the motorcyclist and, when it was fully dark, leave unseen and cross the fields to safety. In that way I could use my tent as a decoy. It seemed like the only option.

With the powerful light of the motorcyclist now trained on my back, I set about the task. It only took a few minutes, and I was careful to keep the open side of the tent facing away from the road. As the shadows began to lengthen I threw my rucksack inside, scrambled in, and with my penknife cut a small slit in the fabric. I squinted through the gap. And there I sat, waiting for him to turn off his headlight, waiting for the right moment.

The light went out. I had to go *now*.

I picked up my rucksack, turned, and edged it out the flap. I crawled back to the front of the tent and peered through the slit. Good. The guy hadn't moved an inch.

Feet first, I started to back up into the gloom. I paused at the flap and tried to control my breathing. Still no sound from the road. Once fully outside, I rose cradling my rucksack, slipped it over my shoulders, and began to stumble across the heavy clods.

I'd only travelled about fifty metres when I saw a flash. As I looked to the rear I could see my tent illuminated by torchlight. The small triangle of plastic was literally surrounded by figures. One turned to face me. An arm rose in my direction.

And that was when I started to run.

I ran hard. I ran deep into the night. I ran across the uneven dirt, feeling my ankles twist and turn in between the clods. The thought stirred. *A snap here will be fatal.* As I spun round, gasping wildly, I thought I saw a figure fall, then rise again and stumble forward with outstretched arms.

Instantly, they were upon me.

Rough shouts rose to my left. I couldn't understand it. How could that be? I sensed danger straight ahead, and I realised that the road, back to my pursuers, was the only way out. I charged to the right, driven by pure instinct.

I halted before a screaming corridor of piercing light. Solid yellow beams drilled the dark. Shouts from all directions moved closer. I paused for breath. The feeling was unmistakable.

There was a hand on my shoulder . . .

I felt an arm snake around my throat. With a cry of my own I twisted violently, somehow pulled free; then my assailant staggered back, appeared to trip and within seconds I was dodging cars, dancing with death in the ultimate lottery.

I crashed out the other side, smashing into a knee-high wall of plants. I began to push through the fields. Had they followed? Had my pursuers made it across the road?

The suffocating reek of crushed tomato leaves began to taint the air. I moved forward into the blackness, half-walking, half-jogging. In what appeared to be a lucky break I managed to find a fence to hide against, but within minutes the familiar yellow headlight swerved into view, probing the gloom. These people seemed relentless. What had Father Harron told me?

'Your value to these people, to terrorists, is very high.'

I scrambled to my feet. As I backtracked towards the road I found myself struggling between a pile of giant boulders. Disorientated and off-balance, I clambered forward, missed a step, fell and smashed my knee on a rock. I rose bloodied, stifling a scream with a fist. Eventually, I swung right to parallel the road. I found a new fence to rest against, and there I sat in the dark.

Listening for the slightest sound. Waiting for whatever might come.

Dawn broke at 5 a.m. I'd never been happier to see a new day. With barely an hour's broken sleep I rejoined the road half expecting a last-minute assault. Once again, I was lucky. Perhaps the previous night's action had been the last roll of the dice. Perhaps my assailants figured I was too close to the border and would soon be gone. I didn't have any complaints. I was just glad to be alive, and I knew I would never know the truth of these events.

Two days later, I finally reached the Jordanian border. It was early. Birdsong swept the broken fields, giving life to dead earth turned by dead metal. The horizon flickered crimson, waning yellow on the lower clouds and jagged grey on the heavens. I glanced about, spotting a hotel-cum-restaurant. A few minutes before eight I took a strange breakfast of what appeared to be custard laced with strawberry jam. I emerged into the sunshine sticky-fingered with a heart light and free. Despite facing the greatest danger I'd ever known, I'd travelled the length of Syria on foot. It seemed like a miracle, the first of a new life waiting to be discovered.

I felt it again during these moments, the momentum of the journey building and the weight of past events pushing me on. In the heavens I sensed unseen threads being pulled together, like plotlines in a book. God, the supreme author of life, was busy scribbling my future. Each tiny step formed another word, each act of kindness a comma and each country a completed chapter. How would the story finish? If my pilgrimage ultimately provided me with a new sense of purpose, as I hoped, would I have the courage to follow it? Only God could say. Only God knew the direction I would take. As each day passed I patiently waited for a sign—my *Damascene moment*—that one irrefutable statement of God's intent that would answer all profound questions and deliver certainty in the twinkling of an eye. So far nothing like that had happened. I was still convinced it would.

Gradually, the first checkpoint came into view—a drop-down barrier guarded by a single soldier eyeing me from a distance. I stopped about fifty yards away to pull my passport out of my shorts and generally psyche myself up for the challenge of walking alone through another country. For the last time I looked back toward Damascus.

Had Syria ultimately been a positive experience?

I remembered, then, the endless cups of coffee, the wonderful hospitality of those early days, the friendly Armenian grocers of the coast and entire families who had happily signed my stick. Before I could take another step, a small boy sprinted out from the desert fringes. He came to a breathless halt, broke into a lopsided grin and with a single sentence all the good feelings came flooding back.

'You are welcome in Syria!' he cried.

I looked down into his expectant face and gave him the coins left in my pocket.

I don't think God himself could have authored a more fitting ending.

Chapter Fourteen

Jordan, Israel and
Jerusalem

The Land of New Beginnings

Syria hates Israel. Jordan's a friend.

Syria is dangerous. Jordan is peaceful.

In Syria the secret police and dubious individuals will harass you for days. In Jordan the army serves cups of tea.

It's not hard to figure out which I preferred.

Between 2 and 9 November I spent eight days in the Hashemite Kingdom making the most of that comparison. Like all previous journeys through foreign lands it began with the process of gathering passport stamps and navigating stern-looking officials eager to expose enemies of the state. It was the Syrian side that bothered me the most. Given all the unwanted attention, I was half expecting some last-minute hitch featuring big Arabs wielding thumbscrews and an unscheduled detour into a side room. Once again, I was fortunate. I smiled at everyone in sight and managed to get the hell out.

Despite growing pretensions to worldliness, I'd never been to Jordan before. As a result, I didn't know a lot about King Abdullah's little piece of Middle Eastern desert. The only information that readily came to mind concerned Abu Musab al-Zarqawi, a Jordanian terrorist notorious for beheading hostages in post-war Iraq. The censored television reports broadcast at the time had made grisly viewing—night after night of haggard faces in orange jumpsuits begging for their lives. People like you. People like me. People like British engineer Ken Bigley murdered in 2004. It may surprise some to learn that Islam considers Jesus an important prophet. I'm inclined to think Zarqawi would have done better heeding the words of Matthew 26:52:

Then Jesus said to him, 'Put your sword back in its place, for all those who take the sword will die by the sword.'

On 7 June 2006, the murderer Zarqawi was himself murdered by an American F16 laser-guided bomb. I know Jesus has his detractors, but he didn't get many things wrong.

From the Syrian border it's a hefty 86 km to Amman. Once free of officialdom, I wasted no time in making for the capital's choicest hotels. I won't apologise for nurturing the thought. My foam roll mat had been disintegrating for weeks, and more than once I woke impaled on the needles of some spiky desert plant that had found its way into an unfortunate crevice. If that's not a Legionnaire-style invitation to 'March or die!', then nothing is.

Loaded up with bottled water, I immediately set off for the delightfully named Thughrat Al Jubb. Ten hours of dusty light disappeared in a procession of tatty poster-column sheikhs and several hundred zipping cars. The famed 'romance of the desert' was strangely absent, though towards the end of the first day I did encounter some marvellous hills, swirling like cornets. At dusk they acquired a lovely golden orange tint and sparkled like a million rhinestones. No camels plodded among them, but the sight did encourage me to walk on a bit longer.

Then came the second day, and it was easily the worse of the two. In 1966 the now very-dead Zarqawi had been born in an ugly concrete maze called Zarqa. I could see why he'd embraced jihad and fled to Iraq. The city that bore his name was a gigantic honeycomb of black dots—literally a sprawling tomb on a hill. As I battled my way around the seemingly endless Zarqa, fleets of cigar-shaped petrol tankers came streaming toward me. Clouds of black smog darkened the sun. Exhaust seared my throat. The hot, acrid air was full of dust, petrol fumes, camel dung particles, screaming rubber and heaven knows what else. I decided to keep to the left of the highway, meeting the heavy six-wheelers face on. There was little choice. Walking on the right meant risking traffic from behind, and with Jerusalem only a week away I didn't fancy being squashed flat. Two hours later, I was still circling the tomb-like Zarqa. Each rumbling tanker was a hammer blow in the face. Vicious tailwinds quickly followed, pulling me backward like a riptide dragging a swimmer out to sea. The rest was a heat-induced blur: garage forecourts casting oil-slick rainbows; someone handing me a glossy copy of Emirates' in-flight magazine; coffee and stick-signing with a group of teenage boys, all machismo and easy grins.

I marched on, taking five-minute breathers and gulping water on sandy mounds. When the car pulled up from behind, purring like a leopard, even twenty feet away I could see it was a beauty. Virgin-white, open-topped, grey leather seating—the sports car reeked of oil dollars, and plenty of them. The driver waved me over, a bearded, baby-faced millionaire floating in a white robe.

'Hello!' he said. 'So, you are English?' And then began to clap his hands with the biggest grin I'd yet seen. 'Oh, wonderful! Wonderful! Is there anything I can get you?'

Hmm. My own private oil well would be nice . . .

Two minutes later, he gunned the engine, the car uttered a deep-throated purr, and he spun away toward Syria, punching the sky. 'I just wanted to welcome you to Jordan!' he shouted back. Jordanians: yep, they're friendly like that.

At sunset the highway between Zarqa and Amman is not a great place to be. Both are large cities, and the open desert that supposedly lies between doesn't really exist. Fed up with peering hopefully at shoebox houses on shadowy hillsides, at eight I decided to call it a day. With no hotel in sight I hurried across a footbridge, dodged a pair of barking dogs, scuttled down a dirt slope and threw my roll mat onto a rocky ledge overlooking a chasm shrouded in gloom. The pitted rock above my head was probably scorpion city, but I tried to ignore the thought.

Soon the muezzin broke into mournful song: 'Allaaaaaah ~ uAkbar! Allaaa~AA~aa~A~a~A~aa~AAh ~ u ~ aakbar!'

One, two, three, then a dozen strong Arab voices began to echo around blackened hills aflame with tiny orange lights. 'God is greater!' they cried, as far below, howling dogs commenced their inevitable serenade, and warm drizzle spattered my face.

I lay quietly in my sleeping bag, listening to the now familiar chorus. Tomorrow I would wake half an hour before sunrise. I would talcum blotchy feet and check carefully for the menace of new blisters. I would eat scraps saved for breakfast and curse myself for not being better organised. Then, while millions slept and millions pondered, I would place my few possessions in a fraying rucksack, pull out a map and calmly walk into my eighth capital city. For a little while longer I was still a pilgrim walking to Jerusalem. I honestly couldn't imagine life any other way.

* * *

Excluding the fear of kidnap and an untimely and thoroughly undeserved death, of all the old aspects of myself symbolically discarded by the roadside, it was ignorance that departed last. I have to confess, my expectations for Amman had always been pretty spectacular. I pictured blue-tinted skyscrapers funded by billions of oil dollars, lush lawns beside dancing fountains, and regal headscarfed sheikhs in Ray-Ban sunglasses and billowing white *dishdashas* strolling down waving palm-tree boulevards. I was convinced chauffeured limousines lined every kerb.

The eastern part of the city, known locally as 'downtown Amman', was happy to disappoint. Before dawn I was on my feet, yawning mightily, and with Efendi in hand striding purposefully through awakening souks. When the sun finally blessed the city I was already deep in the suburbs. Young men with razor haircuts and glum faces lurked in shadowy doorways. Canary-yellow taxis prowled the streets searching for easy fares. I was lost in Arabic squiggles and poster sheikhs. Desperate for local currency, I spent a futile fifteen minutes in the Cairo Amman Bank arguing with a grey-bearded buffoon in a black waistcoat.

He waved the cheque in my face and with reddening cheeks spluttered, 'We need at least one month's notice to exchange American Express!'

Yeah. Right . . . and Elvis is alive and well flipping burgers at McDonalds. Gotcha.

I left the bank in disgust and went outside to hunt down some Jordanian dinars. The main road was frenetic: pink baby clothes and blue jeans dangling chaotically from rafters, steamy kebab shops and sizzling spits, women in white *hijabs*, women in black, grizzled old men in chequered headscarves huddling beneath the soaring minarets of al-Husseini Mosque. The air seethed with harsh tongues, rough shouts and the growl of yellow taxis. By now I was pretty light on my feet; I danced between the crowds like a two-footed gazelle. After swapping some AMEX cheques at a seedy exchange office, I made straight for the nearest hotel.

'Twenty-four Jordanian, sir.'

The receptionist was a young man, late teens, smartly dressed in a black suit and white open-neck shirt.

'Twenty-four? Are you sure?'

'Sir!' he cried, sweeping his hands outward as if to embrace the entire building, 'this is the finest hotel in all Amman, perhaps the whole of Jordan! For a man of your sophistication, I promise you, this hotel is ready to give you the very greatest pleasure!'

Excellent, I thought, in defiance of my budget (plus astonishingly accurate intuition). I soon regretted the decision not to look elsewhere. There are a lot of places to stay in downtown Amman, but the one no tourist should ever choose is the flamboyantly named 'Amman Palace' on King Faisal Street. I don't know about other guests, but in my palace I like the hot water to be hot, the room not to smell like a drain, and the ice-cubes drawn from the Russian-made rattling fridge not to be a) yellow and b) entombing a cockroach like a Jurassic fly imprisoned in primordial amber. When faced with such unpalatial pleasures I might be persuaded to calm down if presented with a decent breakfast. Which nicely brings me to the bizarre.

I never did work out why most of the guests had the appearance of being patched up by trainee doctors. Taking a boiled egg and tea at the Palace was like participating in a badly written hospital soap opera. Each morning they all came shuffling down: two guys on crutches (one in a splendid full-length plaster cast) and a tiny bloke with a head bandage covering one eye. Our prize guest—the 'mummy'—typically arrived half an hour later. I was sitting at my table hammering a hard-boiled egg senseless when a towering six-footer meandered past. I looked up and was confronted by a torso knitted together with safety pins and flailing bandages. Why? I have no idea. But during my entire stay I think I was the only resident that could walk unaided to the lift.

I munched on, one eye on a new tourist map. Away from the breakfast tables I normally devoted the afternoons to exploring the city's cultural treasures. This being the eastern flank of the Mediterranean, you might have expected the Romans to turn up here eventually with their unique agenda of conquer, plunder and build. They did, arriving behind Pompey's dusty sandals in 63 BC. Without doubt the architectural highlight was the amphitheatre just minutes from the hotel. It's a superb arrangement of old stone. Row upon row of chalky-grey seats steadily rise to form a delightful cockleshell pattern. Museums on either side provide cartoonish mannequins and the amusing spectacle of smiling plastic camels. The best of the entertainment probably lies in the adjacent gardens. Clutching their trademark aluminium kettles and with sprigs of mint tucked inside their belts, ninja-ish tea vendors creep among fluted Roman pillars looking for innocent tourists to ambush.

'Tea, Mister?' said a voice behind my shoulder.

'Eh? What?' I spun round to find a steaming polystyrene cup hovering two inches from my face.

I dropped some coins into his hand and sipped gingerly. The proffered cup was no Earl Grey, but it was drinkable—in a warm, minty, overpriced kind of way.

I continued with my investigation of the city, embracing the positive and trying to avoid the pitfalls that await any traveller. If the tea had been passable, I didn't gel so well with the fast food served from the city's many *shawarma* stands. Of the four days I lingered in Amman, limbering up for the final assault on Jerusalem, two were spent sightseeing and the two after wondering if I was going to die. I was quite surprised by these developments because I'd always counted myself lucky, particularly as a child. Consider these impressive escapades:

Age three—bowled over by a freak twelve-inch wave while paddling on Southend beach. Result: saved at the critical moment from a grim and premature reaping by mother's outstretched hand.

Age five—crashed into a wall-mounted gas fire while clowning around with friends. Result: glass held firm. Jelly babies confiscated for two weeks. Rejoined society chastised with a slightly singed bottom.

Age nine—for reasons only known to the pre-pubescent mind I decided it would be cool to ram my head through a glass door. Result: picked up a few scratches but nothing else. Catholics two doors down began crossing themselves. Such was my indestructibility there were unsubstantiated reports that the Vatican was preparing to investigate.

Then came the sternest test of all—my infamous eleventh birthday party. It was a touching family scene: Aunt Gerty in a rainbow shawl and 1940's hairnet with brown stockings bunched at the ankles; Uncle Vic, red-nosed in a green bobble cardigan complaining about his Dunkirk shrapnel ('You know what, lad,' he wheezed, 'I'll pay a visit to that damn hospital one day.'); three kids wearing paper hats, hoping that today is the day they could stay up late (late being after 8 p.m.—yes, my parents were a strict lot) and Great Aunt Matilda, freshly arrived from her mansion in Sussex, dressed in a black taffeta gown, looking like a Victorian dowager and holding a steaming plate of . . . well . . . what?

'What's that?' we chorused brightly, banging spoons on the table.

'Now don't complain,' she said. Our faces dropped. We had our eyes on the strawberry jelly and ice cream. 'You're going to love it. It's my special tuna surprise.'

Rarely has a tin of tuna chunks caused greater surprise. Aunt Gerty went down first, felled by a monstrous burp and an urgent need to visit the toilet. All but myself and the equally indestructible Great Aunt Matilda swiftly followed.

'Oh my God! Oh my GOD!' she twittered, as chairs crashed and everyone turned green.

In the end, forty-four years of mostly good fortune had to run out somewhere. It was my bad luck they ran out on the road to Jerusalem. On my third day in Amman I started to feel ill. Then I started to feel very ill, and two hours after *that* I began to travel down a tunnel of light towards whomever, or whatever, might be waiting to embrace me. As I lay 'dying' I fervently prayed it wouldn't be old Fred—my neighbour Bill's deceased brother. The unsmiling scrooge had checked out in the winter of '99, and I still owed him twenty quid. Knowing that miserly family I could almost see him hovering in a halo waiting to collect.

A troubled twenty-four hours ensued. Vomit, nausea, stomach cramps: I had the lot. Unable to leave the hotel, I rolled about listlessly under a wafer-thin blanket, sleeping when I could, fiddling with my MP3 player when I couldn't. Perhaps the most important consequence of the illness was the dent it made in my extended travel plans. I'd been gradually warming to the idea of taking a bus to Petra—the ancient Nabataean city in southern Jordan. The pictures I'd hunted down on the Internet looked marvellous: rose-coloured temples dipped in shadow, secretive tombs honeycombing the rock. Reluctantly, I let the idea go. At this late stage it seemed too risky and, in any case, I needed all my remaining strength for Jerusalem. In the heavens someone finally gave the green light.

By dawn most of the mysterious illness had disappeared.

An hour later, I'd run out of reasons not to climb out of bed.

The city of Christ that had drawn pilgrims and armies for centuries was a short hop over the King Hussein Bridge. Swinging rucksack over shoulder, I picked up Efendi, closed the last hotel door of the journey and strode out into Jordanian sun. The wheel of life had come full circle.

It was time to finish what I'd begun.

For a backpacker approaching on foot from the east there aren't a huge number of ways to enter Israel. In fact, if you've been joylessly crouching over a vomit-spattered toilet in Amman the only logical place is the Allenby Border Terminal standing on the west bank of the River Jordan. I was there on 9 November, shoving heartily with the best of them, and so many toes were mercilessly crunched that morning I'd be wracked with guilt if I didn't offer this survival guide to lessen future pilgrim pain:

1. Disembark chaotically from coach. Avoid tripping over the suitcases littering the ground and subsequent melee. [Note for British travellers: don't bother looking for a queue; there isn't any.] A look of mild bewilderment is strongly advised.
2. Navigate legendary Israeli security. Unscrew any metal legs (or other protruding body parts) and place them in the trays conveniently provided for immediate X-ray. Try not to look too undignified as you hobble through the metal detector frame.
3. Bluff your way through immigration. Unwavering eye contact is best. Maintain British stiff upper lip at all times, and never say anything good about the Palestinians.

4. Collect passport stamp. Ensure that all-important smudge is on a bit of loose paper unless you want to be denied entry to Saudi Arabia, Bahrain, Kuwait and a bunch of other fun Middle Eastern playgrounds.

5. Bluster furiously at Customs. Don't waste time declaring excess cash unless you're
   a) Incredibly stupid (like me); or
   b) Palestinian, in which case your luggage will be ruthlessly examined for Qassam rockets, pocket penknives, paper clips or other illicit items that might threaten the state of Israel.

6. Step out into the daylight. Celebrate your good fortune by purchasing overpriced snacks and a bus ticket you don't really need, just to leave the heavily fortified compound that not even a five-kiloton nuke could dent.

And that's all there is to it, folks. Well, very nearly . . .

Despite leaving a pint of vomit in the toilet, I arrived at the Jordanian side of the river a mere two days after leaving Amman. The journey to the border was smooth enough: find road to Naur, take afternoon tea with the Jordanian Army, sleep in crumbling gun emplacement, then march on past fields heavy with ripening tomatoes and flanked by ribbed irrigation pipes the width of a man's waist. The continuous demand for water had turned the once mighty River Jordan into a pathetic dribble. Now I could see why.

At 9 a.m. I trudged up to the first checkpoint. I halted at the barrier: hot, unsure, unshaven, clutching a generously proportioned five-foot walking stick and wondering how the hell this was going to play out.

'Excuse me,' I said. Arab eyes holding a rifle refocused forty-five degrees downward. I was a boy standing in front of a black-bearded giant. 'Is it possible to walk to Israel?'

Ha! Ha! Ha? Notwithstanding the nurturing hand of hope, I had a pretty good idea I wasn't going to be allowed to march unaccompanied toward one of the most sensitive borders on Earth. You kind of get a feeling for these things.

The giant Arab in khaki peered down at me, scowled, waved his finger in a disapproving kind of way and silently pointed to a clutch of buildings to the left.

I spent about forty-five minutes there, eager to restart the dream. To reach the Allenby Border Terminal it's necessary to cross the River Jordan via the grand-sounding 'King Hussein Bridge'. The departure lounge where everybody waits for the coach is a light and airy place where the chairs face each other in a tight square. Once you've paid the five-dinar 'exit tax' for the privilege of leaving Jordan, you'll end up there like I did, gazing anxiously at fellow departees, munching on expensive crisps from the vending machines and generally trying to get your shit together for the legendary Israeli security that naturally awaits. And by the way, don't expect to see many European faces.

Because there won't be. Most Westerners who have any sense opt for the swanky Jordan River Terminal at Irbid in the north. Only the 'locals' and the adventurous take on Allenby. I flopped on a seat and scanned the assembled faces: an Arab woman with heavy jowls, sweating in a silver-and-black headscarf; two pale-skinned American girls in flowery dresses—twenty-somethings with perfect teeth chatting excitedly at the start of a magnificent adventure. Beside them sat an old Orthodox priest in a black stove-pipe hat, resting his gnarled hands on a silver-topped cane. The thirty or so Palestinians clinging to their children looked more nervous than all of us. In fact, they seemed terrified.

I think it was just before ten when the order came. As one we piled onto the coach, taking our places by tinted glass windows and fussing with little squares of orange curtain. Vroom, vroom, VROOM! The driver shoved the stick into reverse; we lurched backwards with a tremendous jolt, then turned sharply to the left and began to career down the dusty tarmac. Excited chatter rose to mingle with cheap cologne. Snippets of English floated through the hot and stuffy air.

'So, Peter,' said a male voice two rows down, 'have you been to Jerusalem before?'

'They like to repeat questions to try and catch you out,' whispered a woman two rows back.

Yes, I mused, Israeli immigration could be a problem. I'd spent twenty-four days plodding around Syria. What would they make of that?

The two American girls had taken the seats opposite. While they fiddled with the air nozzles I sat with my nose pressed hard against the window, overcome by schoolboy curiosity. When the King Hussein Bridge finally arrived it was something of a disappointment. I'd envisaged a girder-and-cable spectacular like America's Brooklyn Bridge. Reality was very different. The latest version of what the Israelis call the Allenby Bridge was a short sliver of boring M-sided concrete. We zipped across in seconds.

On the Israeli side there were fences everywhere. Entry to the Jewish state was obviously a serious business. After the bridge we slid past a parade of welcoming palm trees, pulling up smoothly outside a large hanger with a green-edged roof. The experience of getting off the coach lent new meaning to the cry 'Every man for himself!' The American girls rose first, squealing like throttled mice: 'Oh my God, Chelsea! We're here! We're here!' Everyone piled out into the sun. Suitcases tumbled onto the pavement, tossed from above. Shouts filled the air. Toes were mercilessly crunched. It was complete pandemonium for at least ten minutes.

Totally bewildered, we entered the arrivals lounge, a herd of bobbing headscarves, taut smiles and glistening lips. The pedantic Israelis are renowned for their security. At Allenby they were on top form. At some point a young Palestinian woman in a wheelchair came forward, smiling serenely. Her leg was made of steel below the right knee. Could this disabled woman bypass the metal detector frame? Nope. No way. Absolutely not. A green-shirted guy simply knelt down and spun it off like a mechanic changing a tyre. The leg was unceremoniously dumped into a tray and then trundled through the baggage scanner with a pile of loose change. I had to see it to believe it.

Immigration was the next obstacle. Five pairs of blue-panelled counters stood before us. Behind the bulletproof windows sat stern young women in sky-blue shirts and matching neckties eager to root out the gibbering enemies of Israel. Our arrival sparked a bout of nervous coughing, myself included. What is it about crossing borders that always makes a person feel guilty?

Gradually, the coughing queues began to thin. When my turn came I walked up to the counter and slipped my passport under the glass. She was the epitome of Jewish womanhood: flawless olive skin, silky black hair drawn up into a tight bun, eyes like liquid almonds. After nearly nine months on the road this pretty young woman was going to decide the fate of my entire pilgrimage. Funny how it had all come down to this.

'You have been travelling a long time in Syria . . .' she began. Her voice was gentle, casual, almost disinterested. Those cunning Israelis; was she trying to lull me into a false sense of security?

I gulped hard and wondered how best to respond. This didn't seem like the right moment to bang on about man's inner search for meaning, the many blessings of God, the incredible power of synchronicity and all that mumbo jumbo which would probably takes ages to explain. I threw up an enormous prayer and just told it straight.

'That's right,' I said, with only minor quavers. 'I'm a Christian who started walking to Jerusalem from Holland. When I reached Turkey I had to walk through Syria because there is no other way to reach Israel on foot.'

'Okay,' she said, without a trace of surprise, 'but how will you leave Israel?'

'By return flight with Turkish Airlines. I've got my ticket right here. The date can be changed if need be.'

Almond Eyes glanced at the e-ticket, smiled, pushed it back. Returning her gaze to the keyboard, she said, 'Are you travelling to the Occupied Territories?'

Of course, it was another obvious question. Unfortunately, I was a trifle hazy on Israeli geography and hadn't thought that far ahead. Actually, wasn't Bethlehem in the Occupied Territories? Crikey . . .

Gibbering tourists tend to irritate officials. So do the indecisive. Noticing the obvious pause in proceedings, Almond Eyes stopped tapping on her computer and fixed me with a businesslike stare.

'Do you understand the question I have asked you?'

I nodded quickly, not wishing to antagonise further. To end what was fast becoming a sticky moment, I starting talking up a possible day trip to Bethlehem. (But only, I declared solemnly, if it was expressly permitted by the authorities. Most officials are power-crazed nutters; it never hurts to flatter them.) Then, with a surprisingly warm smile from Almond Eyes and a 'Welcome to Israel!', incredibly I was waved through.

Outside I didn't have long to celebrate.

'Walk out of the compound?' said the bus-ticket vendor. 'Do you want them to shoot you?'

I'd prefer it if they didn't.

'No one can walk out of here! It is absolutely forbidden!'

The vendor sat scowling behind a desk piled high with little towers of shekels. A tanned and puffy-faced youth in a patriotic 'Stand with Israel!' navy T-shirt, he had the kind of facial blandness normally associated with shopfront mannequins. I watched mesmerised as a purple vein throbbed in his bloated neck.

'You must pay me thirty-three shekels for a ticket,' he decreed, and after ten further throbs I was handed a bus ticket to Jerusalem. My face fell faster than Icarus. Walking every step of the way really was impossible.

I received poor value for my money. Fifty metres after clearing the compound, the minibus pulled up with a start. Everyone was thrown back. I scrambled out the side door, grabbing Efendi and my rucksack from the hatch springing open at the rear. Palestinian hands waved frantically, then the bus spun away, kicking up clouds of dust. When the sky cleared I found myself gazing speculatively westward upon the swirling hills of Judea.

And it was then, that I finally saw it.

I'd walked nearly 6,000 km to see a Jerusalem road sign. The officer standing in the road beside me was a bull of a man in an army baseball cap. He cocked a blond eyebrow. 'Really?'

'Yep, I actually started in Holland about eleven months ago.'

'Do you know how far it is to Jerusalem?'

'Not really. I've just crossed at Allenby.'

He was thoughtful for a second. Then he beckoned me closer. 'Come over here.'

I trotted round to the front of the jeep. The officer twisted a few buttons on his tunic and wrestled free a substantial map. He spread it across the bonnet—a two-dimensional Israel drawn in grey contours and shades of arid brown. The colour scheme was nearly as forbidding as the bleached hills looming in the west. If Jesus had roamed those, he was a better man than I.

The officer ran his finger across the map, paused, tapped it lightly, then looked me straight in the eye. 'For you it is about thirty-three kilometres.'

Only thirty-three kilometres . . . could it really be true?

I was totally drained by the time I reached the monastery. Lugging a 30 lb rucksack was only partly to blame. Whatever junk I'd swallowed in Amman had felled me like an oak, and it still wasn't out of my system. 'St Gerasimos is five kilometres along this road,' were the burly officer's parting words. He was right. It was visible even a kilometre away: a ribbed silver dome edging a splash of hazy green and splintering the best of the afternoon sun. Conditioned by months of travel, my response to any monastery was almost Pavlovian. All I could think about was finding food and shelter.

There was a buzz about the place that day. The Cappadocian saint who'd plucked a thorn from a lion's paw had spawned a leafy oasis of scattered tables dotted with pretty orange urns. Diners nibbled on croissants and sipped from white china cups;

children licked pink ice-cream cornets. The ambience was more Parisian street café than smoky chapel. There was no denying the Greek influence. Blue-and-white flags, striped like spearmint, hung from every arch. Olive-skinned tourists, round like beer barrels, streamed past clutching silver cameras. Orthodox clergy crowded several tables. They sat chatting—Rasputin figures in black cassocks, with hooked noses, old-growth beards and un-blinking mesmeric eyes. 'There is a big meeting here today,' said the Arab boy beside me. I smiled at him and waited patiently.

I spent most of the afternoon there, waiting and eating prodi-gious quantities of overpriced toasted cheese. All the spare beds had been taken by visiting priests or Arab boys scampering about in the employ of the church. I felt the usual disappointment, but not as much as the early days. When darkness fell I left the grounds and its street café atmosphere, walked on fifty metres, then for the last time threw my roll mat onto the dirt. *Cling-clang! Cling-clang! Cling-clang!* At seven prompt the church bell began to peal. Rotating yellow light from a shadowy watchtower swept the night like a barnacled lighthouse on the Cornish coast. The sky was a velvet blizzard of warm drizzle. I fell asleep dreaming of all that was yet to come.

Damp and trembling with anticipation, I rose before dawn and rejoined the road for the final time. All that was yet to come . . . yes, it was a tantalising prospect. How would I feel at the end? Triumphant? Relieved? Dejected at the climax of something that had become my life? Some crazy mix of all three? There was no way of knowing. Not yet. And of course it *had* become my life. For nine months I'd been living, eating and sleeping pilgrim-age. I'd overcome every obstacle, faced down every threat, stayed open to whatever each day held.

Just after midday, along an incredibly quiet road rising from the Dead Sea, the final kilometres began to unwind, and Jeru-salem drew near. The yellow sun of Judea once tested saviours and sandaled saints. Two thousand years later, it tests the right-eous and sinners still. Hot sweat dribbled into my eyes, stinging like acid. I rubbed them savagely with my sleeve and plodded on. From sentry boxes Israeli soldiers clutching rifles nodded warily, flashing brittle smiles and stabbing with gimlet eyes. The sleeve of an Arab's robe flashed white against a wilderness of orange stone. His distant hand was swaying bronze reaching for turquoise blue; I waved back wildly and continued to climb.

Among arid swirling hills I glimpsed shapeless Bedouin camps, hovels of wood and carpet. Higher still, jittery Jews hid beneath roofs of scarlet clay, finding comfort in stout wire fences, in padlocks, in burning bushes, in the menorah and the Torah and babes in baskets crying among the reeds, in mighty staffs that parted mighty seas and the promise of their jealous God. I saw then what Moses never saw, and once again I felt it. I was a Christian, in Israel, walking the final kilometres to Jerusalem. The air seemed to shift with quiet triumph. I picked up the pace, sensing the end and with it the promise of a new beginning.

I'd changed. Only with victory finally at hand could I see it. I'd begun timidly, like a pet mouse suddenly let loose from its cage. Where would I sleep each night? How would I overcome the Austrian Alps? Would I 'disappear' in the forests of Bosnia or enter Albania and never return? I'd even doubted the advice of Johanna: 'Tony, people will invite you in.' She was right—so many had. Since then, eleven months had passed. Throwing off the old, I'd embraced the new, finding peace in flaming deserts, humility in the gifts of children and an acceptance of the world as it really is. Above all, I'd discovered courage, the quiet knowledge that I could do, be, *achieve* anything I wanted if the will was really there. It was all a matter of belief. In the end, it was all a matter of *faith*.

The last hill was an absolute monster, a mini-mountain of Alpine proportions dumped in the middle of Palestine. Slowly, doggedly, I continued to climb. Using Efendi I dug hard into the tarmac. Traffic zoomed by and upward, oblivious to my plight, oblivious to my struggle. The words of St Paul thundered in my ear: 'When I am weak, then I am strong.' My lungs were on the

verge of bursting, and *still* I climbed. When the road at last levelled out I found myself staring down the barrel of a gun.

The soldier yawned. 'Jerusalem that way,' he said, cocking a
thumb over his shoulder.

Jerusalem? Where? Here? I can't see it! He pointed again, and
I glimpsed the black gape of a tunnel. I took back my passport and
pressed on. The tunnel drew close. Cars swept by in a noisy blur.
The past bore down on me. I'd given up my job. I'd abandoned
family and friends in the pursuit of a dream. I'd put my life on
the line risking everything in one massive gamble. And yet at
the entrance I finally hesitated. At the start I'd been terrified of
failure. Now, I was almost too afraid to succeed.

You must go into the tunnel to see the light.

Instinctively, I knew the truth. This was the end. This bleak
tunnel of dancing lights would be the final journey.

Forsaking all doubt, I hurried forward into the unknown. How
far could it be? Surely not much further? In the dark the faces of
friends drew near. I saw them then. I see them still: Johanna van
Fessem handing me a cross of plaited string; Frans and Heleen
waving my astonished face through the door; seventy-year-old
Kornelius Moll, who admired tough guys and marched 20 km
through German mud to prove it; Stanislav the Bosnian Serb
sitting on his porch, waving for me to join him as the heavens
poured and white lightning split the sky. There had been so many
countries and so many gifts, I could scarcely have asked for . . .
Wait! Was that light up ahead?

Hot blood pounded my eardrums like thunder. Traffic roared
by; someone tooted their horn in bloody anger. I ignored them
and hurried on.

Unseen in the heavens wheels of enormous power were turning, moving into position, fulfilling their purpose, as I fulfilled
mine. Something amazing was happening, and I was right at the
heart of it. Expectation was in the air. It was the second before
the first peal of thunder, the adrenalin before the starter's gun.
Six thousand kilometres from home a lone figure approached

the holiest city on Earth. The waiting was over. The universe was turning. Everything was as it was *meant* to be.

'Have courage,' Johanna had told me. 'You will make it.'

As the darkness fell away and I tore through the tunnel it all suddenly seemed worthwhile. The heat and the snow: I braved it. The loneliness of the road: I took it. The hunger and the thirst: I shrugged it off. If I never did anything worthy again, I would always have this moment.

At 1:45 p.m., on Saturday, 10 November 2007, the sun broke before me like the first dawn. After a 251-day march through Europe and Asia, I emerged breathlessly into the sunshine and looked across with wonder at the golden Dome of the Rock. I'd achieved my goal in nine million steps of two-thirds of a metre.

Above the City of Peace, the next step had just begun.

I stayed eighteen days in Jerusalem. The impossible journey that started in Holland on 14 November 2006, that had faltered in muddy fields east of Dordrecht, restarted the following March among crackling frost and come to a triumphant halt high above the sawtoothed battlements of the Old City, turned out not to be the end at all, but rather a new and challenging beginning.

It honestly didn't seem so at the time. Upon arrival I took a room at the busy Jaffa Gate Hostel. I hadn't had a decent chat in English for weeks, but not even the camaraderie of biblically named Americans reared on corncobs and Corinthians could lift the mood. As a pilgrim I belonged outside on the road. My job was to shower rarely and walk until my feet bled. When hunger struck I picked up interesting things from the ground. Accepting cups of tea from strangers was essential. As each dawn broke I threw back the sheets ready to march to the next dot on the map—but now there were no more towns to conquer. My walking boots that had served me well since Ankara stood idle and useless in the corner. I sat down on the bed and looked at them, remembering.

I took it easy for a couple of days, mostly washing clothes and making phone calls home. Then, with renewed hope and considerable excitement, I began the ritual of sightseeing. Jerusalem and its environs are packed with religious sites. Having shed at least a stone and destroyed four pairs of boots in the process, I was determined to see as much as possible. Like millions before me, I began with the Via Dolorosa—the traditional path taken by Jesus during his trial and crucifixion. One by one I ticked off the Stations of the Cross, peering in at smoky chapels, lighting votive candles in sandy trays, halting by ancient oak doors studded with arcane strips of black metal.

Did Jesus touch this? Did Christ really stumble here?

I moved slowly through the crowds of swarthy Arabs and pale-skinned Westerners using imagination to augment the eye. I'd walked across Europe and Asia Minor to reach these hallowed stones. I expected to be rewarded with a deeply moving spiritual experience. I expected the suffering of Christ to literally reach out to me across the centuries. Perhaps it was the rampant commercialisation of Christian Quarter Road with its massed ranks of leering shopkeepers trying to flog mass-produced mugs. Or perhaps my expectations for pilgrimage had always been unrealistic. To my surprise the great spiritual high never happened. I felt confused and disappointed when it didn't.

My last memories of Israel are of the old port city of Jaffa on the coast of Tel Aviv. In the chilly afternoon of 29 November I toured the art galleries, the souvenir shops, the narrow alleyways hemmed in by sandstone buildings, and took photos of churches, though all were closed and it was impossible to enter. As dusk fell I found myself on the Wishing Bridge. It's a short, wooden structure etched on the balustrade with the twelve signs of the zodiac. Legend states that anyone who touches their sign and makes a wish will see it come true. It seemed too good to pass up. I stood alone, hand on my own sign—Libra, the scales. The heavens were twinkling. The morning star had blossomed into life, smudgy yellow and white. I prayed that I would finally get the new direction I'd worked so hard to find. The star continued to twinkle without obvious reply, and yet I walked away a little more hopeful than before bearing a small share of its great and dancing light.

At the end of November I flew back to London. Home, then, to England and all I'd left behind. Naturally, it was raining as we disembarked. Heathrow was as Heathrow is: huge, impersonal and daunting. I have no idea what foreigners think, but the scale of the place always terrifies me. Before leaving the concourse I decided to offload some dollars at the exchange office. The rate was diabolical, but I thought what the heck.

Julie was behind the counter that night. Blond, blue-eyed and bubbly, she had a plastic nametag clipped to her white blouse to prove it.

'. . . and here's your receipt. That's sixty pounds and ten pence for you.'

I tapped the glass. 'Excuse me, what's this?'

Julie looked up from her computer screen, all doey-eyed and helpful. 'It's a twenty-pound note.'

'Is that true? I've never seen one of these before.' Suddenly, I felt like a stranger in my own land. An odd feeling indeed.

'Yeah,' she said, planting her elbows on the counter and resting her plump chin on interlocked hands, 'yeah, you know, it's one of those new ones. They've been out for quite a while now, months in fact. How long did you say you've been away?'

'It must be about nine months,' I said, still suspiciously eyeing the purple-tinged banknote.

'Really? I bet you must have some stories to tell.'

'Well, I—' And before I could finish, the smile on my face had spread from ear to ear.

'What's so funny?' she asked.

'Oh, nothing,' I assured her, momentarily amused by a vision of myself fleeing a Turkish madman on a donkey.

'It's just that, I'd need to write a book to explain it all.'

What I Would Do Differently

One of the few advantages of destroying four pairs of boots is the acquisition of hard-won wisdom. If I ever pull on a rucksack again, here are the ten changes I would make:

Don't take travellers cheques. Commission charges can be steep (20%+), and some parts of the world are totally locked out of the system. Difficult to exchange in Jordan and Syria.

Keep money and passport separate. It's worth reiterating, unless you want to lose $200 as I did.

Train right from the start. This is an arduous journey, and the challenge deserves respect. Few people would enter a marathon without preparation. This shouldn't be any different.

Walk more slowly. The desire to keep piling on the kilometres is commendable but can be overdone. Consider Cologne. In the afternoon I walked straight in, and the next morning I walked straight out. Skipping the World Heritage Site cathedral wasn't my greatest decision.

Manage hydration better. This is a difficult one to get right as water is heavy, and there's only so much you can carry in one go. However, I could have done better.

Wear a hat. In the hottest countries some kind of headgear is essential. Failure to wear one may see you spending a lot of time nibbling chocolate bars in Montenegrin petrol stations . . .

Vary the photos. After returning from Jerusalem, my first idea was to compile a picture book accompanied by a smattering of amusing anecdotes. Unfortunately, for some countries I hadn't collected enough photos. Also, I had too few of myself and the local population to make the project work.

Shoot a movie. Video footage makes a great souvenir and will look particularly good on your online travelogue and YouTube channel should you decide to use it for informational or marketing purposes. With recent advances in technology, HD quality is readily accessible from smartphones and tablets.

Invest in a three-season sleeping bag. From an equipment point of view, this was the biggest mistake. A two-season bag won't cut it in winter, and it was never going to.

Buy a waterproof cape. A combination of rainproof jacket and trousers works okay, but in warm weather during a shower you will sweat like hell. A plastic cape lets the air circulate and is considerably lighter.

And that's it. For a complete kit list and comprehensive travel advice, visit my website:

www.iwalkedtojerusalem.com

Acknowledgements

When you're sitting at home contemplating a 6,000 km trek to the Holy Land, you never think that one day you'll be writing an acknowledgements page. Now I've arrived at the moment, I'd particularly like to thank:

Paul Versteven, for visiting me in Rotterdam and letting me blog on his website; Thijs Postma, for advice on long-distance walking; Mony Dojeiji, for sharing her experience of travelling to Santiago de Compostela and Jerusalem; Barbara at Antakya, for letting me enjoy the peace of the old quarter; Johanna van Fessem, for inspiration, my talismanic cross and meeting me at the Hook of Holland; my editor, Imogen Lees, for her diligence and many insightful suggestions.

Final, and very special, thanks must go to the scores of Good Samaritans who gave directions, money, or hospitality, and who encouraged me to walk on.

Index

12454486R00203

Printed in Great Britain
by Amazon.co.uk, Ltd.,
Marston Gate.